Trends and Techniques in Contemporary Indian English Poetry

For

My Students

Trends and Techniques in Contemporary Indian English Poetry

edited by

RAMA NAIR

PRESTIGE

PRESTIGE BOOKS
3/28, East Patel Nagar
New Delhi 110 008

ISBN: 81-7551-114-1

Printed at Chaman Offset Press, New Delhi 110 002

Contents

Individual Studies

Regional Interface

Preface

This anthology, a modest survey of the trends and techniques in contemporary Indian English poetry, was compiled for a variety of reasons. While Indian Fiction in English has made considerabie forays into the realm of international literary criticism, Indian Poetry in English remains by and large a relatively unexplored field. It is commonly assumed that Indian Poetry in English has no voice of its own, and that its relevance and validity within the literary scene of the country has a doubtful and dubious authenticity. In fact, post-Independence Indian Poetry in English is generally known through a few well-established poets like Nissim Ezekiel, R. Parthasarathy, A.K. Ramanujan, Keki Daruwalla, Kamala Das, Jayanta Mahapatra and Arvind Mehrotra, to name a few. In the 1980s and 1990s there has been an upsurge of poetic talent which, however, has remained less evaluated and even lesser appreciated. This is partly due to academic apathy, lack of publishers, and the inordinate desire to venerate the 'old masters'. A critical perspective of the poetic development over the last two decades (1980s and 1990s) is essential to promote a greater self-awareness, a more accurate knowledge of native traditions, and a greater insight into their modern transformations. These are initial preconditions for initiating relevant and useful debates about the function and practice of contemporary Indian English Poetry. With this in view, the Dept. of English, O.U. College of Arts and Social Sciences, Osmania University, Hyderabad, organized a two day UGC National Seminar on "Trends and Techniques in Contemporary Indian English Poetry" on Dec. 20 and 21, 1999. Its main objective was to formulate fresh and meaningful insights into the nature and context of contemporary Indian Poetry in English. Most of the papers that feature in this volume are those that were presented at the seminar. The success of the seminar proved that Indian Poetry in English is very much alive and thriving in spite of its marginalized status. A positive result of the seminar was that it brought to the forefront certain issues that lay outside the canonical fold. Gay and lesbian poetry, dalit poetry, poetry concerning feminist issues provoked animated discussions and fiery debates. Another interesting aspect of the seminar was a session devoted to the study of contemporary poetry by Indian language poets. The objective was to apply a comparative perspective in the study of the poetry of Indian language poets and Indian English poets of the last two decades. By analyzing the process of creativity, an attempt was made to offer fresh insights into the relationships between literature and society, and the development of human imagination and intellect. A study of the trends and techniques in these poems can lead to further insights into the well-known cultural traits of Indian history such as eclecticism, multi-lingualism, and multi-culturalism.

If a more reliable poetic theory is to be postulated, it is essential to have a holistic perception of both the earlier and later poets. It will be necessary to examine closely the role played by younger Indian poets in English in establishing a uniquely Indian poetic tradition. The process of assimilation of western 'modernity' into Indian 'tradition' calls for careful scrutiny. In the essays that feature in this anthology, Western paradigms of intellectual enquiry have been minimized as far as possible, and an attempt has been made to draw on modern Indian intellectual discourse. A significant development has been the emergence of women poets. Women poets like Eunice de Souza, Tejdeep, Imtiaz Dharker, Meena Alexander, Sujata Bhatt, Gauri Deshpande and Melanie Silgardo are some of the poets who have managed to secure a place in this largely male dominated sphere. Amongst the younger male poets, Prabhanjan Mishra, Sudeep Sen, Agha Shahid Ali, Vikram Seth, Sultan Padamsee, Ranjit Hoskote,

Vijay Seshadri and Jeet Thayil have made significant contributions. Most of them have remained by and large unknown since their chances of entering mainstream Indian English Poetry appears remote. This anthology proposes to partly rectify this omission by critically assessing, evaluating, and surveying the intellectual and stylistic innovation in their poetry. But by and large one hopes that this anthology will augment and enrich the inadequate body of existing scholarship in this vastly complex and interesting field.

As the Director of the Seminar, and as the Editor of this anthology, I have been fortunate to receive assistance and encouragement from many friends and colleagues. My thanks go to Prof. M. Sivaramkrishna for his exceptional generosity in sharing his insights and ideas. I owe a special debt of gratitude to Sudeep Sen, poet and critic, for his cheerful and spontaneous assistance in sending me books and material from London. These helped me considerably in formulating the course and content of the seminar, and this anthology. I thank Jayanta Mahapatra for his active participation and interest. Thanks are also due to SCILET, Madurai, for providing me with the necessary source materials.

I am specially thankful to my colleagues, Prof. Meera Manvi, Head, Dept. of English, Osmania University, Prof. B. Gopal Rao, Prof. Bala Kothandaraman and Prof. D. Venkateswarlu for providing me with a congenial and amicable atmosphere to work in.

Finally, I would like to take this opportunity to thank all my renowned contributors who, in spite of innumerable pressures, commitments and engagements elsewhere, helped me successfully complete this anthology.

Rama Nair

Contributors

M. Sivaramkrishna, Osmania University, Hyderabad.

Jayanta Mahapatra, Cuttack, Orissa

Mohan Ramanan, University of Hyderabad, Hyderabad.

Sudeep Sen, London, U.K.

Laksmisree Banerjee, Women's College, Jamshedpur.

Hoshang Merchant, University of Hyderabad, Hyderabad.

T. Vijay Kumar, Osmania University, Hyderabad.

C. Vijayasree, Osmania University, Hyderabad.

E. Nageswara Rao, formerly at ASRC, Hyderabad.

P. Laxminarayana, Osmania University, Hyderabad.

Shirish Chindhade, M.U. College of Commerce, Pimpri, Pune.

Girija Nambiar, Marie Stella College, Vijayawada.

K.S. Sunita, Osmania University, Hyderabad.

Pramod K. Nayar, Kuvempu University, Shimoga

B. Gopal Rao, Osmania University, Hyderabad.

Sumita Roy, Osmania University, Hyderabad.

Rama Nair, Osmania University, Hyderabad.

Annie Pothen, Osmania University, Hyderabad.

Alladi Uma, University of Hyderabad, Hyderabad

M. Sridhar, University of Hyderabad, Hyderabad.

G. Tirupathi Kumar, Osmania University, Hyderabad.

Alpha Joseph, Osmania University, Hyderabad.

Tutun Mukherjee, Osmania University, Hyderabad.

Sachidananda Mohanty, University of Hyderabad, Hyderabad.

S. Khalid Qadri, Osmania University, Hyderabad.

Variety No Hierarchy

M. SIVARAMKRISHNA

In the face of the enormous variety and spatial diffusion of Indian poetry in English (IPE hereafter), it is naïve to be—or try to be—comprehensive about the plurality of expressive modes and strategies of absorption. The geographical range itself makes homogeneous Indianness anachronistic. Along with the pioneers based in India, we have the poets from, of course, US and UK but also from Copenhagen, Frankfurt, Nairobi, Fiji, Adelaide. Perhaps what Margery fee felt about the authenticity of the Maori literary tradition sums up the situation: "How do we distinguish biased and oppressive tracts, exploitative popularizations, stereotyping romanticizations, sympathetic identifications, and resistant, transformative visions?"[1]

Part of the problem is demythicised: there is visible receding of the earlier obsession with authentic indigeneity. I think we do not ask if it is Indian: we ask whether it is poetry. The transition is in keeping with global economic plurality: brand names count, diffusion through hype matters but we ask does it work, before we buy. Are we spending precious resources on a real product? I can invoke the insightful insistence of Srinivas Rayaprol, a Hyderabad-based poet, largely ignored since he was hardly expert at the promotional manouevres that you need these days to sell and swell your wares: "I have been asked," he says, "about the Indianness of my poems. And I am puzzled and do not know what to say. I've never thought that a poem required racial characteristics."[2] He admits, though, that the senseless hurt inflicted in Indian ethos affected him.

Nagarjunakonda

And you my father
who did not let me see you then

now face me in your old age
as I feed you with my hands.
Love and pity will not explain
the hurt of my then young pain
and what I feel for you now
is but a token of thanks
for your sperm that gave me root

You my father
that gave me being
can you see me now
as you were then—
strong as these stones?
Or do your tired eyes
see in me the vision of your broken dreams
as I counter my impotence
with your infallibility?

And you old man
hungry yet for the pleasures of life
Lean thy strong body
on my frail arm,
And lust for the world
while I face the shame
of being thy son
full of the love that I cannot share with you.[3]

The poem is called "Nagarjunakonda" the famous Buddhist centre. But it hardly seems to matter to me whether the locale is Indian or not. What does matter is the realised, actualised emotion of—can we call it—the 'Daddy cool' motif?

This brings me to the first of the 'stays' against the obsessive intrusion of indigeneity. If the poem works, it does so because it is just that, a poem. It is a poem not due to but in spite of the poet's ethnicity, his/her cultural specifics, his/her ideology. Perhaps, the classical assumption of *apaurusheya* approximates to this. The text is authorless, it has no signature to help boost the CV for the inevitable disaster of academic promotion. I know the notion is indigenous but it is generic too. The death of the author, perhaps, is a necessary precondition for the poem to move in its own autonomy. If, as Adrienne Rich put it, "language is a map of our failures" then poems are successes to the extent they transcend notions of inviolate individuals and cultures and undefiled foundational languages. Another way to express this is: we can affirm the hinterland of the poem even while questioning it in our appropriation of the poem.

We can cross boundaries at this stage and seek help from Roland Barthes: "The text you write must prove to me *that it desires me*. This proof exists: it is writing. Writing is the science of the various blisses of language, its Kama Sutra (this science has but one treatise writing itself)."[4] The discourse of desire is central to poetry but the centre is quite often questioned in the name of privileging. Perhaps Sudeep Sen's lines come to my rescue in expressing the implicit ambiguity:

> But it is this sacred darkness that endures,
> melting light with desire, desire that simmers
> and sparks the radiance of your
> quiet femininity, as the female dancer
> now illuminates everything visible: clear,
> poetic, passionate, and ice-pure.[5]

One way to get out of the nearly irrepressible urge for magisterial hierarchising is to look at this idea of text as desire closely. It could accommodate several things ranging from the compulsive desire to get good grades in a testing context to the desire to clasp the poem as a lover does the beloved. Often the beloved doesn't yield easily but then one persists. And even if it is hard to crack the apparent resistance, the crack itself may yield a poem: Then we welcome the very torture as prolonged agony, necessary for the eventual and longed for absorption. The predicament is articulated with exasperation but with effectiveness by a Telugu poet about another intolerably difficult, obscure poet:

> Torture us, please,
> impossible poet,
> with your exuberance of stunning words
> and delicious feeling slightly mixed
> with bitter dryness. We need jaws of stone
> to grind the elevated phrases you utter with ease
> as you tease us through your labyrinths,
> books cooked to the texture of rock.[6]

The process is the stock-in-trade of most of us who teach poetry. As Amos Ox, the Israeli writer, put it "Only the pleasure of reading do they castrate—just a bit—so it doesn't get in the way: so that we remember that literature is not playing games, and, in general, that life is no picnic."[7]

I think you can guess my game: covering up the (colonial?) anxiety to make oneself acceptable by quoting authors whom I never met from countries I have remote chances of visiting. That quoting is analogical: it happens quite often in our responses to IPE. So and so has Eliotic preoccupations, Audenesque oddities, Poundian ambiguities and finally the poet wore jeans made in US which were greatly admired! Such comparisons seem to me part of the history of early responses to IPE: we can call it the juvenile delinquency phase. But, this is not denigrating comparisons: the problem is privileging in the name of comparing. But what a poet—an Indian poet—can do with such a context is at variance with what evaluation does with it. An example:

> Let us be going then, me and Baljit,

when the evening is spreadeagling the sky.
Like Mrs. Gandhi etherised by Sikhs;
Let us be going through certain Chandigarh streets,
The Rajneesh retreats
Of restless thighs in all-right ashrams
And stripper coolies with saffron lingerie,
Chanting in sawdust restaurants
With oyster shells, the smell of incense in hallways.

Aré do not be asking "what is it?"
Let us be avoiding Bombay shit.

In the room women coming and going
Talking of Swami Satya Govind

There will be time, there will be time
To time the ball like Sunil Gavaskar;
There will be time to murder a lascar
And time for all the works and days of hands
That lift and drop pakoras on your plate.

HURRY UP SAHIB IT's TIME
To finish the samosas and start the curry.
HURRY UP SAHIB IT'S TIME
Got to marry a woman with a fat dowry.[8]

And so on it goes. A comic and agonising parody of Eliot: the comedy is born out of the agony of the rootlessness of responses to IPE. The situation is comic: maturity of a demonstrable quality in poetry goes along with naivete of reception. Is this some sort of nostalgia for a largely constructed past, constructed ideologically through exclusion undermining the very ground of reception: choiceless awareness which is concentration without elimination? See what Jayanta Mahapatra, "a melancholic modern day dervish," as Keki Daruwalla called him, says:

You say you are a poet;

you sit next to me
and talk to me from a distant country.
Yet your own past is too large
for you to talk sensibly about it.[9]

Two categories of people talk sensibly about the past: poets and mystics. Their modes of discourse are revelatory and visionary. They balance each other, the one revealing what words do not, the other envisioning what the Word underlying the words can. The seventeenth century Telugu poet Vemana put it perfectly:

> Unless words are shed
> the Word is unattainable;
> Until the word itself withers
> the mind remains wayward;
> Unless the mind focusses
> where is freedom?

The poem posits not the rejection of any of the previous frameworks but recommends what Antonio Nicolas called "changing to a transcendent 'viewing' of the world implicit in the internal dynamism of the languages themselves." In short, "a complimentarity of languages is suggested under a transcendent and unifying language; and each language is torn from its opposing demands of exclusivity in language in exchange for a way of viewing and acting in the world which is eternally (*nitya*) efficient."[10]

With due and much deserved disrespect to Derrida, let me be more explicit: the complementarity of Indian languages under the canopy of the evident element of transcendental signifier seems to me a richer way of enjoying IPE. We have poetry in the Indian languages, Indian poetry available in English translation and our own IPE. The correspondences are striking. We have now a situation in which English and Indian languages are comparable to displaced Sanskrit and Indian vernaculars. One can juxtapose the other tongue and the mother tongue to reinforce the prisonhouse of language. Scoring off is common: Dasu Sri Ramulu (1846-1908), the Telugu poet, for instance is too mocking in tone:

The Other Tongue

The village elders gather on the porch of the Rama temple
to recite *Mahabharata* and talk of other things.

"Telugu is a good language," they say.
"This hissing—spitting *Englis*
that our boys are speaking
goes no further than their lips,
even if they pass F.A., B.A., or some other A"[11]

Read in translation, this transcends the insularity of its original production and that, manifestly, is an advantage. But beware of cultural anthropologists for whom all patterns of perception are constructs. Then, the IPE poem and the vernacular poem deconstruct without endless relativism. In spite of variant physical landscapes and mixed myths, often an implicitly strident critique becomes a signal poem. The signalling is all the more enjoyable if it is a woman's voice. Let us take Meena Alexander in English, Jayaprada in Telugu, both women, and Tabish Khair—all three evoking the mythic figure of Draupadi with, expectedly varied stances. Since Meena Alexander is known widely in English let me give Jayaprada's poem in translation first: It's called "That's why they are called Rishis."

When the folds, one by one,
were being stripped
what exactly happened
in Draupadi's mind
the Mahabharata doesn't tell;
married to five persons
how outraged her
fiery, burning body felt

when Keechaka dragged
her by hair defies
Vyasa's correct comprehension;

better to steer the story
towards Dharmaraja, for,
one does not know how
fatal it is fouling
wifely virtue!
And for Vyasa
the archpolitician and the
author of the Mahabharata
is it too difficult
to strangle the story?
That's why they are sages:
wives they do not have,
daughters they do not have;
born in sky vessels
they do not, of course, have
even mothers. (My translation)

Juxtapose it with Tabish Khair's "Dushasana's Temple."

His evil could not be explained.
Dushasana
His name still fire to Indian ears,
echoing beyond Sanskrit to Hindi:
'Dusht'; wicked.

More Iago than Lucifer, he
thrilled in the act —
Disrobing innocence
Dragging helplessness by the hair -
Simply because.
No envy of earth-shaking Bheem,

No lust for Draupadi,

Nothing
But the need for action. Any act.
Even evil.

He was not Ravana
Who would abduct but not rape
For him there were no Gods
To be fought, but absurd
Men—

Who could be tricked at games,
Cheated, bullied, beaten, killed;
Or women who
could be disrobed,
Raped.

Evil and good were garments
That the act wore after
A cleansing bath. Only the living

Had the power
To name;

The only truth was being.
Dushasana,
Unlike Ravana, has no temple
In my all-worshipping land.
His name's an echo.[12]

And Meena Alexander sees Draupadi as a referent for mixed mythic waters resulting in "The Art of Pariahs" the title of the poem:

Back against the kitchen stove
Draupadi sings:

In my head Beirut still burns.

The Queen of Nubia, of God's Upper kingdom
the Rani of Jhansi, transfigured, raising her sword
are players too. They have entered with me
into North America and share these walls.

We make up an art of pariahs:

Two black children spray painted white
their eyes burning,
a white child raped in a car
for her pale skin's sake
an Indian child stoned by a bus shelter,
they thought her white in twilight.

Someone is knocking and knocking
but Draupadi will not let him in.
She squats by the stove and sings:

The Rani shall not sheathe her sword
nor Nubia's Queen restrain her elephants
till tongues of fire wrap a tender blue,
a second skin, a solace to our children

Come walk with me towards a broken wall—
Beirut still burns—carved into its face.
Outcastes all let's conjure honey scraped from stones,
an underground railroad stacked with rainbow skin,
Manhattan's mixed rivers rising.[13]

Looking at the three poems—the obvious way in which they hinge on Draupadi as the nucleus of cultural configurations is striking. Gone are the self-conscious days of Manmohan Ghose and the attempt to provide glossaries for who Draupadi is. The colonial hangovers assume new avatars.

All the three hinge on Draupadi as the nucleus of cultural construct. Two are obviously women's voices but not obtrusively so—though the poem in translation appears a more trenchant critique than Meena Alexander's or Tabish Khair's. But then all the three approximate to poetry of an enduring quality. The linguistic distinction, it seems to me, can hardly be abstracted from the implicit view expressed. The one is inseparable from the other. Moreover, one remarkable feature—particularly in Meena Alexander is the absence of self-consciousness regarding myths. Perhaps, what we have in contemporary IPE are, to use Joseph Campbell's idiom, heroes and heroines with a thousand faces. In retrospect, the self-conscious Manmohan Ghose, seems quaint, even a curio in this sense.

Perhaps, the need is to site IPE in translated texts. Whatever the polemics of translation are, they do not prevent us from enjoying a poem in translation. The implicit logic is interesting: for one who knows the original, the translation is a second sight; for one who does not have access to the original the original is the only sight. Hence, either way, it could be made into a mode to enrich the responses. Situated between languages and cultures, the poem's job is not to mediate but to dramatise. Out of the absence of choosing arise the peculiar pleasures of poetry. The construct of the poem is experiential in its immediate and ultimate concerns. All other considerations are bound to be there provided the poem sticks to its *swadharma*: a language event that turns cultural assumptions upside down only to set them in the right perspective. The right perspective is implicit in the unconscious that the poem uncovers. But to read the poem for absences alone is to miss the presences. It is, for instance, analogous to opening the Pandora's box of ideologies: gender bias, however authentic, can hardly engender a poem. In that case newspaper reports of gender injustices would qualify for poetry.

Meena Alexander does not make or take an explicit view; the Telugu poem seems to do. Khair re-visions the poem to evoke—to put it simplistically—the notion of an immutable self. But whatever the content, the question has to be faced delicately and decisively: ideological underpinnings, unless they form the intricate texture of the *dharma* of a poem, are to that extent sources of propaganda for which versification is an *alamkara*. To be true to itself, the poem has to be the community's sharing of the startling potential of words to explode into triggers of consciousness. A good example is from Arun Kolatkar, the bilingual poet who, interestingly enough, bases his poem on

Old Newspapers

Beware of the old newspapers
Stacked
on that little three-legged stool over there.

Don't disturb them.
I know it for a fact
that snakes have spawned in between those sheets.

Don't even look in that direction
It's not because of the breeze
that their corners are fluttering

It's alive, that nest of newspapers,
New born snakes, coiling and uncoiling,
are turning their hoods to look at you.

That white corner has spread its hood:
A forked tongue
shoots out of its mouth.
Keep your eyes closed.
Get rid of the whole goddam pile
if you want to
in the morning.[14]

The poem, originally in Marathi, is translated by Kolatkar himself. And that brings me to the final aspect I would like to mention. Translation from Indian languages has made available a uniquely significant collection of Bhakti poetry. Kannada *vacha-*

nas, Tamil *Saivaite* hymns, Telugu classics like *Kalahastiswara Mahatyam* (translated as *For the Lord of the Animals*: Hank Heiftz and Velcheru Narayana Rao, Delhi: OUP, 1987) and above all the *sant* tradition of the north—they constitute an astoundingly multi-layered quantum of poetry that turns, as most of us do now, faith and belief upside down. They are adorations in tension with interrogations; iconoclastic they are yet fiery with a faith that is agonisingly uncertain. Working within tradition bound rigidities, they yet dislocate the social hierarchies. In other words, these translated poems offer vantage points to learn for oneself what a poet does with the past as it impinges on his present preoccupations. Perhaps, A.K. Ramanujan puts it best: "A medieval Sanskrit epigram about the past says, 'If you have not read the ancients, how can you write? If you *have* read the ancients, why do you write?' One cuts through the dilemma by translating the past. Translation then participates in our dream of making out of a historical past a contemporary past, creating out of the so-called linear sequential order of history a simultaneous order, an active presence."[15] In short as I put it in my own way in another context, "changed contexts require transformed texts. And the transformation is by translation."[16]

IPE, in this sense needs the site and sight of the poetry of devotion in translation from the Indian languages as a comprehensive frame that accommodates and does not privilege the various dimensions. The very tensions engendered by the use of English are questions so far understood in terms of linguistic choices. They are, it seems, actually choices of interior faith which has several ramifications (e.g. "Prayers to Lord Murugan"). This complex gives us a variety which does away with needless hierarchies. Above all, the body of Bhakti contains passion poetry that is most invigorating to the jaded nerves of glazed eyes fed on celluloid erotic titillation!

To sum up IPE *is*, these days, pleasantly threatening to be poetry first and everything else later. Its far-flung geographical diffusion has made it transcend the image of exotica, of alleged archetypes. Nevertheless, a core of uneasy but perceptible Indianness persists. Its very uncertainty is the poetry. Whatever the modes of faith, it is, in every sense of the word *anuvada*. Thus the need to siting IPE in Indian languages, preferably in translation and Bhakti renaissance offers a cultural paradigm in this regard.

Notes and References

1. Margery Fee, "Who can write as other?" *The Post Colonial Studies Reader*, ed. Bill Ashcroft, et al (London: Routledge, 1995), p. 242.
2. Srinivas Rayaprol, *Selected Poems* (Calcutta: Writers Workshop, 1995), p. 39.
3. *Selected Poems,* p. 36.
4. Roland Barthes. *Selected Writings*, ed. Susan Sontag (Fontana/ Collins, 1983), p. 405.
5. Sudeep Sen, "Bharatanatyam Dancer," *Lines Review.* A Selection presented by Sudeep Sen, ed. Tessa Ransford (Loanhead, Midlothian, 1996), p. 30.
6. *A Poem at the Right Moment: Remembered Verses from Premodern South India*, trans. Veleheru Narayana Rao and David Schulman (Delhi: Oxford Univ. Press, 1999), p. 51.
7. Amos Oz, *The Story Begins: Essays on Literature* (London: Chatto and Windus, 1999), p. 114.
8. Sudesh Mishra, "The Loving Song of R.J. Tangaya," *Lines Review*, p. 24.
9. Jayanta Mahapatra, "1992", *Poetry Review: In Search of Kavita: Poetry from the Indian Subcontinent and Beyond* (Vol. 83, No. 1, Spring 1993), p. 16.
10. Antonio T. de Nicolas, *Meditations through the Rig Veda: Four Dimensional Man*, (NP, 1976), p. 89.
11. *A Poem at the Right Moment—Remembered Verses from Premodern South India,* p. 40.
12. *Lines Review*, p. 38.
13. *Poetry Review*, pp. 58-59.

14. Arun Kolatkar "Old Newspapers", *Periplus. Poetry in Translation*, ed. Daniel Weissbort, Arvind Krishna Mehrotra (Delhi: OUP, 1993), pp. 79-80.
15. *The Collected Essays of A.K. Ramanujan*, ed. Vinay Dharwadker (Delhi: OUP, 1999), p. 189.
16. M. Sivaramkrishna, "Engendering Translation," *Translation: From Periphery to Centre Stage*, ed. Tutun Mukherjee (New Delhi: Prestige, 1998), p. 22.

Of the Lowly Potato: Indian English Poetry Today

JAYANTA MAHAPATRA

If you can get to its essence, even a lowly potato would be poetic. What is remarkable is that poetry can prove it. In India, in the post-independence era, innumerable collections of poetry written in English have appeared from various publishing houses. Certainly more than the volumes of prose that have been published so far. The point is: It is an odd situation, because more bad poetry is being published now than ever before in Indian history. And whereas our fiction has made a decisive impact on literary writing around the world, nothing very significant has been seen in the output of Indian poetry written in English.

The reasons for this would appear to lie in the writing of poetry itself. One sees the evidence of poetry's diminished stature even within the practice of poetry. There are very few magazines in our country that publish poetry today. And even in the ones that do, one's heart sinks to see so many poems crammed so tightly together, like sardines packed in a small can. It would be easy to miss a radiant poem among the many mediocre ones. It takes much effort to read these little magazines with openness and attention. Few people bother, not even the magazine's contributors. The sheer indifference to poetry in the mass media has created a sort of Frankenstein—magazines that publish poetry unwisely, with total indiscretion.

The other characteristic that catches the eye is the overwhelmingly *positive* prose that is being written about published collections of poetry. These reviews or comments and essay do not (I stress, do not) provide an objective perspective on new poetry volumes, which is what is required, but simply publicize them. Quite often there are manifest personal connections between the reviewers (or editors) and the authors they discuss. The unspoken editorial rule seems to be: Do not give negative views; they are, after all, our friends and colleagues, and we cannot afford to hurt them.

The consequence of all this seriously affects the thinking and make-up of the beginner-poet in our country. These emerging poets (and we are full of such writers and readers) are seemingly confused by seeing mediocre poetry praised, or never criticised—and in the long run end up doubting their own critical perceptions. Younger poets, therefore, start emulating the work of these poets, writing in the same manner. This is a dangerous process that has only resulted in betraying the integrity of the art of writing poetry. Very recently I came across an editorial comment in one of our larger circulated weeklies, which stated that a particular collection of poems "was easily the best volume of poems published by an Indian in recent years." This is a strong statement indeed. But made in a casual vein. Statements such as these should be substantiated. Books are read, and ultimately, judged by individuals in the privacy of their own sensibilities, and not by committees who talk about cricket and Kargil and poetry in the same vein. Evaluation is always hard, serious work. And by going about it frivolously, we only demean our own art.

But why should anyone but a poet care about the problems of Indian poetry? What relevance does this archaic art form have to contemporary society? If ours would have been a more tolerant, better world than what it is today, then poetry would have no need to justify itself beyond the sheer splendour of its existence. Does our world vindicate the American poet Wallace Stevens's words that "the purpose of poetry is to contribute to man's happiness?" But perhaps aesthetic pleasure needs no justification, because a life without such pleasure is one not worth living.

Poets are expected to make sense of life. If they find life today in fragments, they must not leave it that way. Perhaps they should have that desire to produce poetry that transcends the ills of modern life rather than poetry that helplessly mirrors them. It is easy for me to say this when I know I am guilty myself of such writing. But I am afraid this is a difficult task to achieve.

Indian poetry in English lacks ideas. Again, I realize this is a foolish statement which leaves much room for error. Let us all agree that our poems are characterized by thinness. Somehow all our poems sound alike. And barring the poems of a few, these poems exhibit a one-dimensionality that reveals their meanings, straightaway. Missing are the many levels of meaning that give strength and intensity to a poem. Do our poets ever attempt in Hardy's phrase, "to touch our hearts by revealing their own?" May be they don't do that.

Sadly, Indian poetry in English does not touch us in our deepest, most enduring self.

I believe our poetry—by this I imply Indian poetry in English—will not be held in high esteem until we explore our writing within the context of a unifying outlook on life. It is easy to make poems that are urged by sporadic, individual responses to things—to write a poem on the potato I mentioned earlier; but perhaps to seek an insight into the potato's mind that is haunted by the sinister density of the earth. Perhaps we never try to seek that experience and perception that make up for what we call the poet's "vision." I do not know how to define these things. But this way of going into the meaning of the insight is more likely to be achieved slowly and naturally as a result of *simply living and responding to things in the world,* of reading and thinking, and in the daily work of writing poems.

Every poet seeks to accomplish something like this in the poems he or she writes, or else he or she would not be able to write at all. But he or she should not build his or her life by finding himself or herself in another country, in another history, or elsewhere. Simply speaking, one's own roots are of the utmost importance although one's work is in English. One of the strengths of poetry in Spanish in our time is that it has not lost contact with the past. Quevedo and Gongora are still living presences for poets in Spain and South America, as they were for Lorca and others of his generation.

It wouldn't be wrong to say that there is a distinct absence of vitality in our poetry. All our competence with words and with craft, with images and metaphors, asks for *substance;* and purpose beyond mere versification is what is called for. Our poetry must be involved with us, with the many lives we live. Perhaps our prose just possesses that; it makes us participate in the myth-processes of our people—and this aspect accounts for its success in the present day.

If we accept the fact that English poetry in India has taken a definite direction today, we could trace its influence to a few poets who were teachers of English literature themselves. Nissim Ezekiel could be considered to lead this poetry movement; he was followed by A.K. Ramanujan, R. Parthasarathy and Shiv K. Kumar, if I would name some. Today, we have a number of younger poets who seem to be influenced by the terse craftwork exhibited by their elders. If we examine these poems, we find an excessive use of wit and irony in them. It is difficult not to notice the distance this poetry reveals, as compared to the poems of poets in the many regional languages of India. Also is evident a lack of musicality in the poems. Somehow I believe that music is the most important virtue in poetry, and this appears to be absent. I will not go into the reasons behind this. But it seems right I should speak about my own experiences in this regard.

In the 50th year of our independence, the British magazine titled *London Magazine* appeared with a special issue with the words "INDIA 1997: with affection" on its cover. This magazine is now in its 39th year and is edited by Alan Ross. A look into this issue gives us an insight into the type of poetry the editor likes to publish. I am afraid I have to admit that the poetry here conforms to the qualities I mentioned earlier. I should like to confess that my poetry didn't find a place in this issue. The fact is: I didn't send my poems for this issue. And if I had sent my work, I am certain the editor would have rejected my poems, as he had done twice before, twenty years back. The ironic mode has never suited me, and I have chosen to write what I wrote, straight from my heart. Maybe this isn't good, well-crafted poetry—the poetry I write. I could never respond to the sight of Nandi in the manner a poem "Pashupatinath" goes on to depict the scene (pp. 178-79).

> A bull of beaten gold
> balanced on balls
> so large they dwarfed
>
> the nesting crowds.
> With hands full of money,
> flowers and prayers,
>
> our unruly lines
> mobbed the priest.

Or, as in the poem "One or Two Places" on page 63 of the issue:

> If you love your country, he said,
> why are you here?
> Say, I am tired of hearing about
>
> all that wonder that was India
> kind of crap.

And incidentally, I remember Alan Ross, the editor, having written me on a 5 cm by 10 cm rejection slip, when he had returned my poems, that my work was unsuitable for publication because it tended to be philosophic. My own writing has always reflected an Oriya sensibility and I have felt myself to be an

Oriya poet who happened to write in English. I suppose our sensibility, the Indian sensibility, is different from the Western one, and this fact stands in the way of the Western reader. This is an area where space and time, sound and silence, motion linear and cyclic, word and symbol, become one—and one is unable to distinguish between them. Or perhaps the Indian mind turns its antennae toward the unknown, the *beyond*; making the resulting poetry lose its concreteness, and the verse becomes dependent on suggestions of meaning. This is one reason why some of my work comes back from editors of foreign journals.

However, it was in the eighties or early nineties that a change was seen in much of the English poetry written in India. The discerning reader no longer wanted to read merely a well-crafted poem of an Indian poet in English, a poem which could have come as well from the pen of a poet living in Britain or Australia. Neither was the poet interested only in the dry wit and irony most Indian English poems exhibited. The prevailing poetry scene was witnessing a subtle change. Poets, younger poets, from various parts of the country were coming out with their poems; suddenly, English poems were being written differently in Kerala, in the Northeast, and in my own state of Orissa. It was the native culture showing in the poem of the Indian English poet. It was a poetry which eased itself from the earth the poet inhabited, nurtured and nourished by the soil and the air of the place. There was a distinct sense of belonging; it couldn't be mistaken:

On a warm day at the start of spring
men in the fields feel winter
melting in their blood too,

they smell the seed of ripeness in the air
and nod to each other happily,
or take up the children, kiss their

dusty heads and let them go again.

Evening comes. Everything happens naturally
as leaves closing, or the breaking of stars,

hesitant and white, as if long ago somebody
was hurt by their pleasure.

Or, as in this poem:

We heard whatever is not lost.
We speak of a mythic time.
Let us speak of what we found:
In the place of gold-dust we found still
golden ears of rice beneath that copper haze
of dying years, dancing to the valley's
wind-borne music;
beacons of wild fires we saw on dry autumn nights,
mountains signalling the fates of trees and grass.
Instead of pages of heroic deeds or undying love,
we read parchments written in blood, our history
stained by illicit love and betrayal;
we found our alphabet buried with the shrunken heads
of enemies, ghosts who died long ago laughing
at the attempts at civilization.

Here, at last, the poet is speaking to me. This is poetry one likes to read, to hear. A poetry that should last.

The Society of the Indian English Poem

MOHAN RAMANAN

I have chosen a theme which was dear to Jonathan Raban, who spoke of the society of the poem in a well-known book. What I mean by society is that there is an internal coherence in the tradition and one can see the whole tradition as basically united by common concerns, motifs, techniques and attitudes. There is a view of Indian English poetry which looks upon it as spurious and inauthentic. Proponents of this view are certain that it is only in fiction that our writers have done well. Poetry at best has been a peripheral activity and in any case the output of significant verse in the tradition is quite thin. I agree that in terms of bulk the tradition is not large—our novelists have done better and continue to do well, but if poetry as Roy Harvey Pearce put it, is an interior signature of a culture, the quintessential expression of the life of a community, these Indian English poets have definitely captured the nuances of a particular class of society having to do with English educated people in India. I am constrained to bring in this notion of English educated people, Aijaz Ahmed would term it a 'collectivity', because writing in English does have a limiting quality. This limitation is felt in fiction where the very expansiveness of the genre brings out the limitations dramatically. Take the question of caste. When, to give one recent example only, Rohinton Mistry writes about caste in *A Fine Balance*, one simply does not get a sense of the nuances of social relations in rural India, or for that matter any idea of where in India the particular characters are located. When he is talking of Bombay or of Parsi life, Mistry is inward and on strong ground. On caste he is out of his depth. Writing in English (and I am now thinking of English both as a language and an ideology) brings on this inauthenticity. Compare this with an English translation of U.R. Anantha Murthy's *Bharatipura* and we immediately sense the difference. Here there is specificity and particularity of apprehension. It has surely something to do with the fact that Anantha Murthy was writing in Kannada. However, the fact that there was this quality of specificity in an English translation, though not in a novel written originally in English, has its own story to tell. English it seems to me *can* be a fit medium for true expression, but then Indian English writers must have that sensibility and vision in the first place. It is my view that though Indian English poetry is limited in scope and cannot express 'India' and her 'fragments', the 'nation' and its 'collectivities' in a grand epic sweep, it has nevertheless in its modest way, in its occasional lyric outbursts, in its small poems, expressed the deep structures of thought and feeling of a specific class of Indians who speak to a specific audience. This audience is middle class, and comprises Indians who have been educated in English and who know the language well. This coherence, I believe, makes for the unity of the tradition, a unity underscored by recurrent motifs, concerns and attitudes.

Of late some people are reviving that old belief that the experiments with 'Indian' themes done by nineteenth century writers like Toru Dutt or Madhusudan Dutt, or later ones like Sri Aurobindo and Sarojini Naidu have greater value than the work of the modernists like Ezekiel, Ramanujan and Parthasarathy. It is tempting to accept this and indeed the work of these 'seniors' is noteworthy. That 'slip of a girl', to use Professor Narasimhaiah's catchy expression, Toru, did galvanize our poetry by resorting to Indian myths, legends and folklore. Her sonnet on the Lotus is a classic case in point. And surely Madhusudan Dutt's English poems with their epic sweep before he began to do wonders in Bengali cannot be ignored. Sri Aurobindo's theory and practice of 'mantric' poetry has resonances for anyone at all deeply engaged with the spiritual life. And can anyone mistake the pleasurable jingle of the much anthologized Naidu poems? I cannot agree with Arvind Krishna Mehrotra's dismissive remarks about either Sri Aurobindo or Sarojini Naidu. It is a measure of the arrogance and superciliousness of Mehrotra, and I think he represents a particular class of 'secular' 'English' intellectuals, that *Savitri* can be dismissed as a 'worthless epic of 24000' lines. Mehrotra's poem to Bharat Mata surely is no substitute for the harmonies and metaphysical stirrings of *Savitri*. However, having acknowledged this, one must point out that the real problem with our seniors was the use to which they put the English language. They tended to be 'romantic', gushy, florid and fond of the large gesture—qualities we in our time do not much care for. Professor Nadkarni speaking on Sri Aurobindo recently made some amusing references to the 'lean and hungry' poetry of the modernists and though he intended this pejoratively he indeed is able to point to a real strength. For a moment I shall ignore the narrow and restricted 'vision', if it can be called that, of the 'modernists' and concentrate on the quality of their language. There is, in my opinion, much virtue in being 'lean and hungry'. For purposes of contrast here are two passages:

I She sat upon her palfrey white,
    That damsel fair and young,
And from the jewelled belt she wore,
    Her trusty rapier hung;
And chieftains bold, and warriors proud,
Around her formed a gallant crowd.

II Add now, at thirty-nine to the old old fear
    of depths and heights,
    I father in the bedroom,
            insects, iodine
                    in the eye,
sudden knives and urchin laughter
    in the redlight alley,

add now
the men in line
behind my daughter.

The first passage is from the quaint poetry of Hur Chunder Dutt. The poem is entitled "Tarra Baee", who is the Princess of Bednore and who is fighting for her land taken away by Lilla, the Afghan, from her father Sootan. The Romantic atmosphere is apparent in the description which instead of giving us 'inscape', to use Hopkins' well-known idea, gives us adjectival excess, circumlocutory collocations and a heavy musky fragrance of an unreal world. The images used are stock ones from Romanticism–'palfrey,' 'rapier,' 'jewelled belt' and so forth. Compare that with the sinewy strength of the Ramanujan lines in my second passage. Ramanujan has sharp edges to his poem which is about identity and the stripping of masks and illusions. Clearly for us in the modern age this toughness is preferable and I am quite unabashedly with the Imagists who want the poet to feel his thoughts, give concepts concrete expression, and poetry itself a material substantiveness, free from sentimental gush or imprecision.

I do not wish to be misunderstood. It might appear that my position is not different from P. Lal's when he attacked Sri Aurobindo's apparent imprecision and mystic obscurity. I understand Lal's position but he chose the wrong example for his attack. H.R. Dutt would have been a better candidate for his attack than Sri Aurobindo whose mystic poetry has a specificity only an initiate can recognize. Lal is guilty of a gross error of judgement and this is particularly surprising in one whose own poetry has mystic and metaphysical longings. Indeed in some ironic way I would look at Lal as Aurobindonian—an important aspect of the coherence I am talking about. Here is Lal's excellent rendering of one verse of the *Teja-Bindu Upanishad*:

Brahman:
The All

The Supreme
The Full Void
The Nothing-Beyond
The Unimaginable
The Beyond-Consciousness

This is not to say
that devotees of truth
do not know the truth
of the nature of Brahman

This is not to say
that the gods do not know
the nature of the Supreme

Expressions like 'supreme', 'void', 'consciousness', 'truth' are-exactly what Sri Aurobindo would use. Admittedly this is a translation but Lal's point against Sri Aurobindo was that he was obscure in his mystic world. In fact Sri Aurobindo is using such expressions in as concrete a way as it is possible to use it in the field of discourse of the Oversoul, and Lal's own translation is of that order.

There are other Aurobindonians in the tradition. Take these lines from Amal Kiran (K.D. Sethna) who is a devotee of Sri Aurobindo but whose poetry, one will find once one has entered the field of consciousness, learned, allusive and superb:

What country shall I take as mine? Iran
  Is but the perfume of a rose long dead;
While India that has moulded me a man
  Whose heart goes throbbing with a sunset red
And straining towards a mystery beyond eyes
  Makes deeper yet the homelessness of me.
I move a stranger whose horizon flies
  Hither and thither, settles on no sea.

Guarding and lulling one dear land alone.

Fire-cult that neighboured the Greek world of thought
Burns through my Persian blood to Europe's large
Earth-richness, India's infinite Unknown
Lures up the same fire-cry-both stay uncaught.
My country's a future where all dreamlights merge.

There is, what Matthew Arnold describing great poetry called, benignity, largeness and, I may add, a quality of vision here which lifts Sethna's poetry to Aurobindonian heights. This is poetry which consoles us and sustains us.

One could multiply such instances. Indeed I wonder at the plentitude of the Aurobindonian strain in our poetry when everything around us seems to promote a godless secularism. I shall leave out, only for lack of space, consideration of the verse of poets like Prem Kirpal or Subrahmanyam or K. Srinivasa Sastry and simply note that Kamala Das is a poet who rises to Aurobindonian heights in her Annamalai poems. In these poems she is evoking her sense of the formless Brahman and she brings it off with considerable control over her medium. She is a deeply religious poet and while her love poems to Krishna in the mode of our Bhakti tradition are an important part of her oeuvre, I do believe that in the later Annamalai poems her intimations of spirituality are tenderly dealt with. Here is an example.

Beyond the bone and the marrow
into that invisible abode of pain,
yes that deathless creation tethered to yourself,
and constantly struggling to wrest itself free,
tethered to your soul
as your shadow is to your form
your siamese twin no surgeon can cut away from you.

If the Aurobindonian strain is a major source of continuity, I must also add that the 'modernist' strain in conscious opposition to the Aurobindonian has given Indian poetry in English a 'voice,' to use M.K. Naik's distinction between 'voice' and 'echo.' Modernity is both a question of technique and attitude. To a large extent modernists like Ezekiel, Ramanujan and Parthasarathy, the three 'seniors', followed by Daruwalla, and Mehrotra, have cultivated the ironic, less deceived, dry and witty style. It is a poetry of wit, symmetry, intellect and ratiocination and all of these have a concern for the well polished image. Here is Ramanujan's "Self Portrait":

> I resemble everyone
> but myself, and sometimes see
> in shop-windows,
>   despite the well-known laws
>   of optics,
> the portrait of a stranger,
> date unknown,
> often signed in a corner
> by my father.

Here I think questions of identity, illusion and reality, parental authority and rebellion against it are all held in check by a superb spareness of cerebral writing, not lacking though in metaphorical force.

Another example is Ezekiel's lines in "A Poem of Dedication":

> There is a landscape certainly, the sea
> Among its broad realities, attracts
> Demoniac life within,
> Hardly suggested by the surface facts . . .

The pressure of inner life is captured through symbol, but Ezekiel is aware of the illusions in reading and as he puts it he is able to see better when he closes his eyes. Not sight, but insight is what he has.

The same coolness and unsentimentality is seen in Daruwalla's descriptions of scenes. Here is "Night Fishing":

A shorelamp drops
its lighted tackle.
On the hook
no fish-snout spin.
Night fishing
sad as night rain
alone as the mind
before the dreams crowd in.

Poets of the 'modernist' variety attempt to craft poems with imagistic precision. This tradition clearly is a dominant one and to a large extent the society of Indian poetry in English has been strengthened by this modernist strain, providing as it does a balance to the romanticism and metaphysical strain of the older poets, both in terms of a balance and a contrast.

I do not, of course, imply that all modernists are the same. I am only concerned here with large strokes of the brush, with delineating prominent trends which offer continuity of the tradition and perpetuation of the society of Indian English poetry. Clearly there is much difference in the wit and irony of an Ezekiel or a Ramanujan and the somewhat pared down writing of a Parthasarathy or the more expansive writing of a Mahapatra. Indeed Mahapatra who likes to call himself an Oriya writer who happens to be using English is given to mixing the abstract with the concrete, the philosophical generalization with the concrete apprehension of these generalizations. Here is "Hands":

Between them
a silence occupies the whole place.

Slowly my body has walked
into deep water.

As a boy I learned to come in
by the back door. Sad
houses now, clean and leaning
against one another, full of sleep.

My old rag elephant is
smothered with small screams.
From the dark surface,
waving like grass–
when the last boat crosses the lake.

This is a good exemplification of what I think is Mahapatra's characteristic style. But on balance we can put Mahapatra into the 'modernist' slot and link him to that strain in the tradition. There are other variations too. Mehrotra can combine passionate social verse in "Bharat Mata" with witty and taut writing and the poem of occasional lyric intensity. Saleem Peeradina who in a line about Bandra–"your mud is versatile"–came up with a beauty, is a poet of domesticity and personal feeling. Paranjape writes of love in terms of Siva and Krishna, one austere, the other gay in abandonment. Hoshang Merchant writes of male bonding and is the author of several volumes of poetry, making him a major contemporary voice. Menka Shivdasani and Eunice de Souza, to mention only two women poets provide a gendered critique of life. And the tradition gets sustained by these medley of voices.

An important aspect of the coherence I am talking about is the link between the 'seniors' and some of the recent poets, representatively put together in Sudeep Sen's *Lines Review*. One way of seeing this continuity is to look at things from the perspective of the binary relationship of 'Home' and 'Abroad'. An important theme in 'modernist' verse was the idea of home, with Ramanujan, Ezekiel, Parthasarathy and others constantly seeking a return to roots. The post-modernists, for so I consider Sudeep Sen and his poets, are equally concerned with this idea, but home for them is often abroad. Many of the poets in Sen's anthology are diasporic, others divide their time between India and abroad like Sen himself. Life and reality for these writers is comfortable whether it is in Delhi or Tokyo, San Francisco or Suva in Fiji. They are at home in the world. If anything distinguishes these poets from the modernists it is that they no longer agonize about home and abroad. A related concern is the use of English by these poets. The seniors did have some tension in using the language, witness the protestations of Ramanujan and Parthasarathy at any rate. The new writers use English with facility and felicity and they do not agonize about it in the least. They write about books, authors, monuments and a host of things and they are clever and artful. Elsewhere I have called Sudeep Sen an artful dodger but the description would fit many others like Ranjit Hoskote or Sudesh Mishra because of their cleverness with language, the brilliant surfaces of their poems and the quality of slickness and suavity in their writing. One might worry about their lack of depth and profundity—the seniors had this—but then these new and young poets gleefully participate in a post-modernist carnival.

A final point about language and I am done. Ramanujan speaks of English, linguistics and anthropology providing the outer forms of his poetry and his multiple native heritage of Kannada, Tamil, the classics and folklore, providing him the inner form. This seems true of many writers in Indian English and one has only to invoke the names of Mahapatra (Oriya poet who happens to use English), Kolatkar (whose native Marathi pressures his English verse), Agha Shahid Ali (whose Urdu gives his poems a multiple and layered texture), to realize that finally Indian poetry in English is as much about English as it is about native speech and sensibility. This realization is perhaps the most potent factor in keeping this tradition alive and in providing the reading public with a steady output of poetry truly Indian in every respect. Far from seeing decline I should pronounce a valediction forbidding mourning.

Midnight's [Grand] Children: Post-Independence Indian Poetry in English

SUDEEP SEN

Arvind Krishna Mehrotra, poet and editor of *The Oxford Indian Anthology of Twelve Modern Indian Poets*, in a 'Writer At Work' feature in *Gentleman* magazine wrote: "In the author's note to [Jorge Luis Borges's] collection, *The Book of Sand* (1977), he remarked, 'I write for myself and for my friends, and I write to ease the passing of time.' [Many] would have found in Borges's remark much to agree with. This is not to suggest that writing is the only thing a writer does. Indeed, famously so, he has been known to work as an efficient librarian, or as a bank clerk, or in advertising, and he also raises a family and does not allow his insurance policy to lapse. But writing is what animates his days and holds their disparateness together. More exactly, it's the desire to write, which manifests itself only too rarely, in the desired poem. With a mixture of fear and hope, it's what he wakes up to every morning, and as another morning turns into another night, it's what he measures the time by. Without it his life would go to pieces. That it still goes to pieces is another story, one that modern biographers tell with increasing candour."

If we were to examine the terrain of modern Indian poetry in English that forms the interior and exterior landscape of writers born in the post-independence India, one would also have a lot to agree with Mehrotra's piece. Moreover, this succinct piece strips aside any ivory-tower illusion or garret-struck stereotypes some people tend to hold about poetry and poets, surprisingly even in these modern times, more than fifty years after India's independence.

The 1980s was certainly the decade for the 'Modern Indian Novel in English', but the 1990s from all worthwhile published evidence was the decade for 'Modern Indian Poetry in English'. Without doubt, Vikram Seth's novel-in-verse, *The Golden Gate* (1986), marked the watershed for the modern movement in Indian poetry. Not only does the book figure on the center-stage of the New Formalist movement in America, but its prodigious success, followed by an even more overwhelmingly successful novels, *A Suitable Boy* (1995) and *An Equal Music* (1999), has put new Indian writing and poetry on the international map.

The contemporary English-language Indian poetry scene has never been so prolific in its energy and innovation, just as much as it has been in its output (at least as far as the number of excellent volumes that have been published by mainstream publishers are concerned). Added to this, a sizeable number of good poetry collections have emerged from reputed small presses. This is true not only for India, but also for the broad Indian Diaspora—USA and Canada, the UK, the Caribbean, Southeast Asia, the South Pacific, and East & South Africa.

Corroborating all that, the success and interest in Indian writing in English (though so far primarily in fiction), both nationally and internationally, coupled with an ever-increasing audience of book buyers and a new-found interest of the mainstream media, have all contributed to this rather welcome situation. It is especially heartening for the health of poetry, as it has finally spilled out from the closet and graduated to a more widespread audience of readers.

India is the third largest English-language publishing market in the world after America and the United Kingdom. Therefore, it is not unusual that a national interest in indigenous contemporary English writing has been firmly established and is steadily making its presence felt internationally.

In 1976, Oxford University Press (India) published the landmark anthology, *Ten Twentieth Century Indian Poets,* edited by R. Parthasarathy. Sixteen years later, in part to update that volume, OUP-India put out a new anthology, *Twelve Modern Indian Poets,* edited by A.K. Mehrotra. This 1992 anthology retained five poets (Nissim Ezekiel, Jayanta Mahapatra, A.K. Ramanujan, Arun Kolatkar, Keki Daruwalla) from the 1976 volume, dropped Shiv K. Kumar, R. Parthasarathy, Kamala Das, Gieve Patel, and unfortunately rather modestly, Mehrotra himself. Seven poets who found their way into the newer volume include: Dom Moraes, Dilip Chitre, Eunice de Souza, Adil Jussawalla, Agha Shahid Ali, Vikram Seth and Manohar Shetty.

The difference between the two anthologies lay ostensibly in its editorial point of view, and the selection of its poets and poems. Apart from Seth and Shetty, both contain only the first generation Indian English-language poets, i.e. poets who were born in the 1920s, 30s, and 40s. The whole generation of newer poets, those who are born primarily in the post-independence India of the 1950s and 60s, are absent. However, Mehrotra does admit at the end of his introduction that "there certainly is room for a larger, more comprehensive selection, one that will include poets . . . who are virtually unknown . . . and younger poets."

But what is refreshing about the second anthology is Mehrotra's candour, his astute comments on poetics and prosody, and his clear unflinching critical observations. "Much of the poetry... written between 1825 and 1945 [in India], is truly dead," asserted Mehrotra in his introduction to his anthology. Sheaves and sheaves have been published much of it unmemorable, on the history of modern Indian poetry in English which many believe has its early origins almost two hundred years back with people like Michael Madhusudan Dutt, Henry Derozio, Toru Dutt, Aurobindo Ghose and Sarojini Naidu. They "were courageous and perhaps charming men and women," writes Mehrotra, "but not those you could today do business." He goes further to say that, "the origins of modern Indian poetry in English go no further back than the poets in this anthology." In as much as it represents the older and middle generation Indian poets, this anthology is extremely competent but the post-Independence generations go largely unmapped. It is the latter that I'm primarily concerned with in this piece.

This essay surveys poetry in English by Indian poets born after 1950, the year India became a republic. Majority of the poets live in India, a few reside both in India and abroad, and the others live abroad though their work is known in India as well as in their country of residence. The fifteen poets featured in this essay/review include: Meena Alexander, Bibhu Padhi, Vikram Seth, Rukmini Bhaya Nair, Prabhanjan Mishra, Manohar Shetty, Imtiaz Dharker, Vinay Dharwadker, Vijay Seshadri, Sujata Bhatt, C.P. Surendran, Jeet Thayil, Vijay Nambisan, Tabish Khair, and Ranjit Hoskote.

Earlier this decade, I was separately commissioned by *Poetry Review* (UK) and *World Literature Today* (USA), to do exhaustive pieces on 'The New Generation/ New Poetry' for their special Indian issues. I scoured and waded through over two hundred volumes of new poetry (as well as journals). In the end, I short-listed about forty collections (by nearly thirty poets), predominantly from India, and a selection from the broad India diasporas who had produced good, substantial poetry. In an attempt to present the true pulse of new Indian poetry, I was to a certain extent, fairly generous in including a reasonable cross-section from an infinitely diverse group.

Looking back with considered retrospection, taking into account the interim years since then, and having further rummaged diligently through innumerable more volumes by newer or younger Indian poets who have published since then, I would make certain additions and deletions to that original list. There are poets who I would drop and others I would add, poets who have emerged since or who were for some technical reason or the other not included in the earlier pieces. But as far as some of the larger issues are concerned (as well as specific comments on previously published volumes), I have drawn upon the observations from my earlier two essays, especially on aspects which have remained unchanged since then.

The Indian mainstream commercial publishers spurred primarily by the international success of Indian novelists such as Salman Rushdie, Vikram Seth, Amitav Ghosh, Upamanyu Chatterjee, Shashi Tharoor, Bharati Mukherjee, Amit Chaudhuri, Sunetra Gupta, Vikram Chandra, Arundhati Roy, and others, enthusiastically entered the arena of creative writing publishing in a big way, first fiction, and then poetry.

As regards poetry, Rupa, and Harper Collins, certainly led the field in capitalising on the new poetry scene at the beginning of the decade. In 1991, the first year when Rupa launched the New Poetry series, they published six titles, followed by another half a dozen the next year, with a similar number the year after. Their emphasis (for the most part) has been on truly young talents rather than middle-aged writers touted as young. Viking Penguin have been more tentative in terms of what one expects of a major publisher. They primarily stuck to the established safe bets like Moraes and Seth, except for two two-poet volumes and a few first-books. Orient Longman under their Disha Books imprint (marketed in the UK as Sangam Books) have yielded four new collections and an anthology. The Oxford University Press (India) list remains conservative publishing a couple of older poets now and then, though they did add one new poet to their list. Ravi Dayal (formerly of OUP) has published two titles under his own imprint. As a postscript however, one has to say that especially in the last few years, the mainstream publishers have significantly cut back their poetry lists.

Among the small presses—Aark Arts, Har Anand, Konark, Praxis, DC Books and Seagull—deserve mention. The Writers Workshop in Calcutta continues to spew out sari-wrapped handbound volumes with more efficiency than a motorised modern press. One wishes that they concentrated on quality rather than quantity. Of course, there is no denying that P. Lal's press is of historical importance because he published many of the older and middle generation poets at a time when no one else was publishing poetry, especially in 1970s.

In what seems like a perfect or neat closure for the century, like the early 90s, the last year of the millennium has seen the publication of a dozen new books of English poetry.

The most striking feature of the post-independence generation of poets is their range of concerns, themes, and the use of language. They use English as an Indian as well as a global language, without the "peculiar hang-ups" many in the earlier generations had, whose work went "under many ludicrous names—Indo-English, Indian-English, Indo-Anglian, and even Anglo-Indian and Indo-Anglican" (A.K.Mehrotra). Thankfully, the last traces of archaic forms of British English have finally vanished. The new generation poets are unafraid, motivated, clear-sighted, and they use English with a sense of ease. Their language, style, rhythms and forms are inventive, original, and contemporary.

Even the poetic climate among fellow younger poets seems to be changed. No longer are the dividing lines between different camps and centres (Delhi, Bombay, Orissa, the North-East) starkly demarcated or distinct; no longer are the antagonism or group loyalties so severe. A fairly professional and keen 'friends in war' attitude seems to prevail among the younger poets from different cities (or indeed, other parts of the world). In my personal experience, the poets of my own generation seem relatively open, supportive and interested in each other's work, at the same time possessing an acute sense of vibrant criticism.

Even some of the older-generation poets are now rather forthcoming and encouraging and treat the young poets as colleagues in the same trade. This is a marked difference from the earlier attitudes of some of the older writers, who possessed a condescending attitude toward younger practitioners. Many of them then were busy praising and publishing one other—i.e., writers of their own generation—with the result that from the mid-70s to about late-80s, hardly any new work by young poets was allowed to flower. Some who did publish consistently were publishing abroad. For an average young Indian poet, however, the task was an arduous one: first, the general lack of support; then the exorbitant process of sending poems to journals abroad, as there were very few journals or poetry publishing outlets in India and fewer still that were not controlled by the older mafia. Even the anthologies edited by different poets that appeared in the last couple of decades contained more or less the same retinue of poets, with very few, if any, young poets represented.

Contemporary poetry criticism, by and large, has been a weak spot in Indian literature. The material on this subject that has come out, published mainly by poet/editors has either been self-congratulatory or absolutely servile vis-a-vis the compilers' peers within the mafia. Poetry reviewing is in great danger because many of the reviewers operate within the ever-increasing context of 'pop-journalism'. Many of them are general journalists reviewing a film one day, a fashion show the next, and a volume of poems the third. Most seem to lack the knowledge of craft and nuances that goes to form a basic poem, and often times the articles tend to be gossipy rather than critical. Of course I can think of exceptions, though only very few, like Arvind Krishna Mehrotra, Adil Jussawalla, Ranjit Hoskote, Rajeev Patke, Sudesh Mishra, and a few others, who do it with precision and rhythm. In the end it seems a poet is usually the best reviewer of poetry (as long as he maintains the poem as the primary text and keeps his personal jealousies and dislikes aside).

Teaching of contemporary poetry is another weakness both in schools and in the universities. Whereas the teaching of 'classic poets' belonging to the 'Eng Lit Canon' like Milton, Shakespeare, Spenser, Donne, and Wordsworth is of high calibre (albeit in a strictly academic sense), the actual aspect of craft and prosody is almost always left out. In terms of modern poetry, my experience as an undergraduate at the University of Delhi left me utterly frustrated. T.S. Eliot was as modern as the syllabus got, as if to say that nothing worthwhile had been written in the post-Eliot era.

It is time to redraw the literary map of India and Indian poetry. Certainly of late there has been an ever-increasing interest in the poetry from the sub-continent. New anthologies have appeared: Kaiser Haq's in America, Vilas Sarang's, Ramanujan/ Dharwadkar's and Mehrotra's in India, and I am working on one that will appear in India, England and elsewhere. Bruce King's recently revised and enlarged *Oxford Modern Indian Poetry in English* that appears in 2000 does some justice to the post-independence generation.

More and more special issues (or sections) of magazines and journals are being or have been devoted to Indian writing and poetry: *Acumen, Ambit, Agenda, Granta, London Magazine, Poetry Review, Wasafiri* in England; *Lines Review* in Scotland; *Ariel, Toronto South Asian Review* and *The Malahat Review* in Canada; *Chicago Review*, *Nimrod, World Literature Today*, and *New Letters* in the USA. In addition, I am currently on commission to guest edit a portfolio of contemporary Indian poetry for *The Paris Review* and *The Literary Review* in the US.

With all this historical background in perspective, let us sample some Indian English-language post-independence poets who have published in the recent years:

Meena Alexander (b.1951) brings to her work a varied range of landscapes—India, Sudan, England, America—as well as a strong sense of being a woman and the issues that arise from being a minority/ black poet in a primarily white American community. Her first book *Stone Roots* appeared many years back in 1980. She has since then published a book of criticism, a novel, and a memoir.

Her newer poetry is available in the form of two pamphlets, *The Storm* (1989) and *Night Scene: The Garden* (1992). Both these work as companion long poems—the first relating to the tearing down of her father's house (to be replaced by a new one), and the second is about her mother's home. Both these houses are located in the landscape of her childhood in Kerala, only twelve miles from each other.

'After the First House', the opening poem in *The Storm,* begins with a mix of drama and sadness:

> Father's father tore it down
> heaped rosewood in pits
> as if it were a burial
>
> bore bits of teak
> and polished bronze
> icons and ancient granary;
>
> the rice grains clung
> to each other
> soldered in sorrow,
>
> syllables
> on grandmother's tongue
> as she knelt.

Alexander's poems tend to have a languorous feel about them. She uses the sequence-form to build scene after scene—weaving characters with feelings that gradually heighten the further you travel with her. Myth, language, warfare, all collide, "And in the empty hold of air/whispers of children born into this garden" closes the *Night Scene.*

In *River and Bridge* (1995), it is again in the long-poem form, as evidenced in the poem 'San Andreas Fault', that we see Alexander's greatest strength. Here is the opening stanza: "It was too hard to remember/ each grass blade, each burn/ of cloud in the monsoon sky/ each catamaran's sail".

Bibhu Padhi (b. 1951) is a poet who uses language with strength and originality. His first book, *Going to the Temple* (1998) reveals his poetic talent amply. In the 'Indian Evening' he shows how well one can handle local colour with subtlety without getting messy or prosaic or deliberately Indian:

Its quiet puts us in touch
with creatures of dust and heat.

The crows fly about the pale sky
with a homely noise,

while the gods float by effortlessly
with the first evening chants.

There is peace here, regardless
Of every single, separate pain.

His second book, *Lines from a Legend* (1992), and his third, *A Wound Elsewhere* (1992), appearing almost back to back, confirmed his strengths further. Padhi's concerns range from the local Cuttack winter to America, and from peculiarities of power-cut in the summer to a dead sparrow. Some of his best poems are ones where he uses sparse couplets, such as in the 'Trees', 'Pigeons', 'I Hear a Small Voice Speaking', 'Footprints', and, 'The Farther Shore'. Taste, for instance, the first half of 'Pigeons':

They embody a consciousness
that shines among light-grey rocks.

In their bodies old stories of flight
repeat themselves, refresh memory.

During the long Indian afternoons
they rest upon our polished floors,

their bodies refracting the warmth
of close contact, their small heads

forming a community of wisdom

His next book, *Painting the House,* is forthcoming, and one looks forward to more pleasure from his quill. Padhi's individual signature, his deft handling of language, and his quiet sensibility, all add to make up a distinctive voice, one that is very much his own.

Vikram Seth (b. 1952) is one of the very few contemporary authors, who with every new book, tries something different—travelogue (*From Heaven Lake)*, novel in verse (*The Golden Gate),* pure poetry *(Mappings, The Humble Administrator's Garden, All You Who Sleep Tonight)*, children's verse *(Beastly Tales),* play, poetry translation *(Three Chinese Poets)*, two prose novels *(A Suitable Boy* and *An Equal Music)*, and libretto (*Arion and the Dolphin)*. His choice of genres, as is evident, spans the whole literary spectrum, and each one with his unique signature and a definite formal necessity. *The Golden Gate* was set in tetrameter Onegin sonnet-stanzas, the play in alexandrine couplets, and not entirely unbelievable, Seth is contemplating writing his dissertation in economic demography in sestinas.

Since all his other books have been reviewed widely, I'll take up the least-discussed of his poetic oeuvre, *Three Chinese Poets* (1992). This volume contains new translations of poets in the period between 701 and 770 in China—Wang Wei, Li Bai, and Du Fu—three Tang Dynasty poets who lived in the period of "great cultural glory interrupted by a disastrous civil war" during the eight century A.D. This triumvirate of lyric poets, even though they share the same period in history, are very different in their sensibility.

Wang Wei is a poet of introspection and seeks recluse in the quietude of nature:

Empty hills, no man in sight –
Just echoes of the voice of men.
In the deep wood reflected light
Shines on the blue-green moss again. ('Deer Park')

Li Bai's (or Li Po in older transliterations) poems on the other hand are full of energy and show, his canvas is wide ranging and grand. Bai's indulgence in epicurean delights invites the vastness of the galaxy, as 'The Waterfall at Lu Shan' plunges three thousand feet "As if the sky had dropped the Milky Way". Elsewhere, he drinks with the moon as his company:

> A pot of wine among the flowers.
> I drink alone, no friend with me.
> I raise my cup to invite the moon.
> He and my shadow and I make three
>
> ('Drinking Alone with the Moon')

Du Fu (or Tu Fu) writes poems that are reflective and sometimes sad, commenting on the Confucian times with "wry self-deprecation." In the changing political climate of the time, he reminiscences "I've heard it said Changan is like a chessboard, where/ Failure and grief is all these hundred years have brought. . . . My ancient land and times of peace come to my thoughts." ('An Autumn Meditation').

Seth's translations are fresh, precise, and moving, adding to the worthy list of works by other important translators like Gill Holland, David Hawkes, and Pauline Yu, and of course Jeanne Larsen's *Brocade River Poems* of the Tang Dynasty.

In 1995, a sort of 'collected poems' appeared under the title, *The Poems: 1981-1994* that included all his 'pure' poetry. But Seth's newer poems can be accessed very rarely. But two such instances include: the poem 'The Fever Bird' in his novel *A Suitable Boy,* which acts as a kind of invisible refrain in the book; and the other one can be found in the recent special Indian issue of *Granta* magazine. Its editor, Ian Jack remarked with a mischievous wistfulness, "It is the shortest [and narrowest] poem by a man who has written the longest modern novel." Seth's Petrarchan sonnet based on a character in the *Ramayana* is titled 'Sampati': Why/ do/ you/ cry?'/ 'I/ flew/ too/ high / Un-/ done,/ all/ see/ me/ fall'.

Rukmini Bhaya Nair's (b. 1952) debut collection *The Hyoid Bone,* brings to light another poet of talent, another poet where the woman's point of view is discussed with authority. Nair also brings to her poetry, her background in linguistics, fusing lexical rules and variations, in unusual ways. In the poem 'Genderole', all of this is displayed with great skill:

> Considerthefemalebodyyourmost
> Basictextanddontforgetits*slokas* I
> Whatpalmleafmscandoforusitdoes
> Therealgapsremainforwomentoclose I

There is no flinching as far as her questioning stance is concerned as she challenges: "Sankarayouoldmisogynisttellme/ Whatssocontemptibleaboutfleeting/ Splendour? . . . Itmaybebeneathyoutopriseapartthisgimmick/Butrememberthethingawomanchangesbestishersex." Nair's endings are always unpredictable, and sometimes quite witty. Another interesting aspect of this poem is its form, the way the 'couplets' are used in the Sanskrit *sloka* tradition with the *poornaviram* or the 'full-stcp' marking the end of the two-line stanzas.

In 'Moondrop, Javadweep', we see the effectiveness with which she paints the fury of the equatorial rainstorm: "Drenching rain, and the blindness/ That goes with it, pushed us down.// We went so quickly on our knees,/ The long soak of road squelching.// Closest thing to stoning it was—/ Small, stinging pebbles of rain// And then—fist-sized rock-hammers/ Loosed wrath of some invisible mob." Her skill, with words and patterns is evident in poems such as 'Word(I)d', '(W)omen', 'Convers(at)ion', 'Ma(i)nstream' where she uses parenthetical puns, or with linguistic and visual arrangements on the page as in 'Language Lessons* Related Reading' and 'Malviya Nagar—Sissinghurst'.

In *The Hyoid Bone,* Nair uses mythology, everyday life, travel experiences and her imagination with power. Her poems 'God From Bankura', 'Maya-Mriga—California', 'Flame', 'Perchance to Dream', 'Quartet', are some of my favourites. She is a poet whose work is exciting and demanding and I look forward to her poems in the forthcoming collection titled *The Ayodhya Cantos*.

Prabhanjan Mishra's (b. 1952) first book, *Vigil* (1993), contains poems that arise predominantly from an Oriyan sensibility, his interest in local folklore and myth, and his experiences as a twentieth century suburban Bombay dweller.

The rural landscape of Orissa, where "The smell of ripe paddy/ churns hungry stomachs", we see the farmer's "sad buttocks/ and shrunken breasts/ peer through the tattered cloth." In this poem 'Peasants of Orissa', the stark reality is brought to sharp focus in a sad vein: "Only daydreams sustain their smiles".

The post-colonial response to a colonial past is ironically and effectively explored in a poem such as 'The Foreign Tourist':

> For you to come and plunder,
> rape and massacre
> and return centuries later
> to applaud the splendid ruins.

Quite in contrast, the plight of metropolitan suburbia are explored vividly with an underlying ironic ring: "It is not Bombay/ unless one looks/ at the postal addresses,/ the varicose city growing elsewhere/ like a pestilence.// In the east the salt pan bask./ The creek, languid in the north, is a well-fed boa; having swallowed the city's garbage/ at the mouth of the belching drains.// At the nearby station/ tired trains stop for a drink or smoke./ One hears them grunt and gasp,/ the announcer urging them to take to the tracks" (Suburb').

But when Mishra chooses to be lyrical, he can be a pure delight. Consider the opening stanza of 'Weeds of Hope':

> The night is an impenetrable mask,
> the sharp shapes of feminine footfalls
> cut slices of nostalgia.
> Across a quiet pool of waiting

the numb senses crawl
on the bellies of turtles.

The jacket blurb of his book highlights his "one-page poems" where he "puts across one basic emotion or feeling in each poem." I tend to think that Mishra is much more complex than that. In fact in his six-part long poem 'Moon is a Neon Lamp' (not in this book), his real strengths with the narrative are displayed—rich use of imagery, lyricism, tension and specificity.

Manohar Shetty's (b. 1953) poems in his three books—*A Guarded Space* (1981), *Borrowed Time* (1988), *Domestic Creatures* (1994)—uses the spatial element that pervades everyday life with unusual effect. Whether in a cramped train "the lines/ Rustle unchecked through his hands" ('Epitaph'), or, looking inward the poet says, "i weave myself/ a cocoon breathe/ the air in the inky/ gloom" ('Cocoon'), or, opening the lid a cockroach "tumbles out/ Like a family secret;/ Scuttles back into darkness" ('Domestic Creatures'), Shetty has full control of the movements of his characters in the areas he has outlined.

In the poem 'Floorshow, Bombay' executed in tight tercets, the performer feels a sense of trap laid by the leering eyes of the audience:

Her unpeeled costume is heaped
Like fishscales, and she
No longer glistens, a mermaid.

Smoke-screened sighs escape
From the redly-lit audience when she bends
Crabwise instead, unwinds a ream

Of ribbon from the cleft
Of her sex, the tantalising yards
Cheered like a victory parade.

Away from the vicarious climax
Her suppleness swaddles her waist,

Her facial a pink mash.

The sense of claustrophobia the dancer feels is finely juxtaposed as an antithesis to both the visual energy of her pirouettes as well as the movement created by the lines' internal rhymes as "Her unpeeled costume is heaped." This poem like many others in his books, uses metaphors refreshingly.

Shetty's poems involve very detailed and exact spaces, areas once painted by the poet's metaphors, can be inhabited and savoured time and again. The last collection, *Domestic Creatures* (1994), contains poems from his first two books that have been thoroughly revised, along with a few new poems.

In both *Purdah* (1989) and *Postcards from God* (1994), Imtiaz Dharker (b. 1954) brings to her poetry a very specific and tightly-wrought Muslim sensibility, one that is further enhanced in strength by her individual point of view, indeed any woman's point of view.

Consider the opening lines of 'Purdah II': "The call breaks its back/ across the tenements. 'Allah-u-Akbar'. . ./ Your mind throws black shadows/ on marble cooled by centuries of dead./ A familiar script racks the walls./ The pages of the Koran/ turn, smooth as old bones/ in your prodigal hands." Further on, she says, "They have all been sold and bought,/ the girls I knew/ unwilling virgins who had been taught,/ especially in this strangers' land, to bind/ their brightness tightly round,/ whatever they might wear,/ in the purdah of the mind.// They veiled their eyes/ with heavy lids./ They hid their breasts,/ but not the fullness of their lips." The quiet juxtaposition of passion and protest eventually strikes a social note of tension, one that is couched as in the reserve energies of an uncoiled spring.

Added to this sensibility is her innate feel for the visual media, especially the fine arts. Many of her poems—'Living Spaces', 'Outline', 'No-man's Land', 'Image'—contains an inner force that is carefully etched, a sharpline quality of sketches derivative from her own work as an artist.

Dharker's poetry arises out of both the peculiarity and particularity of living in a coupled exile—residing both inside and outside of a culture, within both the Islamic and the Hindu tradition, and eventually resting as much in the traditional as in the modern. The short poem 'Exile', exemplifies much of this:

A parrot knifes
through the sky's bright skin,
a sting of green.

It takes so little
to make the mind bleed
into another country,

a past that you agreed
to leave behind.

Postcards from God re-appeared (along with the poems from *Purdah*, and many fine black and white drawings by the poet herself) as an enlarged single volume from Bloodaxe in 1997. Both her poems and drawings interact, not always directly, but very often as a counterpoint. The grey-scale subtlety is evident in both media, where the common strength is the 'line' itself. A good example is at the end of the book where in the poem 'Minority', there is an atmosphere of finely traced mystery and the light touch of evanescence:

until, one day, you meet
the stranger sidling down your street,
realize you know the face
simplified to bone,
look into its outcast eyes
and recognize it as your own.

Vinay Dharwadker's (b. 1954) debut collection, *Sunday at the Lodi Gardens* (1994), shows him as a primarily personal poet—preoccupied with images of pregnancy and child-birth, imagination of loss and alienation, and the politics of being inside and outside society's field of play.

'Splashdown', a long single-sentence poem for his daughter, subtitled "for Aneesha, when she can read it", cleverly interpolates the concepts of interior and exterior space, the space in the mother's womb and the cosmic space. ". . . in the deep sea drift/ of your infinite/ spherical/ universe,/ you found your own/ properly human form,/ . . . your journey/ through six billion miles/ of multiplying cells,/ your whole body/ shining/ with unearthly/ light/ opening your/ moments/ after arrival/ to look around/ for the first time,/ small,/ frightened,/ and bewildered,// as though/ you'd landed// on the wrong planet."

Another poem, 'Nursing', captures the post-natal stage rather vividly; "in the course of a single day/ your breasts/ are bloated and dry in turn,/ sagging under their weight,/ cracked and sore at the nipples."

Quite in contrast however, we see the "local histories" in 'New Delhi', "Where gold reflections rise, quiver at the rims of eyes" in sprung internal rhymes reminiscent of Hopkins. The influence of Eliotesque imagery is fairly evident in the title poem "In the deserted market square/ I stopped to smoke a cigarette/ and stood in the shade/ of a sagging awning,/ . . . // The afternoon was littered/ with peels and cigarette butts,/ faint cries of children,/ broken pairs of lovers/ in patches of shade." The last stanza plays off the lines used as an epigraph from Octavio Paz's brilliant poem 'In the Gardens of the Lodi': "Into the total blue/ The domes of the mausolea/ . . . Dark, shut round on their own thoughts—/Suddenly send forth/ Birds" (Paz). In comparison, Dharwadker writes the following, concluding in a Beckettian fashion:

> As the sun sloped down,
> the black mouths of the tombs
> spat out streams of birds
> that shrieked across the evening,
> and the final glow of dusk

smothered the air,
and the day came to nothing.

Dharwadker is at this best when he uses sparse free-verse lines, such as in 'Class Conflicts', 'A Draft of Excavations', and the most effective of all—'Her Torso',// turning,/ half-turned:// turning/ slowly/ into a torsion// of charcoal/ lines// on my page."

Vijay Seshadri (b. 1954) has recently published his first book titled *Wild Kingdom* (1996), one that is highly accomplished and shows him as a poet of immense intelligence. His poems are very carefully constructed, both in terms of tightness of language as well as understated lyricism. That he is able to do that without using traditional rhymes or resorting to other obvious methods, makes his poems sing with an even greater flight. The poems themselves use a very contemporary idiom, steeped in American popular culture, using nature in an unsentimental but vivid way, and displaying a sheer flow of unexpected phrases. Take the opening section of 'Divination in the Park':

Under the bursting dogwoods, et cetera,
having just finished a pear for lunch,
I lie over the earth, to feel it swim
inside my posture, and sleep

Further on in the same poem, we see "The winter was mild. In the bulbs and empty hives/ spring rubs the velvet from its new brace of horn,/ and around the drowning rocks/ the feral light of equinox// sheds a pattern on the ocean." The use of language here is sheer magic, and there is such grace contained in it.

One of Seshadri's strengths is the use of the long-poem form. 'Lump' and 'Lifeline' (which also won the *Paris Review's* Bernard Conners Long Poem Prize) are exceptional examples. In both these poems, the poetry and the narrative are sustained with equal ease and power.

Structurally, he seems to be fascinated with two forms of lineation: the four-line stanza, and the one-block one-stanza constructs. Almost eighty-percent of the book falls in either of these categories.

Seshadri was born in India but moved to the States at the age of five. His relationship with India is conveyed both in its sense of the geographical distance from that country, as well as in the couched unobvious display of it: "I said Rajasthan, she said Sahara,/ but we knew beyond question/ it was desert we were after." ('The Lump')

Some of my favourite poems include: 'Of and Relating to', 'A Sketch from the Campaign in the North', 'The Gulley', 'Street Scene', among others. This volume is one of the finest first books I have come across in a long time. There is humour, darkness, motion, passion, emptiness, all pirouetting deftly in his wild kingdom, executed with sheer panache.

Sujata Bhatt (b. 1956) uses free verse with delicacy, poise, and effect. Her lines are tight, metaphors unusual, and range of themes wide. In her first book *Brunizem* (1988), the continents she has lived—Asia, Europe and North America—are used as her poetic landscapes. In 'Udaylee' she explores with haunting sentiment, the state of menstruating women who are deemed untouchable during that period, according to the beliefs and practices in the Gujarati community of her childhood:

> Only paper and wood are safe
> from a menstruating woman's touch.
> So they built this room
> for us, next to the cowshed.

Further she describes, "This aching is my blood flowing against,/ rushing something—/ knotted clumps of blood,/ so I remember fistfuls of torn seaweed/ rising with the foam, rising."

Her Gujarati mother tongue figures prominently in her poems in all her books. In her second book *Monkey Shadows* (1991), the protagonist in the poem 'Devibhen Pathak' says at different points in the poem "(Chaal, Chaal! Sapat payhri lay!) Let's go! Put on your slippers", then later "(aray bhen, tamnay khabar nathi. . . ?) Oh bhen, don't you know. . . ?" Bhatt goes one step further by using the actual Devnagari Gujarati script on the page. It is an aspect that we have come to recognize in Bhatt's poems that highlight her inimitable style. This bilingual quality not only provides an interesting East-West tension but also flavours it with a kind of lyricism that can only be achieved when linguistic scales and registers are controlled simultaneously.

In her third book, *The Stinking Rose* (1995), she not only extends some of the themes and techniques that she has used previously, but builds on them substantially. At the core of the collection is a sequence of twenty-five poems that "explores the various mythologies and the magical and practical aspects of garlic". The title poem 'The Stinking Rose', one of the many names garlic is called by, sensuously evokes warmth, passion, and beauty, all juxtaposed delicately: "Everything I want to say is/ in that name/ for these cloves of garlic—they shine/ like pearls still warm from a woman's neck.// My fingernail nudges and nicks/ the smell open, a round smell/ that spirals up. Are you hungry?"

Included in this volume, are poems that earlier appeared as a chapbook, titled *Freak Waves*. These poems arise largely out of the poet's response and experiences in Victoria, Canada. Not surprisingly, many of these poems are swathed in a refractive wash of maritime colour. Also by extension, we see aspects of belonging and unbelonging, rootedness and transience, physical and mental travel, diasporic dislocation, all explored with power and poignancy.

The world art and literature feature vibrantly in this volume. In fact this collection is adorned with wonderful illustrations by Rolf Wienbeck. There are several poems ('The Light Teased Me', 'Cow's Skull—Red, White and Blue', 'Skinnydipping in History', 'Parrots', and others) that respond to the works of artists and writers such as Georgia O'Keeffe, Paula Modersohn-Becker, Jakobine von Domming, Frida Kahlo, and John Ashberry. Many of the poems in this group ingeniously and successfully employ the use of surrealism and internal dialogue.

Sujata Bhatt has recently published *Point No Point* (1997), which contains a generous selection from her three previously published books, plus one new poem which lends this volume the title. This is a substantial collection of poems, one that allows us to travel, dream, and learn, but one that ultimately moves us by the quietude of stance and impeccable articulation. She is an accomplished poet using her multicultural background to its fullest effect—her growing up in America, her Indian family background, and her German marriage. Her next collection, *Augatora,* is due out from Carcanet in 2000.

C.P. Surendran (b. 1959) inhabits the second half of the two-poet volume *Gemini II* (1994) and his first book-length collection *Posthumous Poems* (1999). His obvious strengths are evident in his portrayal of the grimy underside of metropolitan living. This coupled with an obsessive self-mocking posture lends his verse a hard-edged shape. He uses language that's stripped to the bare bones, lean, distraught, and convincing: "He opens his eyes wide and stares/ At the biggest metal-dawn breaking/ Like a wave through the brittle green/ Of summer. He rearranges the cold/ In his bones and wakes the images/On the TV. He read their lips/ Between the sips. Spent/ By their passions, he remains/ Bedridden, thinking of her thighs/ And things like that." ('Saturday Poems: 2. Bed Time').

Surendran's lines are tightly-wrought and packed, pushing metaphors to their limit. Take for example the opening of 'Malabari: Out of my Window': "June speaks thirty times/ Each speech rhymes in green,/ Praises water where it falls./ Leaves plunge yellow and brown/ Stem the oozing mud with rotting colours."

Many of Surendran's poems are arranged as slide-show sequences, poems in various parts, but each having their own integrity as independent poems. The four-part 'Malabari', the seven-part 'Saturday Poems', the two-part 'Renunciation' and 'Annunciation', are good examples.

> Place of perpetual solar suicide,
> Cordoned off by precise fears. In your street
> The hour is always wild sunset. And in some clock
> Somewhere, I too am already dead. ('Annunciation II')

His poems are hot, both in terms of temperature and sensuality; they are also weather-worn, city-soiled, drunken, ecstatic, depressed, and scaring; and all this is achieved through the use of controlled phrase-making and language.

Jeet Thayil (b. 1959) occupies half the space in the two-poet volume *Gemini* (1992), the first attempt by Penguin India to publish young poetry. His work is mostly urban where unusual angles of sex prevail, and he likes using rhymes. Take the poem 'Oneroid' for instance:

> This woman, her milk is black
> she feeds me lying back.
> Strange countries stop her in-betweens
> lazy with crime, softnesses, sin.
>
> Her phallus is a Chinese pipe,
> I suck upon it hollow-cheeked,
> eunuched in the lamplit dark
> as she sputters and spits and shrieks.
>
> She fills me up with moving space.
> I lie still and I'm gone
> on nodding, neon, perfect dreams.
> I pine for places never seen.

In 'India Mother' we see delightful irreverence couched in innocence as "Her hands round out your anus, a hand/ wets you there and powders you, hands/ busy themselves with your sex."

The *Gemini* volume only served as an introduction, but his first full-length collection, *Apocalypso* (1997), show Thayil's full range. His interest with modern living's darker sides is further explored, as is the world of drugs, rock'n'roll, and sex.

> Mandelstam squeezes sperm from the stone,
> water from the dry sponge, regenerates
> with blood the blanched bone, engages
> in mortal hand-to-hand combat with
> perpetual terror.

In *Apocalypso,* his interest in the actual world of poetry is revealed in a poem like 'On Opening a New Edition of Osip Mandelstam's Poems' (quoted above), and through various others that relate directly and indirectly to poetry and poets themselves. Poems such as 'Pushkin Knew Heaven: A Place Where Nothing Happens', 'Where This One Came From', 'Other People's Deaths', show his taste and inclination, one that includes writers like John Berryman, Delmore Schwartz, Hart Crane, along with the Beat poets.

Thayil's view of the world and relationships are painted with a sense of terse grimness. See for example, the poem 'Wedding Picture':

> The lizard twists we try
> Safeguarding escape.
> How little it would take
> To end this life.
>
> Birds drop from the sky.
> Curling past the cape
> Of no hope, we awake;
> I husband, you wife.
>
> Bees stop, flowers die.
> A testament takes shape.
> These are the signs we make

Before the grief.

One of his best poems in this volume is one that is constructed in clean sparse couplets titled 'The Mercy Tree'. Here is the opening: "Yearning for gleaming glass/ And towers of sleepless steel,// He finds instead a dread/ Of nature's restless flowerings.// A lush chaos, as disordered/ As the random chancings of madness.// The deciding day:/ Stumbling home, he falls,// Wakes up bruised, more broken/ Than before,// Urgently missing/ The comfort of concrete."

Vijay Nambisan (b. 1963) occupies the second half of *Gemini* (1992), sharing the volume with Thayil. Nambisan's poems can appear soft-hearted at first glance, but he has a keen sense of sarcasm, wit and humour, qualities that are lacking in most of the younger poets.

> When my grandfather grew to be an old man,
> he was a little mad:
> his hair turned black again
> and his voice held its own, and his eyes
> asked incessantly for answer, an answer. ('Poetic Licence')

His grandfather, family, friends, and his own people appear frequently in poems, so do smells of alcohol, despair of loneliness, rejection and loss. Nambisan's strength lies in his predominantly unsentimental tackling of such themes. The first stanza of 'Holy, Holy' illustrates some of that:

> The rain threatens this ordinary day
> With magic. Things that grow manifest,
> Plainly, the unnatural: more sure
> And permanent is the unwalked way,
> Lifeless air, stone unencumbered
> With feelings; not obsessed, therefore pure.

This volume only provides a glimpse of what is to follow. If the signs he shows here are anything to go by, then I'm excited to see his newer poems in a full-length volume.

Tabish Khair (b. 1966) brings a reporter's eye to his poems. In his first book *My World* (1991), the sequence 'My India Diary' presents us with a series of snapshots, of scenes he has observed and recorded in plain, simple, fragment phrases:

> II. the stifling heat
> of too many men of too little space
>
> hunched houses on both sides brawling boys
> the anger of being bricked in
>
> IV puja procession
> clay god carried to the ghats
> dancing in the streets
> happiness like a summer cloud
>
> today
> man will triumph over gods

Many of these vignettes (I suppose one should call them phrase-poems), draw upon minute and ordinary details in everyday life, and are used as comments on larger issues in society. Sometimes he achieves this with a haunting effect like in 'Second-hand Books': "There is something sad about second-hand books:/ Their creased covers have seen a little too much,/ Their yellow pages promise yet another story.// If you shake them lightly or shuffle the pages,/ Something is sure to fall out—a piece of paper,/ A letter, a receipt, an unused ticket;// Something that seems to hint at a world you cannot enter." There is always a peculiar kind of poignancy in his poems—sometimes wise, sometimes naive, sometimes fatalistic, but always moving.

In his second book, *A Reporter's Diary* (1993), he takes some of the minute observations further. Many of his poems are personal ('To Gyanendra', 'For Smriti"), others contain experience of his travels ('At Theresienstadt'), and there are those that explore aspects of fear while experimenting with the sonnet form. His language has developed more and we see him tackling certain harder issues such as death ('Nanijan's Cupboard', 'When Someone Dies', 'Death in a Muddy Pond', 'Shraddhanjali'), and the futility of language itself ('Preface').

The Book of Heroes (1995) is a volume which the poet himself subtitles "a collection of light verse and much worse". There are poems that are decidedly irreverent, satirical, and mostly funny. They include send-up of Seth's *The Golden Gate* ('A Headless Tale', 'In the Wake of the Seth'), political satires ('Beejaypee Billie', 'The Caangrassman', 'The Ball-ad of Elections') and many others. Khair has also published a novel, *An Angel in Pyjamas* (1996).

As far as first books go, I would certainly rate Ranjit Hoskote's (b. 1969) *Zones of Assault* among the most promising ones. He uses poetic diction with effective accuracy, images with clarity, and metaphors with originality. In his elegy 'Two Women in Midsummer', he portrays grief juxtaposed in a scene of calm:

> Two women in midsummer
> Sharing their loss
> In traditional white.
>
> Walls, their bricks baked brown,
> Relieved now and then
> By pictures fading into cool green remembrances.

The city of Bombay is presented with post-industrial venom and futility in many of his poems. In 'Reclamation',

> The land is a wolf's grey paw reaching out to grab
> Bay and breakwater. It grips hurt headlands
> Above seabite and claws out
> The grasping promontories of reclamation.

Further in the same poem we see,

> drills drone and shop-basements begin
> To be ploughed.
> The crane vanguards the offensive, advancing
> Boom by beam from the bare angle of the road.
> Its herald the jet blast of asphalt and fuel
> Chokes seatush, grass, breath.

His themes range widely, from political violence to Renaissance art, about figures like Safdar Hashmi and Hannibal, and portray landscapes as different as Kashmir and Hardwar. Hoskote pushes syntax to its limits, and uses word-play with cleverness and effect.

He has also co-translated, with Mahesh Kulkarni, V.A. Dhake's Marathi poems into English, titled *A Terrorist of Spirit* (1992). Hoskote's new poems in his current work-in-progress titled *The Sleepwalker's Archive,* show a lot of variation and exploration of new directions, both in terms of text, as well as context and content.

There are several other poets who have published in magazines, journals, anthologies and in book-form—Diane Mehta, Chitra Banerjee Divakaruni, Reetika Vazirani, Darius Cooper, Melanie Silgardo, Debjani Chatterjee, Shanta Acharya, Maya Choudhury, Suma Josson, Menka Shivadasani, Anjum Katyal, Ruth Vanita, Robin Ngangom, Desmond Karmawphlang, Niranjan Mohanty, Rabindra Swain, Smita Agarwal, Suman Gupta, Leela Gandhi, Arundhati Subramanium, Jerry Pinto, Deepanker Kwiwani, Anand Thakore—some of whom could have just as easily featured in this piece.

If the poets discussed in this essay represent the vibrant generation of post-Independence Indian poets, then the future of modern English-language poetry in India is certainly in reliable hands, a force to reckon with in the wider arena of contemporary world poetry.

Trends and Techniques in Indian English Poetry by Women of the Post-Independence Era

LAKSMISREE BANERJEE

This paper is an exploration of a hitherto marginalized literary discipline, which in recent times, has evolved into a widely acclaimed genre, and has been incorporated into the canon as a definitive index for the study of the variegated life of a nation. Indian English poetry by women has formed a rich ingredient in the fabric of world women's literature, which has now come to the fore on a dual score: a) as a literary and linguistic document of Feminism, Postmodernism and Postcolonialism and b) as a sociological document for the lucid registering of the movements of societies and peoples, their transformations, advancements or regressions. After the Second World War and the dissolution of British imperialism, women's poetry and literature has acquired an undeniable validity as an honest mirror of historical subversions, of universal as well as particular human experiences with regard to gender, race, class, religion and nationality. Its special progression towards realism, transparency and radicalism for breaking out of the prescribed zones or norms of patriarchy, has given it the importance of a socio-cultural and national record of the new age. This worldwide focus on women's writings is a significant phenomenon in the sphere of international subaltern studies. The varied literatures of exploited or peripheral races, minority communities and of subjugated women struggling to have their voices heard, are being included in mainstream literature as a welcome sign of comprehensive development.

For the purposes of critical study, two broad, chronology-based categories are used: a) pre-1950s and b) post-1950s. In this wide, homogenous as well as diverse spectrum, there are two primary points of investigation: a) the Poet as a Writer with the special tools or techniques she uses for the crystallization of her poetic ideas and b) the Poet as a Woman, often a rebel against, a conqueror or a victim of age old societal and gender-based repressions. Women's poetry, hence, becomes a window to both her 'creative' and 'feminist' selves operating at a subtle, literary, epistemological and activist level. In this context the well known poet Eunice de Souza says: "What I am as a poet is a result of what I am in all aspects of my life. . . . Women's experience and socialization as a whole is different. . . . The battle is to validate the material . . . the stuff of women's lives, women's experience, not to 'transcend' being a woman."[1] Hence, the ongoing discussion would be meaningful, primarily, at the intersections of universality and sexuality, of the private and the public, of the intrinsically feminine and the human or even the androgynous. Other than the 'feminine' and the 'feministic' themes, women's poetry also affords a wide area of examination of multicultural and pluralistic motifs. It also leads us to view the psychological fabric of literature, to assess the newly evolving, non-traditional roles and situations of women in a fast developing society, the consequent problems and gender issues and above all, the new postmodernist poetic approaches, innovative language-techniques and stylistic devices. Thus the understanding and interpretation of Women's Poetry and Literature becomes a prerequisite for the evaluation of national progress and its vital linkage with international growth.

In this postcolonial era, with the steady Indianisation and decolonisation of the English language, women's poetry has broken out of the starched, plagiaristic, Romantic fold of yesteryears. The style, diction and technical devices have become more open, free, experimental, often elliptical and fluid enough to accommodate the authentic rise and fall of women's experiences and feelings. This poetry has graduated from being a vehicle for the expression of a repressed creativity of the "Mad Woman in the Attic",[2] from being a reckless outpouring of the "other" alternative self of humanity to an assured and cognitive recording of primary human experiences. The English poetic idiom and form, developed and used by the postmodern woman writer, is convincingly and deliberately close to everyday, real life speech-rhythms. There is no usage of an elevated or stilted poetic style; the meaning emerges clearly and potently as in the following lines:

> Transcend self, you say
> Connect with myth, history
> The world crumbling around you.
> Men can, and do. Beggars survive.
> Destitutes survive. . . .
> Smart arse. Poetess. . . .
> Friend, the histories I know aren't fit to print. . . .
> The perfect book is
> One long cry in the dark.
> A novelist said that
> Who spent his life wondering why,
> When the Nazis came,
> His mother pushed him into a closet
> And let his sister go to Auschwitz.[3]

The concept is as incredibly explosive and revelatory as the syntax deliberately non-conformist and innovative. The point to be noted here is that the poetic language of women has outgrown and broken poetic conventions to accommodate the rebellious and realistic voice against male chauvinism. Women writers have raised their voices continuously against the standardized and canonized language of poetry as being the primary element of male hegemony. The gender-actualisation has come through alternative language-structures to accentuate the movement against marginalisation and towards a democratic inclusion in the mainstream.

Virginia Woolf, in the first half of the twentieth century, had initiated the 'stream of consciousness' modes of writing, specifically to break away from 'the sentence made by men'. The style was not just a psychoanalytic experiment with the writer's mind but a powerful method of exploring the limitless range and fluency of the female pen. Woolf says, "The woman writer must make her own sentence, altering and adapting the current sentence until she writes one that takes the natural shape of her thought." This approach has been further advanced in recent years through Julia Kristeva's study of the revolution of the poetic language of women and through Alice Jardine's poststructuralist and psychoanalytic perspectives. It is necessary to note that Kamala Das was the first Indian woman poet who evolved such radical standpoints, both with regard to language and gender during the 1960s and 70s. Women poets in India continue to generate such contemporary patterns of linguistic revolt and literary originality, to propagate, what the American woman writer Elaine Showalter calls *A Literature of Their Own.* A specific poetics of gender has evolved in the Indian-English scenario with Beheroze Shroff, the poet-artist, declaring "We need to stop seeing each other through men's eyes and language. . . . We have to have a different women's voice." Perhaps it is in the light of this statement that Arlene Zide entitled her edition of contemporary Indian Women's Poetry *In Their Own Voice* (Penguin India, 1993). Consider the articulate, novel and matter-of-fact manner in which Gauri Deshpande analyses the generic traits and bonding between women. In this postmodern style there is no effervescence of a bygone, inflated mode of writing. On the contrary, the esoteric and elitist have given way to a populist, accessible and feminist colloquial idiom:

> Sometimes you want to talk
> About love and despair
> And the ungratefulness of children

A man is no use whatever then. . . .
She sews and you sit and sip
and speak of the rate of rice. . . .
You know both that you've spoken
Of love and despair and ungrateful children

This particular genre has evolved from gender; though distinct, different, chatty and informal, it is gradually being validated and absorbed into formalized poetry. Laksmisree Banerjee, in her poem "Your Mother Told You So" uses a powerful, feminist language to lambast male insensitivity:

You finally came
to me for life and
gave me death.
I felt those million hungers . . .
That you had come past by;
I felt the bedimmed
kaajal eyes flickering out,
waning off
In the regalia of marriage,
in the vacuity of love.[4]

With regard to the new trends and techniques in women's poetry, there is a remarkable movement connecting the domestic with the public spheres of work. Increased metropolitan activities, sophisticated lifestyles, globalisation, urbanized influences of pop, disco and café-culture, Anglo-Americanisation and the convent education of the present generation of women poets have made their poetic language chiselled, sharp, pithy and effortless. The deconstructive strategies of narrative and conceptual frames, along with the simultaneous assimilation of pan-Indian elements, have made this poetry a formidable area of study and research. Other than the skilful use of standard poetic devices, the semiotic, symbolical and metaphorical properties of language, help to emphasise the feminist strategies of interrogation. The fissures and fragments of post-modern life are also questioned and reflected in the highly experimental diction. The problems of sociological vis-à-vis literary politics, of gender inequities, of marginalisation and sub-humanisation of women, of their social and artistic exclusion and of the dominant need for inclusion and democratization, all contribute towards the distinctive character of this poetry. Women poets of today have a holistic approach; an all-encompassing intellect and imagination, which focus on minute details of people, locale, events, background and foreground, making their poems richly textured and dense. Says Bruce King: "The poet's speech and that of the characters is colloquial, direct and contemporary. The collapsing of the distance between the self and the external world, between present and past, between reflection and event creates an immediacy, vitality and drama."[5] The external world is so completely blended with the mental arena, the language is so free from any inhibitive formalism that Women's Poetry becomes a dynamic art form vibrating with dreams, memories, living experiences, anxieties, joys and reflections. Consider the following lines from Nabaneeta Dev Sen's 'Sometimes, Love':

> It comes when you call it. Like a pet cockatoo
> it comes and sits on your finger. It flutters. . . .
> it recites fixed phrases. It says flattering words. . . .
> Then, in private,
> alone . . .
> jingles its glittering chains
> and sheds its feathers
>   in empty space

As in many recent compositions by women, there is a disarming way in which the structure integrates with the theme, the images with the metaphor and the syntax with the lineaments of the thought-patterns. In most of the poems there is a wonderful merging of "woman, image and text"[6] in which the ideologies of the woman poet fashion her art of writing. However, the new generation has emerged from the zone of gender-stereotyping, from both aggressiveness and victimization to a state of a vigorous equanimity connecting the 'feminist' with the 'human'. In terms of aesthetic quality, women's poetry shows faithfulness to the immediacy and authenticity of experience. Objectively speaking, it is not bound by literary or social constructs, which often, make the poetry by men spurious and stylized. This primacy of the feminine element in creative exercise is emphasized by Ashis Nandy in his essay titled 'Woman versus Womanliness': "In the twilight zone in which the creative mind dwells, there is always a certain stress upon the ability to turn inwards. . . A certain sensitivity to one's natural environment and to the latent communication among human beings and the capacity to use self-expression which mobilizes imageries. In the West this has invariably meant becoming feminine."[7] This is the most significant trait of women's poetry today.

Another important trend which became perceptible ever since the mid-1960s when Kamala Das made her fiery entry into this realm, is that of the 'confessional' element. Das has often been compared to the American poets Sylvia Plath and Anne Sexton, in having raged into the male bastion with a highly sexually explosive kind of writing, a transparency and an unabashed candour which has lent an air of freshness to women's poetry in India. Her poem "An Introduction" may well be used as an appropriate introductory text for foregrounding the gender and language issues:

> Don't write in English, they said,
> English is not your mother tongue. Why not leave
> Me alone, critics, friends, visiting cousins,
> Every one of you? . . . The language I speak
> Becomes mine, its distortions, its queerness
> All mine, mine alone. . . .
> It voices my joys, my longings, my
> Hopes, and it is useful to me as cawing
> Is to crows . . . it

Is human speech . . .
He did not beat me
But my sad woman-body felt so beaten . . .
    Dress in sarees, be girl
    Be wife, they said. Be embroiderer, be cook, . . .
    Fit in. Oh, belong, cried the categorizers

It is this element of fierce independence and transcendence of 'categorisation' that set the stage for women's poetry to become a meaningful canon worth the reckoning. Such new modes of artistic expression, overriding sexual connotations and anguished human concerns are reflected in the writings of most post-independence poets like Mamta Kalia, Eunice de Souza, Melanie Silgardo, Imtiaz Dharker, Sujata Bhatt, Meena Alexander, Smita Agarwal, Tara Patel and others. The full complexity of life comes alive in the personal voice of the woman poet, which often goes beyond restrictive technique. The deliberate dismantling of structures for the creation of alternatives is evident, for example, in Ketaki Kushari Dyson's "After Reading the Hidden Face of Eve".

Clitorises? Tongues? Hair?
Noses? Uteri? Breasts? . . .
Words, Silences, Structures we uphold:
those ornate arches
we so love to laud . . .
I implore you. . . .
should a woman
dare to speak out aloud
about how she has been
mauled by love or hate
suffer her to speak.
Do not shut her up

Interestingly, the new experimental forms of women's poetry reveal an emotional and an evocative substructure supporting the main cerebral rhythms and patterns. Laksmisree Banerjee, in her poem "Womb Attachments", asserts the undeniably relevant connections between a woman's sensual, physical and spiritual facets which need to be acknowledged as a whole:

> The wild impregnation of the soul
>   nurtured in my womb . . .
> These are womb-attachments,
>   imponderables to the thoughtless,
> I call them not cerebral love,
>   but ingrafted erotica,
> Completions.[8]

The new resilience of the poetic language allows a poet like Monika Verma to use images like "spider bridge", "mallards in precision flight", "geese honking through sheen of pearl sky" and the "the blaring eyes of a speeding car" to accentuate the potency of an alert mind. Her poem "Semantics" is an exploration of the developing trends of language:

> Is this world a piddock
> a bi-valued mollusc?
> Is our writing a pearl in that oyster
> Or merely an incrustation
> A susurration—a detrition by sound[9]

This progression in terms of emerging themes and unconventional language is evident in the poetry of most contemporary poets like Rajlukshmee Debee Bhattacharya, Sunita Jain, Meera Nair, Nilima Chitgopekar, Lakshmi Kannan and others. The Indian Woman Poet, today, has positively grown out of a cloistered inner space into the larger cycles, labyrinths and chequered network of post-Independence life. In Meenakshi Devi Bhavnani, the new dimensions of life in poetry are perceptible. She speaks of the "surrealistic plastics in our blood . . ./ the hard concrete beneath our high-heeled, metal-heeled shoes pleases us./ We are lulled by the sharp staccato of our egotistic walk through the mazes of the city streets . . ./ and our touch and smell dulled by a billion bombardments".[10]

Diaspora writing by Indian women, traversing across the globe, often subsumed in expatriate experiences away from home, is a feature, which enriches women's poetry today. Poets like Meena Alexander, Sujata Bhatt, Melanie Silgardo, etc, generate densely layered compositions evolving at the intersections of the East and the West, of home and abroad. In her poem "The Peacock", Sujata Bhatt uses it as a symbol of nostalgia, harkening backwards "a blue shadow which (falls) over you" and "a loud sharp call (coming) from nowhere". In "A Different History" she asserts "Great Pan is not dead;/ He simply emigrated to India./ Here, the gods roam freely. . . . every tree is sacred". This craving for one's roots, one's home and mother, is a significant trend interpenetrating the poetic configurations of most women writers. The concept of womanhood is often realized through the usage of the symbol of a tree, which is transplanted in foreign soil. In her award-winning poem "Punarnava", Rajlukshmee Debee Bhattacharya talks of "That home left behind/ as birth-strings snapped/ a refugee, a wanderer, I/ look for you." In her poem "Death of the Mother", Meenakshi Devi Bhavnani reiterates similar thoughts:

> Even the Mother must die
> When from our Mother's bosom torn,
> Adrift, orphaned, alone . . .
> Where then shall we dwell

In this specially pro-matrilineal poetic process, the displacement of women either through marriage or through other societal pressures is latently likened to the migratory pain and angst of immigrant experience. Hence, this becomes an important component of Postcolonial Feminist poetry. The interrogation of patriarchy or of any such establishments of power, becomes a complementary ingredient of such poetry. The female repugnance against an intrinsically imbecile father-figure, comes out in the confessional strain of Silgardo's "For Father on the Shelf":

> The days you drank too much
> I cowered from your smell
> You never knew it hurt. . . .
> And now I'm writing with my life
> The price of an inherited crutch

Along similar lines we have Eunice de Souza proclaiming: "I killed my father when I was three . . ./ I head for the abyss." Mamta Kalia, in her "Tribute to Papa" writes:

> Who cares for you, Papa? . . .
> You're not sure what greatness is,
> But you want me to be great. . . .
> I give two donkey-claps for your greatness

Such poetic writings by Indian women have, undoubtedly, widened the horizons of Indian English poetry and added a meaningful dimension to it. The revolutionary changes in diction and poetic thought, the focussing on everyday realities, the dissolution of poetic myths and traditions and the incisive clarity and intensity of portrayal through the extraordinary use of ordinary speech rhythms, establishes this poetry as an important genre in the world context.

Notes and References

1. Eunice de Souza, "Introduction," *In Their Own Voice,* ed. Arlene Zide (Penguin India, 1993), p. xix.
2. Sandra Gilbert and Susan Gubar, *Mad Woman in the Attic,* 1979, p. 18. (Rereading of Charlotte Bronte's *Jane Eyre* and her alternative self Bertha Mason).
3. "Introduction," *In Their Own Voice*, p. 33.

4. Laksmisree Banerjee, *Fire Offerings* (Har-Anand Publications, 1997), p. 33.
5. Bruce King, "Women's Voices," *Modern Indian Poetry in English* (OUP, 1992), p. 131.
6. *Women Image Text*, ed. Lola Chatterjee (Trianka. 1986), p. 131.
7. Ashis Nandy, *Indian Women: From Purdah to Modernity*, ed. B.R. Nanda (Vikas, 1976), p. 154.
8. Laksmisree Banerjee, *Flames and Flowers* (Writers' Workshop, 1987), p. 65.
9. Monica Verma, *New English Poetry by Indian Women* (Writers' Workshop, 1976), p. 79.
10. Meenakshi Devi Bhavnani, *Poetry India: Emerging Voices* (Hind Pocket Books, 1992), p. 59.

"Why I Write/ How I Write"

HOSHANG MERCHANT

21 February 1999 (Anai's Nin's birthday)

Prologue

It is all a matter of concentration: If you concentrate on knowledge you become a wise man; if on money, a rich man; if on love, a prostitute but if you concentrate on god you become a saint.

S. Radhakrishnan, Commentary on *Gita*

Every great document of civilization is at the same time a document of great barbarism. And when this document changes hands each transfer is marked by great violence.

Walter Benjamin, "Essay on the Philosophy of History," in *Illuminations*

Sex is a way to sainthood.

Anai's Nin, *Diary III*

Why I Write

"As everyone knows by now, I'm homosexual." To write this sentence and to speak it publicly which is a great liberation is why I write. How did I write my first poem? I was beaten up while cruising the streets of a small university town in Michigan, one summer in the early 1970s. The man was a Chicano, a migrant Mexican laborer, nameless, of course. He wanted everything: love, money, food, sex, just as I did then because I was a poor student in the world's richest democracy. I remember the room we made love in. I went into the kitchen to make tea, a light liqueurish Darjeeling which smelt of home. He stole the Nepali knife I had hung on the wall to beautify my rented room and tried it on the writing desk cracking it from side to side. Was this the man I had made love to five seconds before? Was he a brute or a human being? Did I not wish to go over from my effete life into the vitalism of his life? Had I not stolen his manhood by stealth in a bed? Was he not justified in wishing me dead?

"12 red roses splattered the shirtfront of my chest."—Lorca

The next night I could not sleep. I had stitches on my nose which were slowly healing. But I was afraid of the dark. I changed my night-lodgings. I slept in a different room the next night. I did not want my private terror to pursue me. In the morning I awoke to Josephine Jacobsen reading on the radio:

"All need is dry/ Rain is a metaphor."
Sex is a metaphor. A poem is a metaphor.
Love is a poem; a made thing.
And a poem is love; a communication.
I am not mad. I write in order not to go mad.

"Zen is the art of not committing suicide, not going insane, not becoming a cripple."—Suzuki, *Zen Buddhism*

(I learnt much later that Josephine Jacobson, consultant in poetry to the Library of Congress, was crippled at birth).

There are no birds this year
In last year's nest
I'm sane now
Then, I was mad. Basho, "Haiku"

II

I'm in a different room now. My mother has suddenly become a cripple. She cannot walk since the day father left her for another woman. I am 16. I know there is a lesson somewhere in this.

And I go back into this mansion of memory with rooms within rooms. And I'm a child of 5. I'm sick with malaria. It is 1952 and all the quinine won't work for this soul-sickness.

I am in love with my mother.

She has a soft green kimono of mercerized cotton which always smells clean and her long hair is soft. This mansion of memory could be my rich father's house on the sea at Bombay or it could be my mother's womb, the only place where I remember being truly happy.

My mother gives me her breast. A rich creamy soft breast. She lets me suckle long because I'm her only son.

Many years later I had a vision of the Phaeneromeni Mother, in Nicosia, Cyprus while awaiting a visa to Israel. She gave the Christ child a rich creamy soft breast. Phaeneromeni means the One Who Appears. The Divine Mother appeared to me and led me to the Promised Land just as my mother had led me up the staircase of sorrow leading to Bandra's Mount Mary in Bombay.

III

Now I'm in a different room of memory. I'm 23. I'm in Virgil Lokke's office at Purdue University saying "I do not want to die before knowing everything." Virgil led Dante through Hell. Surely there must be a way out of this mess I made of my life at 12! And now Virgil is dead.

He was to me a father I never had. I had a father who laughed at a son who wrote poems instead of making money. He also frowned at daughters who did not marry but praised their money making. My sisters and I were born modern, in independent India. But my poor father who lost his doctor-father at birth to the 1917 world epidemic of influenza was brought up by an adopted grandfather who was a wealthy but illiterate jeweller living in fear of an Avestan god and of Victorian morality.

Before her marriage my mother taught Gujarati in a Parsi school, sang Indian raagas, wore homespun for Gandhi and discussed Adyar's theosophy. Father put paid to all that. I identified with my mother's suffering.

So the first poem I wrote was on a photograph of the woman painter Georgia O'Keefe:

Gnarled, snarled hands
And light on the temple
A world is not given
But is made

It was not about life but about art. I was about life-in-art. Then came along Anai's Nin saying pretty much the same thing. It was the Mother, the woman-artist who caught me and liberated me.

IV

When Venice was a village Isfahan was a world-empire.

Isfahan, nesf-e-jehan

Isfahan is half the world. Now I'm in the Sophy's palace. I wander through the music room. Why was a king called the Sophy? Because he was a Sufi. He owned nothing. He held everything in trust for God.

When I gave up my father's wealth, because homosexual sons don't inherit, I gained the world.

Jalal-ud-din Rumi and Shemsi-i-Tabrizi. The teacher and student as lovers. Shems was murdered on his way to Mecca, and Rumi poured out his heart in poems. "Separation leads to pain," is the first teaching of Zen Buddhism, of Sufism, of Christianity which speaks of a Fall. Rumi was God-drunk and he danced and sang of the Return to Wholeness describing vast circles in space with his body.

I travelled to America, Iran, India, Tibet, Arabia, Palestine, Israel, Italy, Britain, Germany, vaster and vaster circles in space. I travelled like Rama for fourteen years.

I lost my innocence in Iran. My hair turned white almost overnight. I saw killing in the streets with my own eyes. A boy lifted his hand to throw a stone. He was met with the soldiers' machine-gun fire. His hand was blown off. He was brought badly bleeding from the groin to the carpet-shop where I had hid. The stench of fresh young blood oozing purposelessly on those priceless carpets! In Iran, in Kurdistan, in Palestine this same blood springs up as poppies in the fields at spring.

I learnt to love my students as Shems loved Rumi.

V

On 19 February 1999 my teacher was murdered in Bombay. Mehroo Jussawalla lived alone, a spinster from one of the city's leading legal families. She taught us moral values culled from Spenser. She was murdered by a brute in her sleep. I wrote her a poem:

The Loneliness of My Spinster Teacher

The staircase would humorously crack
To bear your load
And you would laugh out loud
at the wooden protest

O that this too too solid flesh
  would melt!
That was no cosmic joke!
And the table groaning
  under mountains of food
And the full belly laughing at noon

There were other things under other suns
The Oxford girl reading Marvell or Donne
These hands were not meant for work
  or the kill
But only to prize a meaning out of a text

Her father's own Penelope

And the cobwebs and the tapestry
The warp and woof of familial love
(Mother dead)
The weevil in the bin at work
The termite in the leather bookbinding

Ruskin, Venice and the honeyed sun of love
Sinking over Malabar Hill
The evenings longer
The laughter sharper
And then the night

(On the map
Bombay is a hand
But it is actually an open mouth)

Coda:
There was this healthy woman
With a disease, so lonely
    that grew and grew

And the working-class thief
Who came up at night to kill
Was really a redeemer. . .

The branch is bent when green
And if not, then—

    So I write to make sense of death.

What was Mehroo Jussawalla's crime? She hurt no one. She was a dutiful daughter, a conscientious teacher. She did social service as the women of her class are wont to do. Miss Jussawalla's crime was that she could not see beyond her hilltop balcony to the slums below. In all probability a mafia landlord hired a slum-dweller to axe her for her property. Walter Benjamin says that it is a fascist society that does not change property-relations between social classes. Nazim Hikmet, whom I quote, writes:

The branch is bent when green
And if not, then—
So I am a teacher.

When Ramakrishna preached throughout India someone shouted from the crowd:

Do something for the suffering people of India
I CAN DO NOTHING

The Master said. "This is the position of the artist," says Anai's Nin, commenting on this episode.

I have taken the warning to my heart. I couldn't, but my students will make the revolution.

"When the revolution comes I will be the first one to be killed." (Nin)

How I Write

I shut my bedroom door, unplug the phone and the radio, sit cross-legged like a yogi in the center of my bed and write. I say:

Knowledge is what comes by osmosis in a bed

Or

My poems are written in bed
They are meant for *other's* heads

But this is just the final process. I write my poems on the streets, in buses, while shopping or teaching, in my head. As a medical student Zubin Mehta said a Brahms concerto was always running through his head as he cut up a dogfish.

Proust had his cork-lined room; Anais Nin her fireproof bunker. It is a luxury to say poets write about nature. They do not. They write about culture. It was a luxury for Kim Novak, the 50s movie-star to bathe in a sea-facing bathroom at her Big Sur home with polar bears for company. But I bet her neighbour, Henry Miller, would bolt at the sight of a bear. In fact he writes Nin from Corfu that he longs to be at the Opera. The modernist poet is a citified being. As I wrote:

> In a city where behemoths
> Compete for space with buses
> The absence of poetry is also a poetry.

Poetry is not about Nature. It is about Homer. The poet ransacks the traditions. If I'm in Iran I read Sufi poetry rather than the Avesta because I need to make sense of the Other, as a Parsi I need to know the Moslem.

Enemy, my enemy I name you friend. (Neruda)

Hart Crane tore around his New York city bachelor apartment crying: "I am Baudelaire, I am Rimbaud, I'm Christ." So the French poetry of Symbolism comes naturally to anyone seeking to revolutionize sensibility. It did to Lorca, Crane, Nin, Ginsberg.

My first published poem, "Circles," was based on the Soviet silent film *Earth* by Douzhenko. Lorca, to Crane, to Nin, to Ginsberg. . . .

> He died dancing
> among harvest fruit
> His widow tore her weeds in grief
> And it rained
> Till the melons rotted
>
> And the landlord who shot him
> for a piece of land
> Was so joy-ridden
> He stuck his head
>   in the mud
>
> And danced in circles

till he died.

I was trained in the West. I was not brought up in the *Shah Nameh* which is the Persian epic nor on the Hindu *Mahabharata.* I read Homer and about the Greek wars at school. I saw my warring Parsi family as cursed as the House of Atreus. At college I found an echo of my condition in *The Streetcar Named Desire* or *A Long Day's Journey into Night,* in *Phaedra* first and only later in the epic of the hapless Siavosh accused wrongfully by his step mother.

It is when we make our lives into myths that we find our true meaning. This is, of course, a paraphrase of Nin who might be paraphrasing Jung.

So our writing is marked by hybridity and mirror-imaging: Echoes within echoes, box-within-box as in a Chinese box, mirrors mirroring mirrors in a fun-house. To parody Leonard Cohen:

Giving head in a hired bed
With the taxi throbbing in the street

How else do I make sense of the boys I bed? No, I do not write to beautify them; I write in order to go over to them, as Pasolini did. So there is this great democracy of sex and death Whitman knew and Lorca and poor Wilde and of course, Pasolini. And the boys we dream of come out of the Old City slums or from the recently bourgeoisified proletariat. They all imitate Shahrukh or Salman, Saif or Aamir, the four reigning Khans of Bollywood. And as I teach *Kubla Khan*, I dream him and become him in my poems.

Just as my mother was the 40s tragediennes Meena Kumari or Nargis with her tears, I was the 1960s gamins Sadhana or Saira at 16 being wooed in Bombay's overcrowded suburban trains. If this sounds weird, I'm conscious of it. Art does not imitate life as Arnold was silly enough to believe but it is life that imitates Art as Wilde saw it in *The Decay of Lying.*

What is the relation of a homosexual artist to his body? Poems are written on the body. Ask the English painter Francis Bacon or the Japanese gay Zen poet, Takahashi. My student Sivapriya writes about my work in the *Deccan Chronicle* in 1994: "Hoshang Merchant has a beautiful body." (You can now, in 1999, change that "has" to "had.") Nin was beautiful into her 60s. Ginsberg was photographed nude by Richard Avedon with his handsome lover placed behind him so that we see the hippie poet's large belly and largish member delicately cut out of the frame. Or, take the gay Mapplethorpe's photographs of the body. Once in a Greenwich Village gallery I saw a gay artist mount a cross in the nude to complete his real-life sculpture entitled "The Crucifixion". In a Japanese film on the relation between silence and the spoken mantra in Zen Buddhism, the entire sutra was tattooed on the live body of a monk to the beating of gongs, lighting of fires, loud chanting, and of course the monk's screams. But these are extreme examples. Yet no one is surprised to read at school that Poe was found dead naked on the city's busiest thoroughfare one morning, a bodily sacrifice to the bitch-goddess who devoured him for hymning the moon goddesses.

The gay Parsi poet's body and language are colonized by Parsi culture first and then by the dominant culture he inhabits in India or Iran or the West; by heterosexist notions of sexuality, by colonial history. Zoroastrianism, Hinduism, Islam, Christianity all forbid homosexuality. The men we sleep with in childhood are married men who are heterosexual or bisexual.

The language we speak at home is a hybrid Parsi/Gujarati born out of the long love of the Parsi for his Gujarati neighbour. We took to English like ducks to water but we lost our language a second time and we stand accused of "chamchagiri" (toadyism) towards the British. The case of Kafka comes to mind. An Austrian Jew, he spoke Yiddish but wrote in German to his eternal shame and glory.

One way for me to rejoin India was translation. I came to Urdu through Hindi, Persian, Arabic: the languages I picked up on my travels.

Art is to be lived, not merely read. Now that is a dangerous proposition leading to the madhouse and to death.

Well, how *does* one write?

I write very quickly. And if it galls so much the better. If it doesn't, *tant pis.* "First said, best said," Ginsberg believed. I rewrite a trauma over many, many years until it crystallizes. This is how I could finally write about my parents' divorce or a sister's abortion. Nothing is laboured, everything is spontaneous. "Poems come like leaves to trees."

I'm 50 and my nation is 50 and we have to make sense of each other. What *is* a gay poet saying to a half-starved nation where rape occurs every 10 minutes and a child is born every minute? Perhaps that sex cuts across caste and class? How do you write gayness when there is no gay culture? How do you create a gay aesthetic for urban India?

I found my answer in Pound, a poets' poet. Pound said that if you can rely on high art to be really high then the tenor of popular culture wouldn't be so low. We wouldn't be subject to a garish TV *Ramayana* which nonetheless funnels Hindu pride. Instead we would have our modern gay lives depicted with all the abandon that characterizes any true epic.

I've always spoken in rhymes. Still do I rely on my blood's rhythm which is the rhythm of our spoken Indian English, the sea-rhythms of my birth, of the tides and the mood-phases . . . the rhythm I first hear in my mother's belly.

Epilogue

"Do not forget the wisdom of our Mothers," Mulk Raj Anand wrote a young Hoshang in Tehran. "Is Hoshang a gay poet or a Sufi poet?" people now ask.

Think of the gay Jesuit who wrote "Windhover," think of the *Divan-i-Shams-i-Tabrizi,* think of mad Sarmad followed by his boy from Sind to Golconda to Delhi, think of Amir Khusro making the Moghul prince Dara Shikoh so mad that Aurangzeb had to kill Dara, think of St. John of the Cross on that dark and lonely night when a stranger pursues him up the narrow steps of his house, think of Takahashi dying of hunger in opulent modern Japan, think of the last poems of Ginsberg gone over to Elizabethan love-lyrics and the sweet Lord Buddha.

So the Urdu ghazal has crept into my Indian English poems.

At the end of his life, Ghalib writes:

> Apart from Allah all is vague
> and non-existent. There is no
> poetry and no poet, no ode and
> no ode writer. Nothing exists
> except God

It seems to me the only god in my books and books of poems is the poem, i.e., it is the poem itself.

Ghalib also writes: Whatever happens to the mystic is good for his soul.

A comment on this is that madness is but the last stage of longing, be it for justice (the rage for it turning into violence) or for love, as with the beloved and blessed Sufi, Majnun.

In Hindu Bhakti literature we have a term "Radha-bhava." It assumes, like all mysticism, that the divine principle is male, all others are female souls yearning for divine union. The Radhabhava suits the spiritually included modern gay writer. It is not an accident that Winston Leyland of the Gay Press, San Francisco, is interested in the Iranian mysticism of Jalal-ud-din Rumi who is currently very fashionable in America in Coleman Barks' translation or mistranslations. This is not feminism: the story of Mirabai comes to mind. Tulsi Goswami refused to see her in Brindaban on the grounds that she was a woman. She sent word right back that she thought the only man in Brindaban was Lord Krishna and everyone else was only a woman. She was promptly granted an audience.

There is a well known thumri:

Tum Radha bano/ Main banoo Shyam
(You be Radha/ I Krishna)

When a man, Bhimsen Joshi, sings this, it is all very well. But when women like Parveen Sultana or Begum Akhtar sing it we get a special thrill. The same thrill when we recognize the beauty and terror of the Picwai painting of Radhaji with Krishna's crown and Krishnaji in Radha's saree. It is the eunuch in my friend Bhupen Khakhar's painting: always naked, always an outcast, but with a sky-blue saree sewn with tinsel stars! Krishna is not a "bhogi" (sensualist), he is India's greatest yogi (ascetic).

At first poetry is transgressive, ultimately it is transcendent:

Bairam Khan was sent on a pilgrimage by Akbar
Then set upon/ So was Shams by Rumi's son
No wonder they never returned
But myths grow around madmen not kings
They've said to become one with god
Their blood waters the Martyr's Tree
Its leaves turn books
Boys become poets/ Lovers become ascetics

Yet people say: Love accomplishes nothing
Sacrifice accomplishes nothing
Politics is all/ Ambition is all

A benediction does not stop a gun
But it shames the assassin for centuries
What arms accomplish is immediate
Ashes are for the whole world for aeons
The pelican feeds its young with its blood
Some call him Christ/ Others, Mother
When Hindu killed Moslem I made love to a Moslem
Listen to me. Do not call me names
Now I've stopped speaking. There is nothing more to hear.

Genders are Genres: Gay and Lesbian Writing in India

T. VIJAY KUMAR

Look here, dear fellow:
I wear these men's clothes
only for you.
Sometimes I am man,
sometimes I am woman.
O lord of the meeting rivers,
I'll make wars for you,
but I'll be your devotees' bride

(Basavanna, translated by Ramanujan)[1]

In recent times marginal discourses have greatly undermined the conventions of 'mainstream' writing, its politics, and its poetics. Slave narratives, subaltern histories, women's her-stories, dalit literature, gay/lesbian writings have challenged the generic categories, and the critical paradigms of the 'main-stream'.

The publication in 1999 of India's first anthologies of gay and lesbian writings—*Yaraana: Gay Writing from India* edited by Hoshang Merchant, and *Facing the Mirror: Lesbian Writing from India* edited by Aswini Sukthankar—by a mainstream pub-lishing house like Penguin Books is not only a significant mo-ment in the history of Indian writing in English but also a sign of the 'liberal' critical environment in which such a venture be-comes possible. The critical and commercial 'success' of these books already seems to have facilitated the 'coming out' of other similar ventures: (see, for instance, Ruth Vanita and Saleem Kidwai's exhaustive book on homoerotic mythologies titled *Same Sex Love in India*).[2]

The publication of these anthologies acquires an added significance at a time when in the body-politic there are resurgent attempts to draw the boundaries of the nation's social, political, religious, and territorial identities strictly in terms of self and other. By interrogating social realities, dalit and women's writing expose the constructedness of our social identities; the body politics of gay and lesbian writing extend the interrogation to challenge the givenness of biological categories.

My paper makes an attempt to read the self-definitions gay and lesbian writers outline in their poetry. My paper also seeks to understand the challenges posed by gay and lesbian writings to categories of gender and genre, even as it notes the affinities between homosexual literature and other counter discourses.

I read gay/lesbian writings in alignment with other counter discourses like dalit and women's writing and see the counter discourses of nation, gender, and sexuality paralleling, criss-crossing, and influencing each other. It is not a coincidence that what little openness there is today even in the academia towards gay/lesbian writing, exists because historiography has been redefined by paying more attention to questions addressed by women's history and social history.

II

If they see
breasts and long hair coming
they call it woman,

if beard and whiskers,
they call it man:

but, look, the self that hovers
in between

is neither man nor woman

O Ramanatha

(Devara Dasimayya, translated by Ramanujan)[3]

In India homosexuality is neither a new nor an 'imported' phenomenon as it is often alleged. Given the strict segregation of the sexes its occurrence is not surprising, and its existence is acknowledged, even if to proscribe it as 'unnatural', in texts reaching back to the late Vedic period[4]. What is surprising, in fact, is that *Yaraana* and *Facing the Mirror* are the first books of their kind in India, at least in English, because gay and lesbian issues have come into public domain at least by the beginning of the 1980s in India. Besides being the first of their kind, these two anthologies are significant for a variety of other reasons as well. One, they have brought into public domain writings that are always "hidden from history", for, as Martin Duberman reminds us, "repression and marginalization have often been the lot of historians of homosexuality as well as of homosexuals themselves."[5]

Two, *Yaraana* and *Facing the Mirror* create a sense of community, and afford the homosexuals the right to self-definitions. As the sociologist Alain Touraine points out "society is a cultural field torn apart by the conflict between those who take over historicity for themselves and those who are subjected to their domination and are struggling for the collective reappropriation of this historicity."[6]

Three, like other knowledge systems, knowledge about gay and lesbian movement/writings has followed the 'centre-periphery' pattern: the movement in a New York city is the best known and the US gay movement in general is much better documented than movements elsewhere. *Yaraana* and *Facing the Mirror* are thus important also for breaking this dominant pattern and giving Indian gay texts a local habitation and history.

As editors, both Sukthankar and Merchant are acutely aware of their cultural and historical contexts. Writing about the task of making the anthology, Sukthankar writes: "There were books and magazines from the West, but even the women with *access to them knew that the niches we have to carve out for ourselves here are* very different—not lesbian cafes and bars and bookstores. We have to shape our own spaces, piecing them together out of nothing more than thin air and the willingness to take a risk."[7] "There is no such beast in zoology", writes Merchant, "as a 'homosexual'. It is an invention of late nineteenth century European science. . . . Such a term does not exist in India where the practice is not codified, only quietly condoned and above all, not talked about."[8]

The 'Indian' context also explains why while Sukthankar's contributors barring a few, choose to write under pseudonyms, Merchant's contributors use their real names. In India gay men face 'legal' risk while lesbian women confront a more dangerous 'social' risk: Section 377 of the Indian Penal Code recognizes as illegal only homosexual acts between men but is not technically empowered to punish lesbianism. Thus, the same law that acknowledges the identity of gay men also ironically criminalizes their existence; while by refusing to recognize lesbianism it denies homosexual women an identity of their own.

History and language are two key elements of one's identity, and it is these very elements that are denied to homosexuals. History is both a remembrance of the past and a setting of itself in a context whereby a group can see who it is, relative to everyone else and, as Sukthankar writes, "living without a history of our own kind is like living without the reassurance of a reflection in the mirror."[9] Sukthankar's mapping of lesbian history is horizontal; it cuts across class and language to challenge those who exploit these as othering devices to divide women and to charge that lesbianism is a phenomenon of the westernized upper-classes. On the other hand, Merchant traces the genealogy of gay writing from ancient Sanskrit texts to medieval Sufi literature, to the work of modern Indian writers in English—from Adil Jussawala to Vikram Seth to Mahesh Dattani. Merchant's vertical, genealogical approach is both a reclamation of the past and an assertion of the present.

III

Language, like history, is a crucial issue in identity politics because it can either grant or deny subjectivity. Judy Grahn's frustration with 'ordinary' language is emblematic: "I am a poet and a gay cultural theorist, not an etymologist. Word derivations find their way into dictionaries after etymologists have gathered information based on the contexts in which the words may have been used. There has been no acceptance and exploration of the gay context that would allow our subterranean slang words to enter the world of dictionaries."[10] Giti Thadani's archival research has shown how there has been a deliberate erasure of lesbian love and *an equally* deliberate misinterpretation of texts describing it. She argues that the terms historically used to describe women who love women—such as *sakhi* and *saheli*—have been purged of their eroticism over time and reshaped into harmless descriptions of female friendship, so that today lesbians find themselves banished from language itself, literally at a loss for words.[11]

In a similar vein, Merchant points out that "Unlike 'hijras' the gays do not have a local habitation or even a name. No word exists yet for the 'homosexual' in any of the Indian languages."[12] It is, of course, one more irony of our postcolonial situation that we derive both the vocabulary to articulate homosexuality and the law that prohibits its experience from the same 'authority: while "Macaulay's Minute" of 1835 gives us English enabling us to 'name' a homosexual, "Macaulay's Law" of 1861 (the Indian Penal Code, Section 377 and also Section 292), makes the homosexual act illegal. Merchant identifies the imposition of Western education, with its single sex convent schools and their "suffering god-on-the-cross" religion, as the beginning of a cultural schizophrenia in modern India.[13]

One of the fundamental insights of Lacanian psychoanalysis is the notion that any identity is founded relationally, constituted in reference to an exterior or outside that defines the subject's own interior boundaries and corporeal surfaces. Heterosexuality typically defines itself in critical opposition to that which it is not, namely homosexuality. To the extent that the denotation of any term is always dependent on what is exterior to it, the hetero/homo polarity is an indispensable semiotic model. The fact that the term "heterosexuality" came into public sphere a startling eleven years after, and as an antithetical term to "homosexuality" is further proof of its relational existence. According to historian Jonathan Ned Katz, "homosexuality" and "heterosexuality" were privately coined in 1868 by the nineteenth century German sodomy law reformer Karl Maria Kertbeny. "Homosexuality" made its first public appearance in an 1869 appeal for reforming the German sodomy laws, "heterosexuality" followed eleven years later in a defense of homosexuality published in 1880.[14] On this delayed emergence of heterosexuality into public sphere, David Halperin wittily observes that "it [heterosexuality] came into being, in fact, like Eve from Adam's rib."[15]

IV

Male homosexuality is 'transgressive' primarily because it is non-procreative, and lesbian sexuality is 'dangerous' because it allows women to escape the social hierarchy. Hence the societal insistence on marriage, and the misery that results from such a marriage. Raj Rao's poem "Opinions" mocks at the neighbourly 'concern':

> Onions and opinions come cheap in Bombay
>
> The Gujaratis in the neighbourhood
> want to *know why you're* still single,
> though eligible. . . .
> Shantibai. . . .
> goes one step further.

She thinks
a man without wife and kids
Is cremated by bombay municipal
Corporation

Upon death.

You wonder whether she's making a pass.[16]

Rakesh Ratti's poem "Beta" portrays the conflict between conforming to familial expectations and being honest to one's self:

I want to fill their eyes with joy,
Yet let *my spirit* run wild.
How can I find the love I seek
And still remain their child[17]

If marriage for homosexual men involves a moment of decision—whether to be a dutiful son and citizen, or declare what Oscar Wilde termed as "the love which dare not speak its name"—women in India very often do not enjoy even that: notional freedom. A.G.'s poem "Wifey" describes the claustrophobia in 'arranged' marriage:

I am shushed and hushed and calmed.
I see red—no—a vermillion gash
stretches across my head.
I can't breathe, I can't think.
I straddle the fence of indecision,
cowardly, swaying on the brink.
He snores. On my side of the bed.[18]

Societal pressure on the homosexuals to conform to norms does not, however, stop with 'neighbourly concern' or a personal conflict. Physical violence is very much a brutal reality of the lives of gays in India, and according to Merchant it has always been so:

Shama-I-Tabrizi was set upon
by his beloved Jalal-ud-din's son
and murdered.
There is no blood on anyone's hand today
when fathers murder their son's beloveds.[19]

In Shalini's poem "womanlove", 'the world' is not some imaginary; it enforces its will through family, through friends.

We did not believe that the world will love us for who we are.
But did we know it would be so difficult?
That there is nothing in the world
which makes it easy for two women
to love and live together—we knew.
That our own will battle us the most,
that friends will claw at this love,
that the pain will come from those
we are loathe to fight
. . . what justice is this, goddess?[20]

In such a world where 'ignorant armies clash by night', homosexuals do not have even the comfort of their friend/lover's embrace. It is not surprising, therefore, that loneliness is the dominant theme in Indian gay and lesbian writing, and schizophrenia the most recurrent motif. Merchant's poignant poems "Everyone Can Use a Friend" and "Secrecy" are just two examples that present the emptiness and the body-mind schism:

Everyone can use a friend
Few know friendship's value. . . .
He who had finally learnt
to use my body
Came to say he couldn't call me 'Friend'.[21]

You share your body
But keep secret your mind

At work we share our minds
But kept secret our bodies

There, clothed we become naked
Here nakedness has become another clothing.[22]

Forsaken by friend and foe alike, gays often find refuge in art. "My pen", writes Merchant, "my weapon of love/With other weapons I find the world destructed" (*Jonah* 50). For Merchant, writing is more than self-indulgence: it is an obligation, a responsibility:

My task as a writer was to give tongue to the dumb ones.
The beautiful boys I have loved were always too silent to tell
their story. I spoke for those who couldn't speak.

I was reprimanded, always, for talking too much.[23]

V

Grammar is the central model for thinking in many Hindu texts. As Frits Stal has said, what Euclid is to European thought, the grammarian Panini is to the Indian. Even the *Kamasutra* is literally a grammar of love—which declines and conjugates men and women as one would nouns and verbs in different genders, voices, moods and aspects. Genders are genres. Different body—types and character-types obey different rules, respond to different scents and beckonings.[24]

"But what does it mean to write as a lesbian?" asks Sukthankar, and goes on to give the answer: "It's writing with the whole self, with personal integrity in every sense of that phrase." She further argues that true lesbian writing will resist all categorization, including her own 'Indian lesbian writing'. "What is remarkable," writes Merchant, "is the number of genres homosexual writing encompasses and the easy transition from one genre to another in a single piece of work by taboo-breaking lives."[25] It can be argued that whether gays write poetry, prose, or drama, they are essentially writing their autobiographies, and all autobiographies are fictions. Homosexual writing defines itself, and validates its identity by frustrating generic expectations, because generic categories are underwritten by ideologies of heterosexuality. "It is impossible to think about narrative", Judith Roof writes, "without engaging ideologies of sexuality."[26] She argues that there is something intrinsically straight, something essentially heteronormative about narrative—all narrative, any narrative that comes (as most narratives do) to closure. Narrative "as an organizing structure . . . plays a large part in the stubborn return of a particularly heterosexual narrativity [because] something in the way we understand what a story is in the first place or something in the way narrative itself operates produces narrative's heterosexually friendly shape."[27]

Gay and lesbian writing undermine the ideological imperative for a man and woman to get together, to make commitments to stay together towards which digetic closure inevitably gestures. The only way, therefore, narratives could reflect and reinforce the pleasures of alternative sexualities would be for them to employ radical innovations in their discursive forms, not just to offer new or different subject matter for narratives that follow the same old established patterns of closure. "What we need," Foucault writes in "Gay Science", is "a radical break, a change in orientation, objectives and vocabulary."

Notes and References

1. A.K. Ramanujan, "Men, Women and Saints," *The Collected Essays of A.K. Ramanujan,* Gen, ed. Vinay Dharwadker (New Delhi: OUP, 1999), p. 290.
2. See *Same Sex Love in India: Readings from Literature and History*, ed. Ruth Vanitha & Saleem Kidwai (New York: St. Martins Press, 2000).
3. "Men, Women and Saints," p. 294.
4. Mina Kumar, "Lesbians in Indian Texts and Contexts," cited in *Facing the Mirror: Lesbian Writing from India*, ed. Ashwini Sukthankar (New Delhi: Penguin, 1999), pp. 217-232.

5. See *Hidden from History: Reclaiming the Gay and Lesbian Past*, ed. Martin Duberman et al (New York: New American Library, 1989).
6. Alain Touraine, *The Voice and the Eye* (New York: CUP, 1981), p. 62.
7. Sukthankar, p. xxiii.
8. *Yaarana: Gay Writing from India*, ed. Hoshang Merchant (New Delhi: Penguin, 1999), p. xi.
9. Sukthankar, p. xvi.
10. Judy Grahn, *Another Mother Tongue: Gay Words, Gay Worlds* (Boston: Beacon Press, 1984), p. xiii.
11. See Githi Thadani, *Sakhiyani: Lesbian Desire in Ancient and Modern India* (UK: Cassel, 1996).
12. Merchant, p. 205
13. Ibid., p. xx.
14. See Jonathan Ned Katz, "The Invention of Heterosexuality," *Socialist Reviews*, 21.1 (Feb. 1990), pp. 7-34.
15. See David Halperin, *One Hundred Years of Homosexuality and Other Essays on Greek Love* (New York & London: Routledge, 1990).
16. Merchant, p. 15.
17. Merchant, p. 101.
18. Sukthankar, p. 85.
19. Hoshang Merchant, *Jonah and the Whale* (Calcutta: Writers Workshop, 1995), p. 42.
20. Sukthankar, p. 294.
21. Hoshang Merchant, *Love's Permission* (Calcutta: Writers Workshop, 1996), p. 10.
22. Ibid., pp. 50-51.
23. Hoshang Merchant, *Hotel Golconda* (Calcutta: Writer's Workshop, 1992), p. 78.
24. A.K. Ramanujan, "Is There an Indian Way of Thinking? An Informal Essay," *The Collected Essays of A.K. Ramanujan*, p. 47.
25. Merchant, p. xxv.
26. Judith Roof, *Come As You Are: Sexuality and Narrative* (New York: Columbia UP, 1996), p. 24.
27. Ibid., p. 26.

Patterns of Female Bonding: Contemporary Indian Women's Poetry in English

C. VIJAYASREE

At the end of the twentieth century, as we undertake a retrospective analysis of the various developments in feminist thought and theory, women's writing—its themes and techniques, we realise that there is no single entity called feminism. Feminists reject the very possibility of fixing stable objective meanings. There have been several feminisms and difference has in fact been the keyword in feminist parlance. 'Difference within' is considerably stressed as various distinctive feminist approaches such as Black feminism, Afro-American feminism and Third World feminism emerged as important currents in feminist thought. Even as the divergence in feminist thought enriched the discipline of Women's Studies, the need to connect, the urge to form a female community, the urgency to forge a female bonding have been among the dominant concerns of women's writing, particularly since the seventies. These two impulses—the impulse to assert the difference within, in terms of race/colour/class/ caste and the impulse to connect and bond have emerged as the two nodal points governing the developments in feminist theory and women's writing.

The need to forge a female networking has been increasingly felt by women in all fields in the last quarter of the century. The reasons for this are obvious. Even as the feminist movement gained momentum all over the world in the second half of the twentieth century, an equally strong backlash has mounted pressure to halt and even reverse women's quest for autonomy and equality. This backlash as Susan Faludi described in her book by the same title, has come in different guises, some discrete, some not so discrete.[1] Scientific research reporting studies of working women concludes; 'Professional women are suffering burn out and succumbing to an infertility epidemic.' Psychologists are upset at the uprecedented outbreak of stress induced disorders among high-powered career women; Sociologists are concerned about the collapse of family structures; they blame it all on feminism. Trend stories in the media subtly suggest that pretty girls are better off at home with kids. The message that comes out is straight and simple: Women are unhappy precisely because they are free. Caught within the vortex of these anti-feminist currents, women writers, thinkers and activists increasingly felt the need for forging strong bonds among women and forming a community of women who can feel contemporaneity across time, proximity across space, equality across class, and sisterhood across race and culture. In fact several women writers reject the notion of special or super women since it works not so much in favour of female empowerment as in creating a class of privileged women thus acting as a divisive and ultimately destructive factor. Texts have often played a vital role in promoting female networking. This apprehension of the female collective manifests itself in a variety of curious patterns in women's literary texts. Now I shall focus on patterns of female bonding in Indian women's poetry in English.

Indian women's poetry in English has traversed a long way from Sarojini Naidu to Suniti Namjoshi, from Toru Dutt to Sujata Bhatt in the last fifty years absorbing a variety of influences, dealing with a range of themes and generating diverse strategies of poetic expression. Each one of them has tried to speak in a distinctly personal voice; yet they form a part of a chorus, a collective voice asserting the autonomy of woman. A quick analysis of the collective aspect reveals crisscross patterns of female bonding etched out in these texts. These range from attempts to resurrect a female tradition and heritage to the forging of a lesbian continuum (most of the findings in this paper are worked out on the basis of a sample drawn from Indian women's writing in general and not women's poetry alone. However since our focus here is on poetry I shall choose my illustrations from poetry).

Women writers assert that the creation of a community of women is the necessary antidote to the excesses of individualism. They believe that women need to explore their collective consciousness and shared experience in order to transcend the fragmentation and isolation of their lives. In order to create a community, each woman must confront her experience stripped of patriarchal myths. Rejecting patriarchal territoriality, they try to retrieve matrilinear family histories and attempt to recover a lost heritage. They often turn to their mothers and grandmothers and co-opt them in this project. The persona in Suniti Namjoshi's long poem: 'From Baby F with much love' asks her mother:

> We loved those kindly gentlemen, I mean
> Your own father and your daughter's father
> But in our long ancestry, where are the women?
> I know I should be proud, but I feel
> Like a beggar. Is my vast vanity wholly illegal?

Looking at a mother-daughter relationship and celebrating this most natural bond of all is another related motif in women's writing. In 'Of Woman Born: Motherhood as Expression and Institution' Adrienne Rich notes the intimacy of this bond as well as its implications for patriarchy as follows:

> The cathexis between mother and daughter—essential, distorted, misused—is the great unwritten story. Probably there is nothing in human nature more resonant with charges than the flow of energy between two biologically alike bodies,

> one of which lain in amniotic bliss inside the other, one which has labored to give birth to the other. . . . Yet this relationship has been minimized and trivialized in the annals of patriarchy.[2]

To recover this bond is an important feature of female bonding. Let us look at this excerpt from Meena Alexander's 'Blood Line':

> My child is rain
> On the tamarind tree.
>
> She is my mother's
> Mother who cries in me.
>
> My line of blood
> Our perpetuity

The poet then goes on to dream about a strong breed of girls to emerge in future:

> In the sky's bowl
> After a season of storm
> We'll watch girls
> With antlers in their hair
>
> Dance confounding
> Ancient hunters
> who stumble westwards
> Broken bows in hand.

As they realise the need for caring for each other, and sharing each other's pain and pleasure, women writers begin to talk about their most intimate personal experiences in their work. For instance, female body and its nuances, female biological processes such as menstruation, pregnancy, childbirth etc. are often turned into poetic subjects. These are experiences common to women and these enclose them as a group with a shared experience. Sujata Bhatt in 'Udaylee' articulates the feelings of menstruating woman in telling images. In 'White Asparagus' Bhatt asks:

> Who speaks of the strong currents
> Streaming through the legs, the breasts
> Of a pregnant women
> In her fourth month?

In writing their bodies into their texts, they are not only articulating hitherto silent aspects of female experience, but also communicating directly with a large community of women who care and share.

The relation between classes and patriarchies is complex and variable. Not only are patriarchal systems class differentiative open to constant and consistent reformulation, but defining gender seems to be crucial to the formation of classes and dominant ideologies. The lives of women therefore exist at the interface of class/caste inequality, and women writers find it absolutely imperative to cut across caste/class barriers and bring women together on a common platform. One of the earliest instances of a poetic protest against class constellation may be seen in Balamaniamma's 1930s poem 'to the servant maid.' The speaker in Meena Alexander's 'A House of a Thousand Doors' for instance is an Indian woman living in the United States. She often hears voices of the village women she left behind. During her birthing pains in New York, these women come in dream to deliver her. In a moment of this primeval pain, all barriers collapse and women come together in mutual sympathy, understanding and concern.

Women poets have often raised their voice against social and cultural conventions that constrained their freedom and perpetrated a sort of institutional subjection of women. Here they view themselves as comrades waging a collective fight in support of a common cause. The struggle itself becomes the electronic field effecting the formation of some of the strongest bonds. Imtiaz

Dharker in her much acclaimed poems on Purdah articulates the feelings of the veiled community of women when she says;

> There are so many of me.
> I have met them, met them everyday
> Recognise their shadows on the streets
> I know their past and future
> In the cautious way they place their feet.
> I can see behind their veils
> And before they speak
> I know their tongues.

They share a similar predicament, familiar rage and resistance.

The feminist movement entered a new phase in 1970 when radicalesbians came out with their manifesto called "The Woman Identified Woman" and penned a new ground for discourse about the understanding of lesbianism. This document viewed lesbianism as an important and essential aspect of feminism. "A lesbian is the rage of all women condensed to the point of explosion."[3] They argue that the basic structure of control over women is that of sexuality or compulsory homosexuality, to use Adrienne Rich's term. It is important to dismantle this oppressive structure in order to make female empowerment complete. The radicalesbians stress the primacy of women relating to women, of women creating a new consciousness of and with each other. This notion of woman identification, that is the primacy of women bonding with women emotionally and politically is strongly articulated in some of the contemporary women's writing. Rukmini Bhaya Nair's 'Homophrodite Longings' is one of the most forceful poetic statements available on the subject to date. The poet pays a rich tribute to Sappho and asks:

> Only Sappho imagined history as a woman
> And who but a woman could own a woman's body?

Then the poet proceeds to conclude: "True histories are histories of women in love. " She then adds that the capacity to love is in itself a female attribute and insists that "a man in love must become a woman." In a subtle transposition of images that follows Nair relates to Sappho the Indian concept of Ardhanariswara, half-woman god and finds in both "the perfect androgynous voice of god."

Suniti Namjoshi directly addresses the need to legitimize lesbianism and argues that a woman's love for a woman is both natural and quite ancient. She complains that books, stories and society all collude in propagating the myths of compulsory heterosexuality and in all these versions men love women and women love men, and men ride off and have all sorts of adventures while women stay at home. In a number of poems included in her collections *Jackass and the Lady,* and *Blue Donkey Fables* Namjoshi celebrates lesbian eroticism. In 'The Arbitrary Order' she questions the logic of asserting the ultimacy of heterosexuality as the only acceptable sexual order. The female persona in 'She turns the Grass' describes:

> She turns the grass to sea water
> And the bed to a mountain slope
> When I lie in her arms dolphin like.

She finds an apt metaphor for lesbianism in the ritual of Maenads. Maenadism enabled women to leave their homes, mingle with their sisters and assert their individual desire, joy and ecstasy. In recreating the violent Maenad ritual Namjoshi points out that women's collective resistance to patriarchy is neither new nor shocking. Namjoshi writes:

> The maenads beat my grandfather to death.
> And my brother, he was caught too.
> Caught like a rabbit in the thorn forest.

In a number of short poems such as 'I give her the Rose', 'An Explanation' and 'Metamorphoses', she celebrates lesbian eroticism in telling images drawn from nature. Lesbian writers prefer natural imagery to signify sexuality to make an important point:

they hold that lesbian love relationship is natural while heterosexuality is a cultural construct. Namjoshi makes a strong case for alternative sexualities when she says: "I don't believe sexuality is a matter of nature or of morality. It is the meanings and symbolism attributed to sexuality that are crucial, and when analysed it's clear that many of these are inimical to women—all women not just lesbians."[4] It is interesting to note Adrienne Rich's expansive definition of lesbianism to include all "forms of primary intensity between and among women, including the sharing of a rich inner life, the bonding against male tyranny, the giving and receiving of political support."[5]

Female bonding in literature has thus taken a variety of forms, the agenda being common: women need to come together and call into question all the divisive strategies of patriarchy. This is a necessary prerequisite if women are to consolidate their resources to resist dogma and to collapse the status quo which generally is maintained by the conservatives to make sure that those in power stay in power and those who are relatively powerless remain so.

Notes and References

1. Susan Faludi. *Backlash: The Undeclared War against Women* (London: Vintage, 1992), pp. 1-2.
2. Adrienne Rich. *Of Woman Born: Motherhood as Experience and Institution* (1976; New York: Bantam Books, 1977), pp. 226-27.
3. Radicalesbians, "The Woman-Identified Woman" in *Radical Feminisms*, ed. Anne Koedt et al (New York: Quadrangle Books, 1973), pp. 240-41.
4. From a personal unpublished interview with Suniti Namjoshi by the author.
5. Adrienne Rich, "Compulsory Heterosexuality and Lesbian Existence," *Signs 5* (1980), pp. 631-60.

Srinivas Rayaprol: A Pioneer in Indian English Poetry

E. NAGESWARA RAO

Srinivas Rayaprol who passed away last year was born in 1925, a few months after Nissim Ezekiel. Unlike Ezekiel and Dom Moraes who went to England to study English literature, he went to the United States to study civil engineering at Stanford University. Rayaprol's father was a trend-setter in modern Telugu poetry. Rayaprol imbibed a love of poetry from his boyhood. Although he was a student of engineering at Banaras Hindu University and Stanford, he continued his interest in poetry, especially English poetry. While in the USA he got acquainted with many prominent American writers such as William Carlos Williams, e.e. cummings, James Laughlin, Tennessee Williams, Henry Miller, and Truman Capote. He carried on correspondence with several of them for a number of years. He published the poems of quite a few American, British and European poets in his journal, *East and West*, in the fifties and sixties. As Dom Moraes says, with the possible exception of Rabindranath Tagore who knew Pound, Yeats and Frost, only Rayaprol seems to have had a wide range of international contacts with poets. Also, Rayaprol was deeply read in the work of Eliot, Auden, Gide, Valery, Kafka, Rilke, Lorca, W.C. Williams, Wallace Stevens, Hart Crane, Tennessee Williams and others. In his own words, these "have filled my mind with their words." (*Selected Poems*, 15)[1]

His poems were published in almost all the leading journals in India and in a number of well-known periodicals including the *Atlantic Monthly* in the USA, in Hungary, in Germany and in Australia. Thus his poems have won editorial approval and appreciation in four continents, a distinction which not many Indian English poets seem to have achieved. In yet another way, Rayaprol is rather unusual as he was a Civil Engineer, who reached the top of his profession as Chief Engineer, but continued his interest in poetry. Here also, his literary forbears seemed to show the way. If Eliot a banker, Stevens an insurance man, and Williams a paediatrician, composed poetry, so did Rayaprol the engineer. He writes in "Lines to a Fellow Poet":

> And while I was trained to build of steel
> I sought for the structure of words. . . .
> Words have both meaning and music
> And nothing will convince me
> That the bones of the one are separate
> From the blood of the other. (*Selected Poems*, 63)

Rayaprol's first poem was written in 1948 and the last perhaps in 1995. It is interesting to know his views on the creative process, more particularly the composition of poetry. He writes: "The creative act, after all, is in itself unique, a thing of beauty not forever but for the moment."[2]

Rayaprol's own view of poetry is rather akin to William Wordsworth's who defined poetry as "emotion recollected in tranquillity." Observe what he says:

> The work of art is a creation, as result of the particular experience. What I mean is that it is necessary to 'live' or 'experience', but it is possible to recreate the same only after the experience is over. To that extent we demand of the work of art a mastery of the craft and the medium.[3]

In his mature years, he likens the birth of a poem to "the first spark of semen that shoots out uncontrollable at the climactic moment" ("Preface" to *Selected Poems*, 9). One may compare this with Wordsworth's statement that poetry is "the spontaneous overflow of powerful feelings." For Rayaprol, writing poetry is an unavoidable physical need:

> Why do I write? Because I like to write, because the words which I use convey the meaning and feeling that I wish to convey and the reader wishes to understand. Primarily the need is mine. I need to write just like I need to eat or sleep or fornicate. As far as readers are concerned, a majority of one is O.K. with me.[4]

Poetry is thus a compulsive act for Rayaprol. A younger poet, R. Parthasarathy, makes a similar point:

> Some days it's a torture
> Not to be able to write. . . .
> A poem shouldn't be
> Kept waiting at the door. ("Two Cheers for the Poet")

Rayaprol's mentor, W.C. Williams, emphasizes the shapes of things when he says: "No ideas but in things." Some of Rayaprol's own poems illustrate this principle:

> By my lonely soul I will only see
> The beauty of an orange on a table
> Or a word in a poem. (*Selected Poems*, 61)

Goethe says that thinking is more important than doing, feeling is more important than thinking, but looking is most important of all. Rayaprol's poem cited above is concerned with "seeing" objects or words, but not so much with feeling, thinking, or doing. Poetry such as Williams's or Rayaprol's, deals not so much with actions, emotions or thoughts of men, but with the poet's own reactions.

Rayaprol's themes are the conventional ones such as love, loneliness, death, but there is a freshness in his poetic presentation. His idea of love is comprehensive. In a poem significantly titled, "I am all that I love," he writes:

> You know, love
> is such a funny thing when you
> feel it most you least can tell. (*Selected Poems*, 31)

He explains in a note that love has nothing to do with sex, that it is difficult to express it satisfactorily, that it is "sad and tender and beautiful" (31). In the poem, "Married Love," he ruefully states that he had forgotten his wife and children when he was at work. On returning home, he disappoints them once again as he has set apart the evening to visit the bars. Ironically, he cannot spare time for the ones he loves. In another poem, "All Kinds of Love," he declares

> The commerce of our bodies
> Will end
> In the meeting of our minds. (*Selected Poems*, 33)

This correlation between physical and spiritual love is expressed beautifully in a poem dedicated to Mulk Raj Anand:

> You hold a fascination for me
> wholly physical
> and your body seeks my betrayal.
> But it is just another way
> to say
> that our minds have met
> a long time ago
> and your words have stripped
> my soul naked. (*Selected Poems*, 34)

Rayaprol wrote a couple of poems on homosexual and lesbian themes. For instance, "Valdstenka Hospada, Praha" is candid about an ex-lesbian's yearnings:

> A once upon a time lesbian
> and now in need
> of a man to tell her. . . .
> A man to rough her up a bit
> with his coarse lips
> and his unshaved-on Sunday face
> to light the candle. (*Selected Poems*, 75)

Loneliness and old age are recurring themes in Rayaprol's poetry. "Middle Age" acknowledges the waning strength and competence of man as husband, father, friend and lover. In "On Approaching Fifty," he regrets that one cannot return to childhood:

> Full circle
> I am back
> at the beginning
> But without the wonder
> of being child again. (*Selected Poems*, 46)

A feeling of neglect at being left alone in old age is voiced in "Diwali Days":

> From tomorrow is another day
> and old people
> are left again
> with each other
> to look at the walls
> and the pictures on the walls. (*Selected Poems*, 43)

In a poem written when he was around seventy, he reviews his life and its unfulfilled promises:

Here now, on the verge of seventy
Unsatisfactory husband, irate father
Ugly, old, much misunderstood man
I begin to philosophise on my failures

And sprout platitudes
That have lost all meaning
On a life that is almost over
With too little to show. (*Selected Poems*, 13-14)

The loneliness of old age drives him to thoughts of death in "Not Yet the End":

In my unborn darkness
I struggled for the world's light
In the world's translucence
I lie awake for Death's other darkness. . . .
I, an old man, hanging between
Two darknesses
See only you who are the centre
of the world's light. (*Selected Poems*, 21-22)

Rayaprol feels that man's life is sandwiched between two darknesses, the darkness of the womb and that of the tomb. One may notice a faint echo of Matthew Arnold's words in reverse in these lines.

However, in the poem, "Gone Now," he comes to terms with Death, the stale and inevitable phenomenon:

And if you live a full life
By which I mean, Raise
A family, love a wife
And generally Be
What is there to fear of Death
Which is but a mere cease
of a heartbeat
The sudden stoppage of Is. (*Selected Poems*, 82)

While still on the theme of death, it is perhaps appropriate to refer to two elegies written by Rayaprol. One of these is for W.H. Auden whom Rayaprol adored. He laments:

> "Your multivalence surprised us all"
> "Perfection of a kind was what you were after"
> "English has had a face-lift in your hands"
>
> (*Selected Poems*, 58)

The second elegy appears to be for Jawaharlal Nehru:

> This was a man whose life has filled my life
> This was a man whose death will diminish me.
>
> (*Selected Poems*, 25)

Rayaprol also wrote a few poems in a lighter vein:

> The Jesuit
> Was an able casuit
> After a discourse
> (on various religions)
> he suggested intercourse. (*Selected Poems*, 39)

He pokes fun at the Capitol building in Washington, D.C.:

> and to the right
> are Democrat dining halls
> and to the left
> Republican restrooms (*Selected Poems*, 71)

"Travel Poster" describes memorable symbols of many nations and ends on a pessimistic note:

> A Geisha
> like a
> fish
> for Japan. . . .

The Golden Gate
or the golden eagle
for the Americans

And all round this world
Eternal dissatisfaction
For the eye of Man. (*Selected Poems*, 78-79)

In many of his poems, Rayaprol's refrain is the failure to accomplish lofty goals and to become a great poet as he set out to do. He seems to have realised around middle age that the possibility of fulfilling his poetic ambitions was receding. Like Wordsworth, he laments in "These Days":

And I wonder now
Where was the fire that burnt me
Where the words that danced on the periphery.
(*Selected Poems*, 85)

These lines certainly remind us of the crisis in Wordsworth's career as a poet when he wrote in "Immortality Ode":

Whither is fled the visionary gleam?
Where is it now, the glory and the dream?

Rayaprol started with several advantages: a great poet as his father, an ardent love of literature, especially English poetry, very good contacts with writers in the USA and India. And yet, in his own assessment he was an inheritor of unfulfilled renown. He started writing poetry in English much earlier than Ezekiel, Dom Moraes, A.K. Ramanujan and others. But that was an inopportune period because soon after Independence, the political, cultural and literary climate in India was uncertain. The future of English in Free India was unclear. The more successful Indian English poets like Ezekiel, Ramanujan, R. Parthasarathy, Gieve Patel, Arvind Mehrotra published their poetry in the sixties when the climate was favourable for the reception and appreciation of

Indian poetry in English. Rayaprol's own explanation for his inability to achieve more as a poet was that he had lived in a second-rate city, Secunderabad, which compared unfavourably with larger cities like Bombay and Calcutta in providing opportunities to interact with fellow poets and with visiting American and British writers. There is a valid point here because the composition and enjoyment of English poetry in India was, and still is, an urban, even elite, pastime. Saleem Peeradina's caustic observation regarding the lack of recognition and encouragement to genuine writers may apply to Rayaprol also: "In India, one of the constant threats to an honest naming of worthwhile writers is the indiscriminate and irresponsible promotion of hacks, dopes and outright frauds, chiefly by ambitious publishers."[5]

Whatever might be the disappointments of Rayaprol as a poet, his poems were, in Dom Moraes's words, "unlike any other Indian poetry produced in English over the last 50 years."[6] Rayaprol has stated that it was not the cleverness or artistry of his literary forbears such as Lorca, Pasternak, Valery, but "their sincerity and absolute lack of pretence in thought or expression" which impressed him most (*Selected Poems*, 92). His own poetry is characterised by an authentic voice and an admirable technical virtuosity.

Notes and References

1. Srinivas Rayaprol, *Selected Poems* (Calcutta: Writers Workshop, 1995).
2. *East and West*, ed. Srinivas Rayaprol (Vol. 5, 1959), p. 1.
3. Ibid., p. ii.
4. Ibid., p. 10.
5. *Contemporary Indian Poetry in English: An Assessment and Selection*, ed. Saleem Peeradina (Madras: Macmillan, 1972), p. ix.
6. Dom Moraes, "Poet Whom No One Discovered" *The Hindu Literary Magazine*, May 12, 1996.

Cultural Cross-Currents and Crisis in Sensibility: A Note on A.K. Ramanujan's "A River"

P. LAXMINARAYANA

The highest cultural achievement either of a nation or a country lies in its poetic creation. Particularly, in the context of India, it reached a crescendo during the Renaissance period, pioneered by the formidable trio, Sri Aurobindo, Tagore and Sarojini Naidu. As leaders of a new creative movement they projected the vibrant culture/ profile of India to the world outside, particularly to the prejudiced West.

Sri Aurobindo's *Savitri* celebrates the unconquerable spirit of India and vindicates the divine destiny of man. Tagore wakes up the Indian mind from narrow domestic walls and lights the way towards a transnational experience and participation. Sarojini Naidu with her romantic sensibility and poetic charm earns the title, the Nightingale of India. Thus Indian writing in English achieved an authentic selfhood of its own. Beginning from pre-Independence to the post-Independence era it has grown more virile embodying far deeper cultural currents and forces. Iyengar rightly observes: "We have seen that the base for Indian writing in English is much wider and stronger today than at the time of independence. It's true literature is the creation of sundry gifted individuals."[1]

The two World Wars rudely shook humanity. As a result a wasteland dominated human sensibility. In India, the post-Independence era presented a shocking spectacle of poverty and squalor. The Indian mind was deeply disturbed by the great betrayal of faith. The whole atmosphere was charged by a revolutionary spirit. This modern revolt was represented by the later generation of poets—Nissim Ezekiel, A.K. Ramanujan and Kamala Das.

They make a decisive departure from idealistic tradition and romantic ideology; and confront a decadent social reality. M.K. Naik points out: "Politics ceased to be an idealistic pursuit and was reduced to a power game, and the new gods of self-aggrandizement and affluence easily dethroned those of selfless service and dedication to a cause. The era of hope, aspiration and certitude was gone, an age of merciless self-scrutiny, questioning and ironic exposure commenced."[2]

Of all the Indian English poets Ramanujan is unique in innovation and technique. His poetry is characterized by a deep crisis of sensibility. It is due to his exposure to the rationalistic West and his own roots lying deep in Indian nativity.

He presents a torn mind caught between two cultural polarities. According to Emmanuel Narendra Lall: "Both evaluations corroborate my thesis that Ramanujan's poetry is the expression of his poetic sensibility in which the Indian subjectivity coalesces with the Western objectivity. In other words, his Indian heritage and experience inspire his poetry, which is given speech and form based on English poetic traditions."[3]

Ramanujan in his search for nativity and roots shakes every idea and institution, which he begets by way of inheritance. He refuses uncritical acceptance. Hence his poetry is mostly a self-probing with ruthless interrogations. As an alienated young man he says: "I resemble everyone but myself." This implies a struggle to repossess his identity attended by a rigorous re-evaluation of tradition. He, therefore, is at once with a new generation of poets representing the modernist revolt. Makarand Paranjape rightly observes: "The new generation which had come of age in the 1950s and 1960s found itself betrayed by its elders. It was impatient for change and fed up with the platitudes of the past. . . A whole generation turned its back on tradition and found itself alienated in the new India. Secondly, they declared themselves opposed to the idealism and romanticism of their predecessors. They wanted a poetry which was without escapism and flights of fancy, a poetry written in clear, hard, unsentimental voice, and in everyday language . . . they wrote about city and its dirty poverty-stricken and dehumanising environs. . . . They believed they were alienated from their society and irony was the only way of expressing their ambivalence towards themselves and their world."[4]

Ramanujan's most popular poems *Obituary* and *Last of the Princes* give us a clue to his essential creative stance and vision. *Obituary* reveals the helplessness of the human situation. It portrays the travails of a typical orthodox Hindu family trying to come to terms with modernity. It brings out the authority of tradition and the absurdity of rituals. H.M. Williams rightly comments: "There is however a more appealing side to this clever poet. He sees clearly and to a great extent accepts man as he is, a limited, self contradictory and often weak deluded creature."[5]

The clash of tradition and modernity is brought out more concretely in the *Last of the Princes.* It dramatizes the mismatch between the decadent aristocratic order and the demands of modernity. The princes are the lifeless, silhouetted objects crushed under the dead weight of the present. Their children go to school on "Half fee".

The poem "A River"[6] represents the consummation of Ramanujan's creative achievement as a poet. It is a bold and searching study of the human predicament as conceived in terms of routine and change. Mark Twain, the American novelist, in his novel *Huckleberry Finn* assigns a profound and powerful role to the River—Mississippi. T.S. Eliot calls it "The strong brown God" while Lionel Trilling considers it as a highway towards freedom. The river dramatizes the protagonist's journey from innocence to experience. But, by contrast Ramanujan's "River" is neither a divine agency nor an elemental power. It is the very image of life caught between continuity and change.

It represents a multiplicity of metaphors and modes. A variety of motifs go into the meaning and structure of the poem. Ramanujan undermines the traditional notion that the river is a nourisher and preserver of life. It is on the contrary the cruel death-dealer. The poem opens with the dried state of the river symbolizing the hollowness within:

> every summer
> a river dries to a trickle
> in the sand

The trickle speaks of the poverty and impoverishment that permeates the entire life process. Nature very grudgingly doles out just the trickle. The insufficiency creates a harrowing existential battle. Life becomes a contest between living and dying. The river exposes its interior; it is empty; the very stirrings of life have gone dry and barren revealing the inner sand and stones. The sleepy crocodiles and shaven buffaloes create a sense of the grotesque. They are the ugly and hideous obstructions to the fluid imagination of the river.

Ramanujan creates an illusion of reality and affirms reality as the unalterable experience of life. The river bares its sandy ribs symbolizing the unfed and uncovered faceless masses exposing their lifeless ribs. It reveals a subhuman state of existence—a typical Indian rural reality.

The subsequent lines of the poem provide a powerful study on the condition of Indian womanhood

> straw and women's hair
> clogging the water gates
> at the rusty bars
> under the bridges with patches
> of repair all over them

By juxtaposing straw with women's hair Ramanujan creates a trifling sense of a woman's life—the insignificance of her existence. The hair clogging the water gates speaks of her victimization over the centuries. She has been held captive within the stranglehold of custom and social regimentation. The worn out rusty bars hold tight the woman's hair. The patches of repair and reforms do not create a tangible change.

Ramanujan introduces the motif of floods against the existing passivity and routine of tradition. Floods symbolize the oncoming modernity and change with an uncontrollable speed. People start talking about its alarming intrusion:

> People everywhere talked
> of the inches rising,
> of the precise number of cobbled steps
> run over by the water, rising
> on the bathing places,

At first, the impact of change is felt at the lower strata of society represented by the cobbled steps. It advances further at the bathing places where rituals are observed. The floods later engulf the unaccommodated and the vulnerable segments of society:

> and the way it carried off three village houses,
> one pregnant woman
> and a couple of cows
> named Gopi and Brinda, as usual

The trauma of change creates an unprecedented havoc. The crop and the cattle of the village are carried away. The pregnant woman symbolizing creativity and motherhood is undermined. The traditional life of farming gets disrupted. Gopi and Brinda, the milk giving cows carrying folklore and mythology are drowned in the floods of modernity. Ramanujan attacks the poets who are not affected by the floods. They are at a safe and respectable distance:

> In Madurai,
>   city of temples and poets
> who sang of cities and temples

Ramanujan exposes the cruelty and indifference of poets towards human calamity and suffering. He castigates the romantic ideology and self-seeking system of life. Hence the poem is dominated by the images of 'stone' and 'sand' symbolizing the very sap of life that has gone dry.

The river represents the clash between tradition and modernity. Bruce King aptly observes: "Ramanujan is neither a nostalgic traditionalist nor an advocate of modernization and westernization. He is a product of both and his poems reflect a personality conscious of change, enjoying its vitality, freedom and contradictions, but also aware of memories which form his inner self, memories of an unconscious 'namelessness' which are still alive, at the foundations of the self."[7]

Ramanunjan as a humanist is quite sensitive to human suffering. His poetry ruthlessly exposes the cosmic and cultural indifference. The sandy sterility and the stony indifference underscore the need for the birth of a new consciousness to respond to human pain and suffering.

Notes and References

1. K.R. Srinivasa Iyengar, *Indian Writing in English: The Seventies and After* (New Delhi: Sterling, 1984), p. 695.
2. M.K. Naik, *Dimensions of Indian English Literature* (New Delhi: Sterling, 1984), p. 9.
3. Emmanuel Narendra Lall, *The Poetry of Encounter: Three Indo-Anglian Poets (Dom Moraes, A.K. Ramanujan and Nissim Ezekiel)* (New Delhi: Sterling, 1983), p. 51.
4. Makarand Paranjape, *Indian Poetry in English* (Madras: Macmillan, 1993), p. 20.
5. See H.M. Williams, *Indo-Anglian Literature 1800-1970: A Survey* (Madras: Orient Longman, 1976).
6. A.K. Ramnujan, "A River," *The Collected Poems of A.K. Ramanujan* (Delhi: OUP, 1995).
7. Bruce King, *Modern Indian Poetry in English* (London: OUP, 1987), p. 212.

A Walk along 'Long and Windsome Streets': The Poetry of Gauri Deshpande

SHIRISH CHINDHADE

To regard Gauri Deshpande as one of the hundred and fifty odd women poets "jostling for space"[1] in contemporary Indian women's English poetry is to misrate and underrate her. In addition to her being an *avant garde* writer of fiction and short stories in Marathi, Gauri Deshpande is a name that the critic and the reader of Indian English poetry cannot by-pass without leaving a conspicuous lacuna in his repertoire. As for her post of prestige in the tradition of the *genre*, she is, no doubt, with Toru Dutt, Sarojini Naidu and Kamala Das, comfortably bolstered up by both the merit and the body of work that she has to her name. The canon of her English poetry so far includes three collections, namely, *Between Births* (1968), *Lost Love* (1970), and *Beyond the Slaughterhouse* (1972) with a total of eighty poems, presumably and hopefully excluding the ones not published and not anthologised so far.

After reading the three collections together one tends to register a clean impact of the poet's highly sensitive and reflective sensibility in operation. As the impressions gradually crystallise, one can even attempt certain generalisations with a view to identifying groups of poems expressing common concerns or experiences, though certainly not as hermetically sealed clusters. Thus we have poems of (a) reflections on life and death, (b) relationship between man and nature, (c) love that man and woman are subject to, (d) sensibility characteristic of the feminine world, (e) inner quest or self search, and (f) memories and experience of loneliness, loss and the pain consequent to it.

The first collection *Between Births* opens seriously with reflections on death for whom the poet is waiting "impatiently/ As I would a tardy lover" because the journey is the "deathward slope of life" on "the sure ground/ of death". (p. 1)[2] The relationship is immediately defined in the metaphor of a tardy lover, further strengthened in the concluding lines of the poem where a characteristically Indian allusion to the *saptapadi* (seven steps), the ritual that confirms a Hindu marriage, is used:

> and walk the seven steps
> with him that'll make him
> My ally. (p. 1)

Appropriate images of colour like brown path, gray blond grass, dusty fall, yellow-tipped leaves, yellow winter, to suggest death are used, finally leading to the overwhelming question—

> How long must I walk
> These long and windsome streets
> Before I meet
> You? (p. 2)

in order to be gathered into the sanctuary of his arms. Further reiteration of this willingness is laconically worded in the haiku "Farewell":

> Death has struck a note
> Clear and blue on the piano
> And I go. (p. 4)

This is not to suggest that there is no trepidation but that it would be indecent to disturb the house by the expression of fear: "I can see the noose wait/ but fear to tremble/ as I may quake the house" ("The Hangman Awaits," p. 8). But familiarity (with death) after all, breeds contempt enough to say

> I got over it
> I got used to it
> All dying and my living. ("The Habit," p. 18)

One even learns to live with the bitter stench, "the smell of a death" hidden in the earth instead of the "baked fragrance" that emanates from the earth after the first rains, as the last poem of the collection "The Renascence" puts it.

The other predominant concern in the first book is one of loneliness and loss: "voyages end when they begin." Therefore, like Hopkins in "Spring and Fall", this poet's (ironic) advice to a child is to keep innocence in order to rise above superficialities and see sorrow and joy in the proper perspective:

> That grief is more than the end of a cake
> And that joy is deeper than the gift of a
> Doll ("Find Not", p. 13)

Loneliness has many faces. In "No More" the waking is "tireless, dull, flat and/ unprofitable" as the Prince of Denmark also found it. The metaphor of separation is quite home-spun with a touch of characteristic feminine sensibility:

> No more is the busy thread of my life
> Linked through the eye of your needle (p. 7)

In "The Perfume" also, the lover's absence is conspicuous through certain intimate associations of memory such as a perfume:

> And yet there you were
> Simply because you didn't like it. (p. 10)

Sometimes it is like a journey with "the thought of you/ before I know the road is through" ("Lonesome," p. 4). It can be "a dry and static brook" ("Disillusion," p. 4) or it can be a night that fails to mask the lover's absence ("Haiku V," p. 4). It can also be a strange reunion like "the wedge between misery and content", bringing a life of "disharmony" and "nightpacing", leaving the mind "empty, barren and bereft," ("The Guest," p. 19). It is, after all, not without its negative rewards or lessons. If parting, loss and loneliness are inevitable, then weep and let go the hold:

> So now I watch arid eyed
> As my fingers open slowly
> And let you go ("I Wanted to Weep", p. 20)

When all communication with the external world of senses and persons fails life becomes a "vast/ Barrenness of your presence" ("Poems in Winter," p. 23).

Memories intensify the pains of alienation, with a charming array of visual images of memory in a poem like "Re: Memories": "an old letter/ Evoking images of laughter and rain/ or a yellow diary/ Pressed violets in its leaves/ In a book a photograph"[3] (p. 9). But they, too, lead to "A heartbreak, a failure/ Otherwise there's nothing." This nothingness makes life a mere "hollow task" as futile as "hoping to grow a seed in sand and on rock." But, then, if living is inevitable, why not struggle to live meaningfully? And meaning is added

> If we could kiss with lips not laced with lies
> And learn somehow our shames not to despise
> Then we may live, not wishing to die.
> ("We Hadn't the Guts," p. 15)

Such resolute will to live and create meaning alone may help: "the eyes will retain/ their joy-cored, dark-souled brimming secrets" ("Find Not," p. 14).

This resolute will it is that creates an intense desire to communicate with someone like-minded. Again with a characteristic feminine sensibility she writes:

> Sometimes you want to talk
> About love and despair

And the ungratefulness of children.
A man is no use whatever then
You want then your mother
Or sister
Or the girl with whom you went through school . . .
You know . . . that you've spoken
("The Female of the Species," p. 12)

And when this is also not possible, then a letter will help, a very peculiar, special kind of letter:

I hold in my hands a note
Anonymous, that touches upon all the most
Silent, blue and flat notes
Of my mind and notes
In the end, "you must've known
Who this is from"–
I'm puzzled and in frown—
The hand utterly familiar—
Mine own. ("The Letter," p. 21)

Like memories, a dialogue with the self is the most satisfactory form of communication that helps one span valleys of alienation and loss. It is, of course, a very sensitive mind that feels all such hungers and reacts feelingly to subtleties of change around.

Nature helps to connect the loose ends of memories and add meaning to an otherwise "empty, barren and bereft" (p. 19) existence. In "Thinking Disgustedly" self-pity and self-laceration can be palliated in the company of "the silly Jacaranda/ that waved overhead/ its purple splendour" (p. 11). (A similar sense of self-pity is present in "Camouflage", p. 21, also). The enigma of pain, almost Ghaliblike, is resolved again by nature:

And I wondered if perhaps I had
    caught something . . . .
Yet nothing happened
And I dreamt in the night of long travels.

When I woke up the sky was heavy
And then it rained. ("A Change of Season," p. 22)

Here, changes in the moods of nature become metaphoric of an inner metamorphosis of the poet's world, and memories make more meaning than humans and their physical company as "Poems in Winter" (pp. 23, 24) show. Like the proverbial silver lining of a black cloud, the Indian treescape brings inexhaustible consolation to the pained mind. One of the finest poems not only in the Gauri Deshpande canon but in the entire repertoire of Indian nature poetry in English, "Indian Treescape" with its lovely crowd of cassia, banyan, temple tree, poplar, bamboo, silk-cotton, jasmine and, of course, the emperor mango, simply luxuriates in a pageant of multitudinous, sensuous imagery culminating inimitably thus:

He is supreme in flower, supreme too
In fruit is this tree the mango.
Snowflake shaped flowers make us drunk in youth,
The firm and sour flavour of pleasure's
in his early fruit.
And his ripe maturity fills our mouths
And runs in saffron rivers down
Our summer-soaked trunks. (p. 6)

It is such buoyant—though very rare—moments that perhaps impose a subtly suggestive design on the entire collection *Between Births* which is sombre in the main, and which begins with death but (significantly) closes with "renascence" despite its prophetic sense and tone of doom. It is such rare moments of unmixed exultation, few and far between, that really contain the subterranean sources of hope and *elan vital*. That is what *Between Births* is about. Though the name of the collection suggests a Trishanku-like hung situation, the terminal points of the journey are clearly identified, and in a normal course the journey is expected to lead forward.

Of course, such a forward motion is not the singularly clean impact of the second collection, *Lost Love*. Even so, the first collection offers a model of poetry that one can look for in the collections that follow. In fact, it is still a situation "between two shores" but with observable resolution to:

Try to reach across
The thick stream of traffic,
Find my way blocked again and again
And your face obstructed from view. ("Poem," p. 1)

The experience of being left between two shores is aptly conveyed through the allusions to Prometheus and Orpheus, one suggesting an inexhaustible spirit of hope and altruism, and the other personifying hope deferred and heart despaired, (p. 3). The sapper in "The Road" has a similar experience while making a road,

Along the shoulder of a hill . . .
There you stopped
For this carefully wrought perfection
Had no place to go. (p. 4)

In the companion piece "The Bridge" which is an obvious symbol of connection and communication, the shadows grow still darker because the solid structure "of pylon and span" (p. 4) will disintegrate. Thus, it is a terrible experience that, on the one hand, the road cannot be built and on the other hand the bridge cannot stand. This disturbing sense of indefinition, indirection and frustration shrouds a majority of the poems in the second collection, and nature imagery helps to convey it effectively. In "In Memoriam, M." (p. 5) desolation is conveyed through the tactile images of heat and cold. In "Sun" (p. 7) the tactile imagery is restricted only to heat: beating, parching, scorching, burning, not allowing even a single moment of pure ecstasy. It is like the different smells of "Jasmine, tar, smoke, nightqueen, henna and dung/All mixed with our isolation" ("Three Poems for

Sudheer," p. 8). Disenchantment is intensified in "Summer" where visual imagery appropriately predominates:

> I saw the usual meagre scape:
> The grass indeterminate yellow-brown
> A few thorn trees dead of thirst
> Or playing dead to escape the sun (p. 9)

Adjectives like dry, dying, arid, drained, empty, blinded, terrible, parched mark the summer heat and its desiccating impact on existence. But it is followed by an earnest invocation for a union:

> So soon return
> And let your dark-running fountain
> Pour over me and seep
> Deep into my soil
> The rain of significance (p. 10)

where one feels a little restless about the laboured metaphor in the lines, though the lovely nature imagery becomes its redemptive grace. (The lines remind one of Hopkins' cry of "Lord, send my roots rain", in "Thou Art Indeed Just, Lord"). But burning in the beloved's company is more desirable than burning in isolation. Instead of burning in drought why not "be burnt/In the glory" of the third eye of Shiva? ("To Shiva", p. 13)—because the poet knows

> that I cannot escape
> This gnawing unrest. (p. 14)

Obvious irony is operative in the title of the poem "Integration" (p. 14) as in the opening of the third eye of Shiva's: it burns the object it looks on but, then, it cleanses and resuscitates the object also. But here, again, caution is called for: it is not any cheap, sensual experience that is the fruit of company and love; it is clearly an extra-sensuous experience that lasts longer than the mundane:

That you go is not my sorrow . . .
I grieve that you should assume
Love is only a function of time
("Departure Time 2.30 a.m.," p. 15)

Yes, Shakespeare, too, tells us that love is not "time's fool"; it does not alter when it alteration finds, and the poet reasserts in the next poem "Meeting" that love is not "the weight of wanton intimacy" (p. 17) though it may be an onerous burden of memories as "In Absentia" which is a deeply nostalgic poem in six short sections conveying various moods redolent with memories of meeting and parting, such as:

I remember you did not lift your hand
To touch lightly upon my head. ("Waiting," p. 26)

The poet uses an unusually striking image of a bird to describe her mental state of loss, shock and bewilderment and irrelevance in: "But can bring to mind only . . ./ the bird trapped in the beam of sudden light." (p. 21)

But there is nothing flippant and superficial in the poet's love; its integrity has the dignity, honesty and sanctity of a worshipper's devotion for Shiva ("December"-1, p. 27). Since no physical pleasures are expected in love, the physical pain in it also does not matter ("December" 2). If devotion is a new dimension of love, an equally noble sentiment of maternal love is also an important part of the poet's world of experience. In "Portrait" (p. 28), on a Christmas Day a beggar and her child suddenly remind the poet of Mother Mary and the child Christ. Barring such moments of revelatory exaltation the lasting lesson of life means, "the only residue is this habit of pain" ("Souvenir," p. 32) including love which is "the harrowing re-enactment of an idyll" ("Love," p. 34). Such hours of tension and tribulation at times inspire suicidal anger:

And tell me

Has not your hand clenched
White on the rail
And your heart leapt flying
Down, down-swooping
Plummeting, arrowing, thrusting
To earth? ("High," p. 38)

This is the feeling with which the second collection, *Lost Love,* concludes. The dominant mood is one of heaviness, uncertainty, despair and nostalgia with moments of revelatory happiness conspicuous by their paucity. However, the greatest achievement of the collection lies in its luxuriant abundance of nature imagery such as the cycle of the seasons, birds (with a breath-taking rare variety of them like the drongo, bunting, kingfisher, golden oriole, cuckoo, peahen, and the too familiar sparrow, crow, parrot and myna), flowers, trees, the cycle of day and night, the sun with its burning and scorching heat, clouds and the rain, of which the last mentioned is a recurring, multidimensional one. The imagery is not decorative; it speaks of the changing moods and the sensitive responses to the changes around. The imagery is also largely tactile and visual.

Unlike its stylised image as a bringer of new life, the rain in Gauri Deshpande's poetry is often a reminder of loss and a witness to alienation, as in "In Absentia":

The rain that here falls on my home
There hisses on your huddled head. (p. 20)

It is only rarely, as in "Waiting"-2 that the rain becomes a harbinger of the lover who actually presents himself:

The clouds had gathered all day long
And absently I had noted them
As I waited. . . .
Until you stood at the door, drenched
Smelling of trees and rain. (p. 25)

Another striking quality of some of the poems in the second collection is the lilting line, occasionally regularly rhymed also ("In Absentia"-2) with a marked prosodic measure that makes itself heard.

One of the most marked musical effects is achieved with internal rhyme:

> it seems futile that the drongo
> In its poised, black, fork-tailed
> Flight should alight for one bright
> Breathless instant. ("The Eclipse," p. 19)

It is achievements of this kind which subtly hint at the 'forward' movement (mentioned earlier) from the first to the second collection. A varied, graphic communicative imagery, a clearer definition of moods, an abler handling of the medium and a greater awareness and use of the poetic possibilities of nature, are the highlights of *Lost Love*. It enables the poet to continue with her poetic journey more confidently in the third collection *Beyond the Slaughterhouse.*

The metaphor of the poetic journey just used above indeed owes its conception to the poetry itself, for Gauri Deshpande herself uses it time and again in her poems. Therefore, the title of the third collection also goes well with the metaphor: the journey oscillates between births, then moves on through the *cul de sac* of lost love and now indeed goes beyond the slaughterhouse which is obviously the house of death. Here Gauri Deshpande claims kinship with Emily Dickinson.

> We paused before a house that seemed
> A swelling of the ground;
> The roof was scarcely visible,
> The cornice but a mound.
>
> Since then 'tis centuries, but each
> Feels shorter than the day
> I first surmised the horses' heads

Were towards eternity.[4]

If the first two collections contain poetry which is largely "centripetal" in moods, the third collection strikes a slightly different note suggestive of a "centrifugal" movement. External realities and stimuli begin to command the poet's attention and indulgence with a very wide range spanning various metropolitan experiences such as the trains, the beggars, the lepers, the schedule of a particular day of the week dedicated to the worship of a particular god or goddess (with a depiction of the growing mass fatalism in cities), "the hills and roofs that smudge horizon/spiked with lighted columns" ("This Fair Isle, A Report") which obviously are the pylons, towers, pillars, antennae and such other objects characteristic of a city skyline, paralleled by the indoor counterpart of "museums, seminars, recitals, films" ("Prisons of Freedom") that provide diversions to diffuse the dusk of despair, memories, alienation and lost identities.

And, above all, the miracle of a safe survival performed everyday in and by "a sea of people":

> No one has picked my pocket
> Nor into my house broken,
> And I am as yet not run over by a bus.
>
> ("People Who Need People")

And despite the hustle and bustle, the facelessness and the absence of a meaningful interpersonal communication, the need and effort to acquire and present a face is unmistakable:

> She changes
> Her rings, brooches, shoes, drops,
> beads and bangles
> To match her dress-approximately. ("A Dream of Fire")

And, therefore, "no one's ugly any more." Thus the opening poem (in ten sections) of the collection sets the tone and the tenor of the other poems to a marked extent.

One cause of the desolation and despair stems from the city's unavoidable palpable pollution, inducing a sickly consciousness:

> the roads are crowded
> The smog makes my head ache
> The flowers damn them
> Bring on allergies
> The air is rheumatic damp
> Or too dry, my lips chap
> Or too hot, my eyes smart ("Still Life"-1)

But sickliness is not morbidity that turns to cheap sex for titillation. It is a psychological triumph that instead of (such) a surrender, there is "inexplicable disgust" ("Reaction to Pornzines") at cheap sex. The mind rejects it to be willingly diverted to a sudden moment of beauty:

> But see! you say, and there,
> Through the smog
> The cars
> The pollen
> The damp dry cold or hot air,
> Beyond your face
> Is a lone white sail. ("Still Life"-1)

This inevitably reminds one of Arun Kolatkar's poem "The Priest's Son":

> Do you really believe that story
> You ask him
> He doesn't reply
> But merely looks uncomfortable
> Shrugs and looks away
> And happens to notice
> A quick wink of a movement
> In a scanty patch of stuffy dry grass

Burnt brown in the sun
And says

Look
There's a butterfly
There[5]

Gauri Deshpande scales equal heights when she describes in a superb image a page from a "pronzine" showing "the half-closed scarlet/Flower of the nude's breast/Being nibbled by the 'nubile' child":

The purple lip's flute
Playing upon the full instrument,
The slow coming together and the slower
Separation. ("Reaction to Pornzines")

In addition to the amazing achievement of the tactile, the visual and the auditory images in a rare amalgam the tremendous restraint contains a universe of suggestion which in a lesser poet could easily have decayed into porn itself. It reminds us of Keats' similar feat of restraint in "The Eve of St. Agnes" where the poet is fully aware of the fine line of demarcation between the erotic and the obscene when he describes the sexual union of the lovers:

Into her dream he melted, as the rose
Blendeth its odour within the violet.[6]

The sickly consciousness in "Still Life" finds an obvious explanation in a poem like "The Man from Singapore" which depicts man's dislocation with nature:

The noise—he said, eyes bloodshot,
    Puckered in fatigue, hot
    Face a rictus of disgust
        Unnerves me, haven't slept

> Nor thought; what you say, what
> I, makes no sense against crash
> Crash crash crash

If this is a suggestion of the psychosis bred by the metropolis, there is an equally healthy awareness of realities amidst romantic experiences, as in the "Rain Poems". The rain is a bringer of kaleidoscopic sensations: it reminds one of the moments of love, it induces unbeatable *ennui*, it creates the excitement of welcome, and at the same time it prompts misgivings and augurs suffering:

> There's still time for chawls to collapse,
> For buses to skid and kill, for trains
> To snarl and for flus to catch.
> Ritually we rejoice before we pay
> Into flood-relief funds every year. ("Rain Poems")

The black mood tends to stay, what with treachery, frustration or fatigue:

> You, not a god, to contain it,
> Slowly collapse ("The Poems on Going Away-2")

> It's venom enough to blacken
> Not kill
> Taint, not end. ("The Poems on Going Away-2")

> Their eyes are vacant and they don't push
> Even to get off the train ("Workaday Women-1")

There is, as it were, a benumbing of sensibilities by the ceaseless buffets of urban life, of hurry and worry: "pushed, pulled, dully/ stared at thick-opaque" ("Workaday Women-2"). So, when the body and the mind get confused and benumbed through the "six long Mondays" of the week, both the flesh and the spirit refuse to respond to the mechanical call of love:

And the too solid flesh
Will refuse
When he demands that it melt
At a Saturday touch ("Workaday Women-3")

A Chinese observation says: There is no hamlet remote enough on the surface of the earth where the rays of the moon do not reach. In the same way, howsoever intense may be the moments of dumps and darkness, a sensitive mind will still find a ray of the moon. Poems like "The Poems on Going Away-1", "Summer Sequence," "It Comes Slow," and "I Shall Arise and Go" are real treasures of health and happiness. There isn't much of good nature poetry in Indian English writing, but Gauri Deshpande has made a significant contribution to this genre. Consider a passage like:

Paddy—swollen, strewn
With silver water, kite-flying, river-grown
Where lazy kingfishers brood upon
Their reflections across fishbacks;
And I recognise the old friends (a lost flock
In a jungle of sparrows):
Drongo, barbet, bulbul, wagtail, tern.
And through these green fields I come.
("The Poems on Going Away-1")

Again in "Summer Sequence-3" we have this riot of nature's plenty and beauty:

This is a summer of flowers.
They went berserk
The blossoming trees: first
It was silk-cottons, staining
With red bursts my sight;
Then mango, fragrant, dripping
Honey on our sated lips;
And laburnum hanging

In great globes of sun;
Jacaranda's deep purple—
Subdued splendour;
Then cassia-coloured love;
Finally gulmohur-flame-fulfilment
of passion.

An unusually original image drawn from nature occurs in "It Comes Slow":

The country like a harsh
Lecherous widow awaits
Rain that comes slow
Reluctant to freshen
Her wrinkled flabby greedy flesh
Optimistic.

It is on this optimistic note of awaiting and expectation that *Beyond the Slaughterhouse* concludes:

bitter and sick as the land
To which we rush back
Even happily, for we are it:
Smooth and bitter and poor
And blessed with nothing
but fortitude.

When one puts all the threads together one sees a very sensitive mind receiving various impressions, reacting to them openly and interpreting the whole experience very maturely and consciously. One rare dimension Gauri Deshpande has undoubtedly added to Indian English poetry is the approaches to nature which are neither stylised nor dated, far less merely decorative. They are the "objective correlatives" of the poet's intimate experiences. They help her to connect and establish a meaningful rapport with the world around. In fact, the entire poetic journey is "along long and windsome streets" of memories, of moments actually lived;

it is a journey on the experiential level, through the thick and thin of life, through shadows of despondency, dullness and fatigue but eventually "blessed with nothing but fortitude."

It is exhilarating that of late Gauri Deshpande has a luxuriant flowering of fiction in her first language, Marathi. However, Marathi's gain mustn't spell a loss to Indian English poetry. Gauri Deshpande has—regrettably—not published significantly after her third collection *Beyond the Slaughterhouse* (1972), rather too long a hibernation.

Unlike an established poet like Kamala Das whose flights are usually circular, Gauri Deshpande's encounter with life is multipronged, subtle, restrained and mature, with a cultivated idiom, making her a more impressive and readable poet.

Notes and References

1. Dom Moraes in his review of Arlene Zide's anthology, *In Their Own Voice*. Quoted by Rajeshwari Sunder Rajan in her article in *The Book Review*, Vol. XVII, No. 12 (Dec. 1993), pp. 13,14.
2. "Death," *Between Births* (Calcutta: Writers Workshop, 1968), p. 1. All page numbers are keyed to the first editions of the collections and are parenthetically included in the body of the essay; titles are quoted in the absence of pagination.
3. Cf. "But the rooms still gaped—/ the green hanger swang empty, and/ the head of the table/ demanded a plate".—"The Wake," Rita Dove, *SPAN*, No. 3, Mar. 1994. Ramanujan achieves a similar effect but in a single assertive visual image in "Still Life": "When she left me/ after lunch, I read/ for a while/ But I suddenly wanted/ to look again/ and saw the half-eaten/ sandwich,/ bread,/ lettuce and salami,/ all carrying the shape/ of her bite." *Selected Poems* (OUP, Second impression, 1981), p. 5.
4. "Because I could not stop for death," *American Lit. 1890-1965*, ed. Egbert S. Oliver (Delhi: Eurasia, 1967), p. 332.
5. *Jejuri* (Bombay: Pras, 1978), p. 26.
6. *Selected Poems and Letters of John Keats*, ed. Robert Gittings (London: Heinemann, 1966), p. 105.

Feminist Concerns: A Study of Eunice de Souza's Poetry

GIRIJA NAMBIAR

The women of today are in a fair way to dethrone the myth of feminity; they are beginning to affirm their independence in concrete ways; but they do not easily succeed in living completely the life of a human being. Reared by women, within a feminine world, their normal destiny is marriage, which still means practically subordination to man; for masculine prestige is far from extinction, resting still upon solid, economic and social foundations.[1]

A significant development in Indian English poetry has been the emergence of women poets. Any study of the trends and techniques in contemporary English poetry in India would be inadequate without considering their contribution in establishing a distinctly Indian poetic tradition.

Indian writers in English have been writing in a climate of shift and change in the historical, political and cultural sense, in a postcolonial society. They have been attempting to re-contextualize the postcolonial response to the search for identity and loss of values. Women writers, in particular, appear concerned about issues such as female marginalization, social discrimination, sexual oppression and liberation from the socio-cultural restrictions of the past. Recurring themes in many women writers are: the women's struggle for self-realisation, her quest for an identity, her pursuit of equality and freedom, her rebellion and protest against male oppression, sex-role stereotyping, experiences singular to women and the consequent evolution of feminine consciousness.

Besides, poets of the 80s and 90s reveal a deep consciousness of local realities and their own roots. Though influenced by the trends set by Ramanujan, Ezekiel and Kamala Das, the rich colouring of local detail give to their poetry a vibrant, tangible quality. The verse grows out of situations that are described in a direct, colloquial, contemporary idiom that make the scenes richer, denser and dramatic. Distance between past and present, self and environment is also effectively bridged, lending an arresting sense of immediacy to the situations presented.

II

Eunice de Souza belongs to the group of young poets like Saleem Peeradina, Manohar Shetty, Melanie Silgardo, Raul d' Gama and Santan Rodrigues who are associated with Bombay and Ezekiel. Their poetry reflects the kind of moral realism he introduced into English poetry in India, with the difference that they focus more minutely upon society. The last three poets, together with Eunice de Souza, share a common Goan Catholic background.

De Souza's verse is built upon her memories of Goan Catholic life in Poona and represents the community's repressions, prejudices and ignorance. Unhappy childhood experiences as part of this community form the stuff of much of her poetry. Her verse expresses her private fears, anxieties, anger, guilt, desires and hopes. Though satirical in tone, de Souza never lapses into sarcasm. The message is conveyed, instead, by ironic juxtaposition of details. No comment is made. Strict economy of expression, abrupt endings and easy diction lend to de Souza's poetry a spontaneity and charm that is distinctive.

Besides, the poems register a high level of consciousness of the situation and problems faced by women, though expressed in ironic understatement rather than in overt comment. Bruce King states: "While it has no affiliations in politics, community, humanistic ideals, religion, it is feminist in its kind of awareness, female vision, and affinities to the mode of other women poets rather than in a proclaimed commitment."[2]

Articulated comment may not be her style, but a close examination of her language is suggestive of de Souza's rebellious resentment of the suppression of the female and gender discrimination. Like some other women writers who follow a trend pioneered by Kamala Das, de Souza repudiates the refined lady-like idiom of earlier women writers to register their rejection of the norms of patriarchy. To protest against their marginalized status, and the social and sexual inequalities suffered by women in patriarchal society, they resort to "the rejection of the language those in power created for the politics of patriarchy."[3]

III

Many of de Souza's poems are concerned with different aspects of male domination and oppression of women. The poem "Catholic Mother" is an ironic denouncement of the traditional role assigned to women as wife and mother, a role that relegates her effectively to the private sphere of sexual relations and family life and at the same time, discourages or excludes her from a public and an independent identity.

> Pillar of the Church
> Says the parish priest,
> Lovely catholic family
> Says Mother Superior.
> The Pillar's wife says nothing
> Naturally—for by "the grace of God
> She's had seven children in seven years."[4]

The rich irony in the image of the man labelled "Pillar of the Church" by the parish priest, whose family is described as a "Lovely Catholic family" by the Mother Superior, and who has fathered "seven children in seven years" and that too, "by the grace of God" cannot be lost on the reader. What of the "pillar's" wife? In her silence one can hear a most eloquent statement against the degradation, exploitation and suffering that family, marriage and motherhood can bring to a woman.

Unlike the earlier generation of women poets who appeared to believe that the problems of life could be solved through a man's love, there are no love poems among de Souza's early works. Instead, poems like "Miss Luise" satirise notions of romantic love, marriage and children promoted by patriarchy and accepted by women conditioned by its institutions. If "Miss Luise", derided in her community as an ageing, eccentric spinster and humiliated for her dreams of love, conquest and children, takes a dig at the ungodliness of the male-dominated Catholic Church, "Marriages Are Made" with its ironical title, draws attention to the reality of a woman's plight. Cousin Elena is in the marriage market. Her family history is scrutinised, her father's monetary situation is assessed, her vital statistics, general health and colouring considered before the boy's family concludes that Cousin Elena will do "justice" to their "good son of Mother Church".

"Forgive Me, Mother" focuses on the mother-daughter relationship and the mother as the inculcator of patriarchal codes of sexual repression in her daughters. The lines:

> It was kill or die
> And you got me anyway:
> The blood congeals at lover's touch
> The guts dissolve in shit

appear to suggest that the mother herself is often instrumental in socialising children into traditional gender roles and acceptance of a value system that serves male interests, a system that believes only men, and that too, foreign men, alone can "air their crotches". The resentment aroused by such sexual prudery is voiced in the concluding lines of the poem addressed to the mother:

In dreams
I hate you

That the poet believes women are themselves responsible, to some extent, for their own victimisation and the perpetuation of the injustices meted out to them is obvious in such lines as:

A novelist said that,
who spent his life wondering why
when the Nazis came,
his mother pushed him into a closet
and let his sisters go to Auschwitz.

Transcend Self You Say

Preference for the male child in the Indian milieu is represented in "de Souza Prabhu" when she claims that she belongs to the "lame ducks" because her parents "wanted a boy". Such poems serve to remind one of a certain willingness in woman to collude with man, arising perhaps from self-contempt and scorn for members of her own sex, a tendency Adrienne Rich terms "horizontal hostility".

Although one can discern a current of anger in de Souza's poetry at the social and moral attitudes of women in general and those of the Goan Catholic community in particular, there is also compassion and sympathy for their victimisation caused by their passivity, conformity, illusions and acceptance of feminine norms set by a society hostile to them. There is understanding for the compulsions that make a woman silent and compliant. Consider, for example, "Women in Dutch Painting":

They are calm, not stupid
Pregnant not bovine
I know women like that
And not just in paintings—
An aunt who did not answer her husband back
Not because she was plain

Eunice de Souza appears to substantiate Simone de Beauvoir's famous statement: "One is not born a woman; one becomes one" when she writes of how she was:

> a burly little girl
> who knocked her sissy cousins down *Visit*

But as she grew, there was Embroidery Sister forcing her into developing "feminine skills", then, she was one of a row of small girls in first communion dresses, and then again, in school, she clutched Sister Flora's skirt and cried "for my mother" who taught across the road. The conditioning to fit into a phallocratic society left her confused and anchorless, so that though people now say of her:

> Now she wears lipstick and
> now she is a Bombay girl

the poet confesses that:

> I am still learning
> to cross the road *The Road*

The "otherness" of women seems to be the chief concern in "Advice to Women":

> Keep cats
> if you want to learn to cope with
> the otherness of lovers
> Otherness is not always neglect—
> Cats return to their litter trays
> When they need to

As de Beauvoir explains, "The situation of women is that she—a free and autonomous being like all creatures—nevertheless finds herself living in a world where men compel her to assume the status of the Other". The consequent sense of alienation and loneliness felt by many women is hinted at in the lines:

That stare of perpetual surprise
in those great green eyes
will teach you
to die alone *Advice to Women*

and again in "Remember Medusa?":

Remember Medusa
Who could not love
Even herself

The marginalized, trivialised woman can only hope for a "full membership in the human race"[5], through revolt and defiance of the politics of patriarchy. There is a need to "transcend self" despite a "world crumbling around", despite the fact that "there's something in this culture" in which a "Padma, widowed at seventeen" is:

Forbidden to see the sun for a year,
allowed out to crap only at night
when the pure were out of the way
Transcend Self You Say

There is a need to "transcend self" despite the ridicule and humiliation the creative, independent woman is subjected to—"smart arse, poetess", despite the "intensities of longing", "self-diminishment", "the insularity of confidence" or "the insularity of isolation". Women must challenge the oppressive structure of patriarchal society. She must forge a sisterhood based on the commonality of woman's experience.

Sarla Devi, Susum Bala, Rama Devi,
all of ill fame

I read your story in
The morning paper:
You refuse to wear ankle-bells

Worn for generations
You study law
You hear cat-calls in the street
Drums and bells behind your books
Sitting alone in a Bombay restaurant,
Listening to the innuendoes of college clerks
And a loose-lipped Spanish priest,
I know something
Of how you feel. *Return*

The women of ill-fame and the sophisticated Bombay college teacher are victims of the same kind of sexual harassment and exploitation, placed as they are in feminine situations arising out of sociological and historical causes.

The solution lies in a determined attempt by women to subvert traditionally held values and structures advantageous to the male. Eunice de Souza seems to suggest this when she writes in 'For S, Who Wonders If I Get Much Joy out of Life':

As a matter of fact I do
I contemplate, with a certain
Grim satisfaction
Dynamic men who sell better butter
Sometimes I down a Coke
Implacably at the Taj
This morning I terrorized
(successfully)
the bank manager
I look striking in red and black
And a necklace of skulls.

The struggle for self-realisation and freedom is carried further in the poem 'I Choose Not to Marry You, Love':

I choose not to marry you, love
There is poison in my tongue
I maul, I calcify, I am a rib again

The operative word here is "choose": the long road from the view of marriage as the only destiny of a woman to the stage of exercising an option has been traversed. But the highly connotative 'rib' hints at the internal conflicts and ambivalence of women forced to choose between feminist goals and traditional codes. Indian culture is undoubtedly at the cross-roads of transition. But the underlying message is evident; the non-conformist, assertive modern woman can surely hope to "live happily ever after" with

> students, friends, mother, aunts,
> not always there,
> but on call, often enough — *And She Lived Happily*

Notes and References

1. Simone de Beauvoir. *The Second Sex* (Harmondsworth: Penguin, 1979).
2. Ibid., p. 30.
3. Bruce King "Women's Voice," *Modern Indian Poetry in English* (New Delhi: OUP, 1987), p. 158.
4. Sumita Roy, "Paradoxes of Patriarchy: Feminist Motifs, " *Indian Women Novelists*, ed. R.K. Dhawan (New Delhi: Prestige, 1991), p. 48.
5. Beauvoir, p. 29

All extracts from the poems of Eunice de Souza from Eunice de Souza, *Women in Dutch Painting* (Bombay: Praxis, 1988).

From Subordination to Emancipation: A Glimpse into Imtiaz Dharker's *Purdah and Other Poems*

K.S. Sunita

Within the patriarchal power structure, the very act of writing poetry by women is an act of emancipation. The restrictive behavioral pattern prescribed by this power structure had a limiting impact also on the discourse available to women in the past. But this closed scenario is fast changing, as Dharker herself suggests in a poem entitled 'The Word':

> It is pure power, . . .
> this may change the world . . .
> And I the keeper, with my
> Small signs and codes.[1] (p. 58)

Therefore, Imtiaz Dharker's anthology *Purdah and Other Poems* is an attempt to expand the margins assigned to women, to move from the periphery and attempt to become "the keeper[s]" of the word, even though the process may be attained through "small signs and codes."

This anthology has established Dharker's distinctive point of view—biographically this circumscribes her birth into a Muslim family, her education in England and her marriage to a Hindu. Such a widening of her horizon—geographic, cultural and linguistic, among others—reveals to her the immense possibilities which a woman can realize:

> You hold so many possibilities,
> Just inside the skin
> You could be any number of things. (p. 60)

Although spoken in a different context, these lines hint at unexplored vistas as do some further lines from the same poem 'Image':

> The image is never really fixed
> Allow, for one moment, your guard
> to slip, and all the world
> will catch a glimpse
> of the thing you have kept hidden
> all this time. (p. 60)

Woman as the 'Other' has been forced to be 'kept hidden' by the stifling shackles of conditioning. And that is what Purdah symbolises: not merely a form of dress, but a custom, a norm of behaviour, an indication of a whole social system. Purdah becomes a symbol of oppression, subjugation and subordination. It reinforces the idea of woman as inferior, as a temptress, the very sight of whom is sinful and distracting to the 'virtuous' male.

Purdah becomes a physical symbol signifying several modes of discrimination. Purdah literally and etymologically means 'Curtain'. Through concealment it constructs a barrier between what it shields and the world outside. Purdah also indicates a 'closed mind syndrome', 'a state of mind' that only reiterates a sad manifestation of the resurgence of feudal attitudes. While it grants proprietary rights to men over their women, it denies women even the basic right to their own individuality.

Imtiaz Dharker is of Pakistan descent, and spent her growing years in Britain. Most of the poetry in *Purdah* (OUP, 1989) narrates the experiences of young immigrant girls confronted with the tensions of adjusting within the conflicting cultures of orthodoxy and a permissive society. To Dharker Purdah hides the body in the same way as the earth covers the coffins of dead men. Vrinda Nabar remarks that 'Purdah means the end of existence: it deadens the woman's capacity to interrelate with the world by inhibiting her sensory perception of it . . . besides rendering a woman's sensory existence dead, or at least confining/ denying it, purdah also makes the woman a non-being, a person who is without an identity or individuality in the eyes of the external world." Women in purdah thus become 'depersonalized' "non persons".[2]

Therefore, a woman must know her place, as Dharker says ironically in 'A Woman's Place':

> Mouths must be watched, especially
> if you're a woman. A smile
> should be stifled with the sari-end. (p. 32)

And the place/ space allowed to a woman is within the confines of the shroud—the purdah or the burqa. This cloister is explicated by Dharker in 'Purdah I':

> We sit still, letting the cloth grow
> a little closer to our skin. (p. 3)

And also

> Purdah is a kind of safety.
> The body find a place to hide (p. 3)

It is indeed ironic, almost pathetic, that the woman finds it necessary in the first place to 'hide' and to seek 'safety'. It is a horrific comment on society where one half has to tread warily of the other—though a mask, a veneer of civilization cloaks this destructive tendency, as the poem entitled 'The Mask' suggests:

> We live with a passion
> to destroy . . .
> Power is not always fanged, . . .

> More often it wears a simpering mask. (p. 59)

To keep the mask intact a woman must maintain decorum, be self-effacing and even wipe out her identity and individuality. Dharker uses the metaphor of the "dark mirror" in which "Our faces [are] beginning to take shape" (p. 59) to hint at the as yet undefined, inexplicable reaching out by women towards life, not mere subsistence. There may be hope of more centrality in "tomorrow's cradles rocking' but to achieve that one has to get out of the coffin-like Purdah. This telling image is expressed in the following oft-quoted lines from 'Purdah I':

> The cloth fans out against the skin
> much like the earth that falls
> on coffins after they put the dead men in (p. 3)

Being put behind Purdah is akin to killing the person and this is done as soon as the girl-child is "old enough to learn some shame" (p. 3). Here the poet's voice is raised in stringent criticism against the negative aspects of this custom which totally denies a young woman the opportunity to grow up normally—with freedom on both intellectual and spiritual planes.

Dharker highlights the constraints of Purdah wherein a girl child is looked upon as an object of sacrifice on the altar of social convention and tradition. Intellectual and sexual exploitation begins with traditional marriages involving monetary transactions and no individual choice. Dharker bitterly recalls:

> They have all been sold and bought
> The girls I knew
> Unwilling virgins who had been taught
> Especially in this stranger's land, to bind
> their brightness tightly round,
> whatever they might wear
> in the purdah of the mind. (p. 7)

Much sociological research has been undertaken on this specific custom of Purdah. For instance in a volume entitled *The Status of Muslim Women in North India*, the author Shibani Roy stated that "Purdah is a male imposed symbol of domination and seclusion symbolizing the eclipse of a Muslim Woman's identity and individuality."[2]

Of course, Dharker does not imply any exclusive culture specificity to female subordination in practice, though linguistically she uses the Muslim equivalent of subordination—that is, the Purdah. This becomes obvious in 'Purdah II' where even the "English boy" keeps the woman on her "knees":

> there you are with your English boy
> who was going to set your free,
> trying to smile and be accepted
> always on your knees. (p. 10)

A woman, in effect, cannot afford to rise, and to pander to the male ego, has to remain on her knees even if she has superior capabilities than her male counterpart.

> In or out of Purdah. Tied, or bound.
> Shaking your box to hear
> how freedom rattles . . . (p. 10)

The mirage of freedom, an auditory fantasy of its rattle, the restriction of Purdah can be compelled both by external forces/ factors or even consciously chosen, self-imposed. Paradoxical though this may sound, Dharker puts it tellingly:

> The haunted house could get you,
> so that's where you went
> because you wanted to be got
> Didn't you, didn't you. (p. 21)

The unconscious realms of the human/ female psyche is gripped so powerfully by the long aeons of conditioning that it may impose its own restrictions upon itself. Then, the relevant question which the poet poses is: are women capable of facing the contradictions within themselves? Once more, the metaphor of the "dark mirror" mentioned earlier surfaces.

With increasing self-awareness, better opportunities for education and free thinking, decision making positions in society and such other progressive steps to empower women, the natural assumption would be that the crippling constriction of Purdah, not physical alone, but mental, intellectual, emotional etc. would loosen. It is an agonised poetic persona which identifies the perpetual battle-line in a poem of the same name to express the continuing checks obstructing the voice of women:

> The place in the throat
> where words are halted
> not allowed to pass,
> where questions form
> and are not asked (p. 47)

And one of the major areas expecting this unquestioning conformity is religion—specifically prayer in the mosque alongside men. Detailed by Raj Prithvi in his study *Islam and Women* it is said: "In the earlier days of Islam, women, it would appear, were free to visit the mosque and pray. This practice was, later, condemned as good men found it difficult to concentrate their mind on prayers in the presence of women; by the third century of the Muslim era, the practice of letting women attend the mosque generally fell into disuse, though among some sections of Muslims it has continued to the present day."[3]

Of course, Dharker's poetic expression is "discreet rebellion" which points to a possible emancipation. In 'Purdah II' the following words may be construed as hopeful, even prophetic

> At last a sign, behind the veil,
> Of life (p. 9)

To rejuvenate this initial impulse is not a small matter and for this she sounds a clarion call "Break cover/ Break cover" (p. 9). Women need to answer this call.

Finally, one may conclude that the very fact that these poems acknowledge that there is inequality—symbolised as Purdah—is a step towards solving the problem. As Dharker suggests, change is needed and "the blazing eye of faith/ can bring about" this change—the desired emancipation. How and when is left to individual choice and effort.

Notes and References

1. Imtiaz Dharker, *Purdah and Other Poems* (Delhi: OUP, 1988). All page references are to this edition.
2. Vrinda Nabar, *Caste as Woman* (Penguin, 1995), p. 134.
3. Shibani Roy, *Status of Muslim Women in North India* (New Delhi: B.R., 1979), p. 45.
4. *Islam and Women*, ed. Raj Prithvi and B.R. Sharma (New Delhi: Anmol, 1995), p. 32.

Bodyspaces and 'Illocationary' Acts: The Poetry of Bibhu Padhi

PRAMOD K. NAYAR

Bibhu Padhi is undoubtedly the most spatial of Indian poets in English today[1]. Padhi's spatial motifs are not mere geographical images, but a psychodynamics of space. The very real integration of an individual's being with her/his topoi in Padhi suggests a philosophy of being as *being-in-place*. This ontopology[2] derives from the Self's relation with the place, a relationship achieved through the body. That is, a place is known through the body and its senses. The body is thus transformed into an imbrex which links Self/ identity and place. *Places* (the body or geographic locales) in Padhi become spaces through practice, and may therefore be termed "body spaces"[3]. The role of the body space in sensing a place, and forging a link with this place/ people-in-place is Padhi's own poetics of space. In this essay I shall focus mainly on the orientations of bodies in space (since this is where a psychodynamics of space and identity begins), and touch upon the spatial practices that Padhi portrays. The exploration of the relationship of this spatial dynamic and identity formation will, for reasons of space, require another essay altogether.

I. The Body in Space

The body's orientation in space in perhaps the most important facet of a geographical sense and the beginning of particular attitude and relationships with places. The location of a house is the larger spatialising of identities (in the house's distance, proximity and access from other houses, people and so on). Likewise the orientation of a body-in-place is the immediate context of the body's (primary) identity. The person's ability to locate her/himself, and the successful completion of such acts of placing the body may be called "illocationary acts" (to parody the term from speech-act theory).

Four essential modes of the body's orientation in space and illocationary acts are discernible in Padhi's poetry. They are order, continuity, enclosure, proximity/separation[5]. In Padhi the body *is* a space which is often contrasted or compared with the spaces of the outside and of language. Frequently, the body is the site of inscription (especially for time or age), or the tool of inscription on an external page. The body's orientation in space is indicative of freedom, sense of escape, claustrophobia, the terror of unknown spaces, and the inability to inscribe one's body/words onto the external space/page. The body's rapid decay that prevents this latter inscription is coterminous (to stress the spatial image) with the intrusion of the external spaces or the shrinkage of the spaces of one's language. As the body shrinks in Padhi, two features of space become evident: (a) The space of language escapes the restricted space of the body and the latter's limited location (frequently imaged as the house in Padhi). Thus language is the necessary addition (or excess) to bodyspace, a space that allows freedom for the restrained body; (b) Language-space may also shrink severely. The spaces of language, the external world may thus be antagonistic to the bodyspaces.

I shall first look at poems that suggest a spatiality of *order* and *continuity*. Order and continuity suggests links—with the family, with the objects around the house/home, and with tradition. Lineage is a comforting thought, for it lends an identity through location (in the family tree, for instance). Padhi's attitude towards such an order or continuity is dualistic and duellistic. The speakers in his poem are unable to decide whether their specificity of location (home, town, profession, family, and relationship) is beneficial or claustrophobic. In fact, a sense of the mutually contradictory claustrophobia and agoraphobia haunt the personae alternately. In "Footprints" (*Wound*: 31) the speaker perceives a spectre in his home. A ghost who, paradoxically, leaves a trail of footprints. As benefits the ontopological poetics of Padhi, the footprints suggest a certain direction in movement and orientation.

> Who cares to walk about this
> Table lacking arrangement, every night?

Later the speaker concludes that the ghostly footprints have redeemed his own disoriented state.

> It has nonetheless shown me the way
> The words are here, firm on the page.
> Looking for other, farther words,
> And footprints that travel along unimagined roads.

Here the bodyspace poetics is brilliant. The disembodied footprints lack a body. The finitude of the body that prevents it from reaching beyond is "corrected", and correctly directed, by one that lacks a body. Suddenly the body is the site of inscription; it is also oriented in space, and driven into movement. The table that lacked arrangement is now the site of a presence that bestows arrangement. Here this arrangement is "purpose". The conclusion of the poem suggests a range of bodyspace themes: the direction of future movement of the body, the sequentiality (that is continuity) of movement (the last word of the poem is "roads", which indicate points of departure and arrival), the sense of exploring with the senses-in/of-the-body ("looking for other"). Here order is sought, and provides some "locational security" to the body, an illocationary act.

"In the Temple" (*Painting*: 6) a different situation arises. If the previous example demonstrated the need for order, this one suggests the very opposite. The speaker in the temple's premises notes various spatial details: the "short entrance", the orientation of other devotees ("stand erect"), the "marbled courtyard", the "polished floors" and so on. The speaker finds the ritualistic arrangement of objects, people and idols unremittingly claustrophobic. The atmosphere of smoke, the slippery floors appear to be *disorienting* the body of the speaker. For, in this sacral space, the body loses control over itself: "the polished floors . . . wouldn't hold my feet". And then the speaker discovers that "[he] can hardly stand upright/in her archaic territory". Two things are achieved here: the effect on the bodyspace, and the sense of loss (of equilibrium, since the feet seem to be slipping away). The orderly arrangement throws the bodyspace into disorder. The speaker concludes by giving us another spatial image:

> my words drifting sluggishly
> in the stagnant air, until they reach
> her threshold of innocence and familiarity.

The symbol of the threshold—both inside and outside, and hence undecidable in its spatial "belonging" is the perfect conclusion to this poem about disorientation. If we take the poem to mean a crisis of faith, the symbol suggests that the body's displacement—actual or potential—indicates the Self's slide towards the threshold of agnosticism. The threshold is the boundary that divides faith from disbelief. The illocationary act (of slipping away from/at a place, a dis-placement and dis-location) of the speaker is an affirmation, perhaps of non-belonging and non-belief. And, as Heidegger suggested, a boundary is not that at which something stops, a boundary is that at which something begins its presence. The boundary here is that which destabilises the body, and the disorientation of the body-in-ordered/ritual-space becomes an important metaphor for the problem of identity itself.

Order, continuity, history and identity come together in the bodyspaces of "Paperboats on the Fullmoon Day in October" (*Temple*: 16). In the expanse of the great Mahanadi, the boats "reenact history".

> Once out of our hands

They fly on the outgoing waves
In a most desired motion.

The "desired motion" is the movement away ("outgoing") from the continuity of history. If history chokes the speaker, the boats represent the freedom he desires. Perhaps the boat is the body that yearns to get away, to erase the inscription/ direction forced upon it, and rewrite it. Yet he discovers that such distanciation—in space or time—may be dangerous. Padhi writes:

They lose
The direction we had given them. . . .
while our hopes
sink quietly in the broad river.

However, the freedom of the boats is offset by the dangers inherent in such a free-floating movement. The speaker is thus caught between the claustrophobia of attachments like family and history, and the agoraphobia of the loose movement. The expanse of the great river threatens to engulf all lives and identities. The body cannot orient itself in the vastness of space.

One of the best poems that detail Padhi's concern with bodyspaces and order/continuity is "Letters not yet Written" (*Choosing*: 43). This poem is very similar to "Letters" in *Lines*: 14). Here time suggests the continuity and order of life. The speaker refers to a person who reads old letters as a method of reliving the past. The entire description hinges upon the notion and location of ordered words, and an *order of words* that triggers (or once triggered) an *order of thoughts* and dreams.

You go back to the letters
You've preserved over the years
Instances of affectionate distancing, or unadorned
Praise. . .

marks of clean typefaces
that once triggered off ambitions

which lay dormant for
a long time
dates beginning with
one long wish and ending with another.

The "natural order" that the speaker describes later has decayed and weakened the hands that wrote these letters. Now the steadiness is gone (Padhi's favourite image is of quivering hands). What the other person hopes for now, even with this weakened body, is a revival-retrieval and continuation of the old affection, of the old order, albeit in a different (new) manner. The change, in terms of time and health, does not appear to alter (or, is it the wish that it should not alter?) the order of past days. Padhi captures this notion of continuity brilliantly and entirely in terms of spaces: of the body and of language. He writes:

Better still
To wait for things to happen
In their natural order . . .
hoping
that the next morning would bring
a letter written with new affection
in an almost illegible hand
that hides far more than
what appears on the page.

Other poems that deal with the theme of bodyspaces in terms of the spatial arrangement of order and continuity are: "Annual Invitation to the Dead", "A Sense of Place" (*Painting*), "Birthplace", "Wish", "On a Winter Afternoon, among Lost Faces" (*Wound*) and "Nightwatch" (*Temple*).

The very first poem in *Choosing a Place*, "The Garden", is about *enclosed* bodyspaces. The human beings order their garden, constantly seeking to impose a pattern on nature:

Each morning and every evening
We put it to shape so that

It may grow in size
To take the whole house in

The speaker yearns for the warmth and sunshine of the outside world, but without leaving the confines of his home. Padhi writes:

I think of a time when
I might not have to go out of
the house at all, in search of
warmth and open fields and green.

The garden regularly attracts birds, who, however, "dream of flying *out* of their home" (emphasis mine). The contrast between the human being's attitude (and anxiety) is sharply focused through the use of space. The man does not want his body to leave the space of his house, and the birds dream of nothing else. For the speaker, freedom is the ability and luxury of discovering nature within the enclosed spaces of the garden and the house. For the birds there are no enclosures. The circumscription of the human bodyspace is offset only by the *aspatiality* of the imagination (the words "dream", "wish", "think" occur four times in the poem, all indicating the freedom of thought from spatial limits). Padhi here continued his exploration of the human dilemma: caught between the sterile safety of enclosed spaces and the vertiginous joys of unrestricted movement. This is symbolised pithily in the oxymoronic psychic state described in the last line of the poem, and which invites the argument I offer here (of the contradictory impulses of claustrophobia and agoraphobia): "the unfinished garden in me"—the vastness of the internal spaces of the body.

"Fences" in *Choosing a Place* (10-11) is a poem that aptly summarises the theme of spatial *enclosure*. The need to hem in, to bound and limit, is contrasted with the anxiety against such a limiting spatiality. There is the "insecurity of place". The speaker is afraid of words. Alongside the terrifying openness of the fields, the words "always move across/the roads to the dark interiors/of conspiring neighbours". The shift of orientation and perspective of vision from the vastness of space to the claustrophobia of inner recesses is crucial. For, here the speaker is unable to negotiate the two mutually contradictory positions. The words that the speaker orders and systematises in order to locate himself seem to escape him.

> Words that I always thought
> I had fenced in by
> The barbed edges of the mind—
> Safe, trustworthy, unyielding?
> Even then it seems there are other means
> Of travel that they know and I do not know.

The conclusion of the poem is the resignation that the security of words is not created by the mind. One cannot order the words by fencing them in. Likewise, private words/worlds (fenced in) do not ensure security. The disturbing disorientation is emphasised when the speaker says:

> I shall just wait and watch
> How words take birth, grow.
> Let them go, find their own fences now.

Thus the paradox of Padhi's spatiality. The need to fence in his world/body (since, as geographers point out, "what is the mind but body")[6]. To simultaneously place language and control the language of his spaces (for language *is* space) *and* let them escape into the neighbour's house (a very similar theme is visible in "Word", from *Temple*: 62). Another non-affirmative illocation.

"Stranger in the House"(*Wound*: 12) is a poem that deals extensively with the closed space. In the confines of the house, the speaker feels the presence of a stranger watching the house's inhabitants. Here the house encloses people, thoughts, feelings, sounds, and more importantly, memories from a distant child-hood/ past. It encloses time too:

> words are sometimes faintly heard,
> or just remembered from a distant year
> when I was small.

Feet "shuffling across/ a dark room on the upper floor" can also be heard. The confined space of the house is almost threatening: this stranger monitors movement and thought. The speaker's movements—that is, the orientations of his bodyspace—are restricted, because he is constantly watched in his house-space. The stranger has inscribed his presence onto the space of the house and its residents:

> I see the dust of my father's year rise
> from that corner where my son plays.

Yet the *threat* of the stranger watching also ensures safety: one hopes that someone stands guard over us, monitors our movements. Thus the speaker ends the poem with a sense of affirmation that someone may be watching over his son too: "Is someone, homeless and distant/ over the years, watching him too?" The paradox is evident: the watcher is himself free, "homeless", but is house-bound to his family. The living people are free to move away, but they are chained to memories and history. The inscription of the bodyspace with memories is also, simultaneously, the inscription of the bodyspace onto the house. Unlike other Padhi poems here enclosure seems less threatening than elsewhere.

In a poem very different in its treatment of enclosures from "Stranger in the House", "The Door" (*Wound*: 32) suggests a claustrophobia. This door is one that has never been opened, and therefore excites curiosity. The whole *body* is oriented towards the door. Sounds are heard, and the speaker's attention is on the person beyond the door. The speaker's bodyspace is fully alert:

> I have stood here for a long time now . . .
> the waiting hours do not seem to matter
> any more and cannot even secure
> the sound of footsteps behind the door.

If the senses of the speaker are tuned into the sounds emerging from the closed-off space, the distances from the door (waiting outside the door) also circumscribe his body. Here the sounds from the outside space seem to write themselves clearly upon the bodyspace of the speaker. He is even able to describe the person inside with certainty, almost as if he is on the other side of the door:

> The goddess is wide awake, I know. Her large
> round eye as hard as some precious stone, her look
> about to bestow a long-forgotten gift.

One could say that a *graf(ph)ting* (in the botanical sense of grafting, and writing/graphting[7]) has occurred: the speaker is added onto the woman inside, and she has inscribed her Self on him. Though he is on this side of the door he infiltrates into her presence. Here enclosure suggests a juncture (just as the door is the spatial juncture that separates or unites), a togetherness across barriers. One bodyspace has been spliced with another. Once more the bodyspace has helped attain a Self linked to other people/Selves and firmly located in space.

In "Sleep" (*Painting*: 9) the child is able to run, free of any limitations of space. Padhi describes the boy as "throwing off the near limits of time/ and space, accommodating other dimension of our race". The boy's excited play of bodyspace reveals a whole new realm (not unlike the dancer/dance in Yeats' famous image): the bodyspace is a new dimension, the movement creates space, and movement *is* the space. In "Midnight Consolings" (*Painting*: 15) it is the body's senses that once more suggest a space for the past and the future, a past that is firmly local, and derived from the atmosphere of the body's present location (again, the house/home). Padhi writes:

Our bodies
are half-dreaming still, while
our generous words issue from
A place far within this night.

Here the link between the body and place is seen as "enclosing" a whole memory (in this particular poem it is a collective memory) and thus suggests an illocationary act for the whole town/community.

Other poems that discuss the spatiality of enclosures are "Among the Ruins", "Kites", "Paper Town", "In This City of Merchants", "Watching on a Summer Afternoon, Children Playing" (*Painting*), "The Undelivered" (*Wound*), and "Sea Breeze" (*Temple*).

Proximity and *separation* of body spaces are perhaps Padhi's favourite spatial images. A summary of my argument—that proximity/intimacy and separation/displacement are spatial configurations that prevent or enable an ontological recognition—is readily available in "All through the Long Night" (*Lines*: 18) and "The Bed" (*Painting*: 1). The speaker describes a relationship in space, a relationship that is first articulated through the body's spaces of intimacy. The proximity enables a graf(ph)ting and infiltration where a bodyspace attaches to another. The lines from "All through the Night" are worth quoting in full:

Your quick and considerate light
plays upon my skin.
As the night grows
into a darker life,
my world acquires
a narrow, emphatic heat.
New forces, subtle
fields of energy
create themselves
between skin and skin

and hold us together
in a dear gesture.
But in due time
a thin flame form within you
starts burning
through the night.
It dances inside my brain,
deep below my skin.
As the night turns thin and weak,
your defeating red is all there is.
Your small body wins.

In "The Bed" a similar proximity that suggests intimacy turns out to be a frightening experience.

Every turn in sleep folds into
The inert lines of a deep deep black.
A friendship built through sweat and dreams,
A stickiness of familiarity. And a willingness
To let all of these stay as they are,
Untampered with, through the years
Of a humiliation that the bed alone knows
Regardless of your common everyday wish
To change the sheets.

These two poems speak differently of proximity. The first one suggests an intimacy of bodyspaces (both poems, of course, carry sexual overtones) where a link may be forged. The second suggests a separation in the same close(d) circle. A ritualistic act (changing the sheets) attempts to reassure themselves that all is well. But the humiliation is visible to anyone who looks. The references to skin, sweat and body texture (stickiness, heat) in both poems are a clear indication of the bodyspaces that are in close proximity to one another. The relationship that bestows identity is achieved through a shared bodyspace (two bodyspaces graf(ph)ted on each other)—"New forces . . . create themselves/ between skin and skin".

Another poem that reiterates the spatial sense of proximity in formulating an identity is "Growing Up in the Dark" (*Lines*: 32). After a description of words exchanged, languages shared across vast spaces ("His words reached me as if from a land/on the sea's farther side"), the speaker discovers that the two share a common identity of space. The geographic metaphors make this clear:

> I sit along with him while others have deserted us,
> Reconsidering what lights shine in his kingdom, what
> unseen waves crash at his sea's periphery, recalling
> from memory what night is his that once belonged to me.

Here the speaker discovers that they once shared a common feature. And now, when he has lost this, another comes into his (the speaker's circle) with the same "condition". Memory triggered by physical proximity unites the two in a shared past.

Separation becomes the central motif in Padhi's representation of bodyspaces in "Listening", "Taking Care of the Dead", "Distances", "Grandmother" and other poems from *Wound.* "Distances", for instance, portrays the sense of sight and hearing (imbedded in the body, of course) that create distances or intimacies.

> The smile that is just about to flash.
> The eyes that should've looked
> In the right direction, the hands wide
> Sweeping gesture that is still to come. . . .
> I may not know these short distances that at times
> Plague one with loss and defeat—
> Between one body and another, two consecutive fingers
> Which other wish might intervene and settle . . .
> Perhaps the obscure, wish-bearing
> Spaces in my heart would know.

Here the speaker suggests the inability to know actual, distances. These distances that may be altered with a tiny gesture prove unbridgeable on occasion. The bodyspaces, with all its mechanisms to bridge distances finds it impossible. The conclusion that refers to the spaces of the heart is therefore ironic: a space that is inaccessible may hold the key to bridging the spatial distance between two bodyspaces. In "Letter to My Wife" Padhi once again sketches the inability of wordspaces to provide any certain bridge across the distances: "we haven't spoken, having lost/ our power to speak". The spaces within a shared language have themselves become inaccessible to the protagonists, and hence the chances of their bridging the psychological distancing seem remote (here the enclosure-separation theme of spatiality also works).

Thus far, then, we have seen Padhi's use of bodies in space, spatially configured and related to indicate actual or "spiritual" distanciation. We shall now move on to spatial practices in Padhi.

II. The Practice of Space

Ontopology, as we have already defined, is being-in-place. In Padhi we have noted how bodies are inevitably spaced, and are themselves spaces. Certain spatial practices are "indulged" in by Padhi's protagonists. Three central modes of practising space may be identified in Padhi: *subjectivity, meaning,* and *changes in symbolic value*. Spatial practice, as Henri Lefebvre has shown, is not simply urban or political, but frequently theatrical, erotic, ambiguous, and full of needs and desires. In Padhi, with his near-solipsist rendering of spaces (spaces only in so far as they affect, or are affected by him) this concept of Lefebvre's is of great importance."[8]

Spaces are practised upon through an emotional attachment to the place. The protagonist in Padhi invests an enormous amount of emotional capital in certain spaces, and, therefore, anticipates certain returns. We have already noted two poems in which a space is practised as near-erotic ("near" because both suggest a failure of/ in the erotic space): the bed in "The Bed" and "All through the Long Night". Here the space of the bed rejects the bodyspace. The geographic space becomes a battleground where the Self wages a battle for its sanity and some security (which it seeks to attain through shared spacing of the bed). In "Rest" (*Wound*: 60-61) death unites two people. They die locked in an embrace, sharing a coat. The space of the coat may be the space of paternal love (the headnote to the poem tells us that it is about a father and daughter who were buried alive in snow. There are references to small feet, soft bones to indicate the child protagonist). Here the space of the coat and the space of their death become sacralised space: for it is the space of "forgiveness and love":

> What can separate us then, when
> They find us tomorrow, our bodies
> Entwined with each other
> In an act of forgiveness and love,
> Except this coat?

In "Trees" (*Lines*: 21) the speaker indicates the investments *they* have made, and the return *he* hopes to derive:

> I hear your kind voice
> Within every subtle breeze . . .
> at the end of the storm I try to locate you
> in the spaces between leaves, among the stars
> have you done your job, now that you leave me
> alone, before these trees, your green kingdom?

The spaces practised as spaces of love and affection now do not provide succour or sympathy. They are distanced. The speaker's subjectivity in poems like "Postscript" (*Lines*: 22), "The Storm" (*Temple*: 57) and several others is predicated upon the emotional attachment with a particular place, a spatial practice that converts places into lived and experienced space.

Desire is mapped onto both bodies and spaces in Padhi. Thus the bed, the house, and the romantic trysting spots are territorialisations of desire. The poignancy of unfulfilled desire transforms the place into a barren space. What is practised here is not fulfilment of desire, but the waiting for the fulfilment of desire. "Among the Ruins" (*Wound*: 46) is perhaps one of Padhi's best poems on this theme. It begins with the specific barrenness of loveless space: "what else is left here?" Then Padhi draws out the tragedy of the space:

> From within the dark, someone calls
> someone who has been always there;
> a woman's face grown thin with waiting
> stares at you, almost imploring you
> to teach it how a smile could be made
> or a lost world restored to its place. . . .
> what else is left here?
>   Proud, forbidding shadows
> playing among the last of the pillars,
> arches, family albums, doors and windows
> that never open?

Meaning is attached to a particular space through labour or achievement in that place. In Padhi this is the practice of versifying. We have noted in the previous section the poet's obsession with wordspaces. The "spots" where versifying conveys a shared sense (of place and identity) are visible in poems like "Growing Up in the Dark". The ritual prayer, also a labour of devotion and love, in "The Island" (*Temple*: 58), "Prayer" (*Lines*: 26) are about the spatial practices of achieving salvation, however limited, in the spaces of the temple, the spaces of the prayer, and the conduct of ritual. These are the sacral spaces. Yet the space is ambiguous, just as salvation is an uncertain state. In "Prayer" the speaker seeks a distanciation from the sacral space. Though he begins with "Will this prayer become a thing—/ this whisper on the edge of words?" he concludes with "gather me with your fingers . . . let me go". We have already noted in our reading of "In the Temple" that the speaker is uncertain about his position within the temple premises, just as his faith remains slippery.

Thus spatial practices that seek to actualise places through the practice of devotion also remain unfruitful in Padhi. Sacral spaces like that of the temple have the same "value" as the erotic spaces of the bed or the house. However, the space of the house is not merely of failure. Numerous poems suggest a spatial practice that changes the symbolic value of the house-space. Frequently this is through the child's body that seems not to recognise boundaries or prohibited areas. "Stranger in the House" that hopes for the continuing disembodied and *aspatial* presence of the father (described by Padhi as "homeless and distant") is an example. In "Watching on a Summer Afternoon Children Playing", "Annual Invitation to the Dead", "Sleep", "House Lizards" (*Painting*) the house acquires import precisely because of the presence of the child and/or the forefathers ("House Lizards" described lizards as "our wise forefathers in enviable disguise"). The symbolic value of corners, vessels, facial features and other bodied or non-embodied space changes with the ritual recall of the people once associated with them. Padhi sums up this symbolic value through active participation in space in "Home" (*Painting*: 63-64):

> The things we think we possess
> Are owned by people we've only heard of
> But never seen, . . .
> our home, perched among our
> children's grudging smiles, hands
> that are reluctant to take or give;
> the dim eventful faces from elsewhere
> that could as well belong to the future
> as they did to the passing and the past,
> staying on in indefinite exile.

Thus in Padhi spaces are read at two levels: as bodyspaces and spaces that need to be embodied through specific orientations and illocationary practices. Padhi's emphasis on the body as a means of knowing a place, of transforming it into space, and the scripting of relationships on them is perhaps a unique move in Indian poetry in English (the nearest comparison to Padhi's spatial poetics is Arun Kolatkar's *Jejuri*). Perhaps it may be fruitful to study the entire Padhi oeuvre for its psychodynamics of space. I will conclude by indicating the directions that such a study might take: spatial relationships, a typology of spaces (theatrical, erotic, gendered, spiritual/sacral, familial, ritual, and in-between or third spaces), the link between space and desire (the mapping of desire onto individual and spaces, and the social conditions in which such a mapping takes place—the family, the town, tradition) and the spatialising of identities themselves. Such a study will be fruitful because, in the postcolonial context, place/ space becomes a major theme for both creative practice and critical exegesis (much Indian fiction in English demonstrates this strain). Let us say that such a topographic criticism will clear a new space.

Notes and References

1. The following volumes of Padhi's poetry have been used: *Going to the Temple* (New Delhi: Indus, 1988); *Lines from a Legend* (London: Peepal Tree, 1993); *A Wound Elsewhere* (Delhi: Rupa, 1992); *Painting the House* (Hyderabad: Disha-Orient Longman, 1999); *Choosing a Place*, MS in progress; I thank Bibhu Padhi for allowing access to his unpublished work.
2. "Ontopology" is Jacques Derrida's portmanteau term to suggest a philosophy of being as *being-in-place*. See his *Specters of Marx: The State of the Debt, the Work of Mourning and the New International*, trans. Peggy Kamuf (London: Routledge, 1994).
3. The distinction between space and place is crucial here. One turns to Michel de Certeau for a definition. Place is the order in accord with which various elements are distributed in relationships of the same location. A place is the configuration of various positions. Space include direction. It is the intersection of the variables (time,

direction), it is actualised with the movements of elements within a place. Thus space is a practised place. The street of urban planning becomes space when it is walked upon by people. See de Certeau's *The Practice of Everyday Life*, trans. Steven Randall (Berkley: University of California Press, 1988), esp. p. 117. "Bodyspaces" is the title of N. Duncan's book on the relation between bodies, spaces and sexualities. See his *Bodyspaces*, ed. (London: Routledge, 1995). Of course, if the body could be seen as inherently spatialised, the body may itself be treated as a site for inscription for the discourses of sexuality, medical, legal and others.

4. Much theoretical work on the link between spatiality and identity is now available in lesbian and gay theory, notably in the writings of Judith Butler and Elizabeth Grosz. For an overview see Heidi Nast and Steve Pile, ed., *Places through the Body* (London and New York: Routledge, 1998). I have analysed the link between space, spatial configurations of the human body and identity elsewhere. See my "Spatialising Identity; Wendy Barker's *Let the Ice Speak*" (forthcoming in *Interventions*, Journal of the University of Calicut, inaugural issue).
5. These concepts of orientation in space are based on the work of Jean Piaget. See Piaget and B. Inhelder's *The Child's Conception of Space*, trans. F.J. Langdon and J.L. Lunzer (New York: W.W. Norton, 1967).
6. Julia Cream, "Re-solving Riddles: The Sexed Body," in *Mapping Desire: Geographies of Sexualities*, ed. David Bell and Gill Valentine (London: Routledge, 1995), p. 32.
7. This notion of graf(ph)ting which combines the sense of both botanical grafting and "graphematics"/writing is adapted from Laura Donaldson. See her *Decolonising Feminism: Race, Gender and Empire-Building* (London: Routledge, 1993).
8. For an elaboration of Lefebvre's ideas see Steve Pile's *The Body and the City: Psychoanalysis, Space and Subjectivity* (London: Routledge, 1977), pp. 156-57 and elsewhere.

The Poetics of Exile in Agha Shahid Ali's *The Half-Inch Himalayas*

B. GOPAL RAO

The theme of separation, exile and loss is a recurrent feature in Indian diasporic writing--be it fiction or poetry and Agha Shahid Ali is no exception. His poems represent the influence of diverse traditions and the very trauma of exile becomes an artistic stimulus resulting in a burst of creativity. Commenting on the literary tradition of a writer in exile John Glad observes: "Does the exiled writer attempt to fit into the tradition of the country which received him, or does he cling to his native roots, writing chiefly for "the folks back home?" For the most part, the internationalists are the exception."[1]

Creative writers and poets like Agha Shahid Ali live on the margins of two societies and cultural theory is today being written by people who live on the margins. Therefore exile literature written by those who live on the margins occupies a significant position between cultures and countries. Their works recreate new theories and define positions as it establishes a new identity which negotiates cross-cultural boundaries and relates to different temporal and spatial metaphors.

Many Indian creative writers migrated to America on account of socio-economic and political reasons. The diasporic Indian is: "Like the banyan tree, the traditional symbol of the Indian way of life, he spreads out his roots in several soils, drawing nourishment from one when the rest dry up. Far from being homeless, he has several homes, and that is the only way he has increasingly come to feel at home in the world."[2]

Abdul Jan Mohammed describes the writer in exile as being one of either the "specular border intellectual" or the "syncretic border intellectual".[3] Some writers are more at home in both cultures and relate to both simultaneously, combining and synthesizing them admirably. The meaning and perspective of exile to Agha Shahid Ali first becomes "unbearable," then in the course of time strong and stable. There are always the recurring images of his homeland in his earlier poems and there is a touch of tender and sweet memories intertwined in those reflected recollections.

Edward Said's predicament as an expatriate in America is similar to that of Agha Shahid Ali, and he shares the bitter and sweet experience in elaborating the journey of the exile from his homeland: "The person who finds his homeland sweet is still a tender beginner, he to whom every soil is as his native one is already strong, but is perfect to whom the entire world is a foreign place."[4]

Agha Shahid Ali's "uneasy sense of temporality" is analogical to Salman Rushdie's notion of "broken mirror" about the migrant. Rushdie generalizes the initial excitement of the "homeless" when he says: "But human beings do not perceive things whole. We are not gods but wounded creatures, cracked lenses, capable of fractured perceptions."[5] Emigrants who have chosen to leave their homeland suffer the guilt of the survivor over a period of time. They sometimes desire to return to that land they thought they had put into the past tense.

By analyzing the configurations of the exile complex and reasons for forced emigration in modern times. Martin Tucker observes: "The diasporas continue in modern times; once started, the stones of the heart they induce cannot be rolled back but must in some way be shattered into the power of transcendent adaptation."[6]

In his comments on Frantz Fanon's *Black, Skin, White Masks* the postcolonial critic Homi Bhabha states that memory is the necessary and sometimes hazardous bridge between colonialism and the question of cultural identity. "Remembering", he writes, "is never a quiet act of introspection or retrospection. It is a painful re-membering, a putting together of the dismembered past to make sense of the trauma of the present."[7]

Remembering enables the mind to come to terms with itself. Memories form the foundational basis of conscious existence. Some memories are evoked to give pleasure, while others—more offending than pleasurable—are deliberately blocked to give the mind an illusion of harmony. These obnoxious memories however have a way of influencing one in inexplicable ways. Many of the traumas of modern existence deal with the mind's inability to accept or cleanse itself of these retarding blocks to psychological stability. When these offending memories are released from their captivity as it were, then there is an attempt at a final spiritual reconciliation. The procedure of analysis theory, recommended here, as Leela Gandhi states, is guided by Lacan's ironic reversal of the Cartesian logic, whereby the rationalistic truth of "I think therefore I am" is rephrased in the proposition "I think where I am not, therefore I am where I do not think".[8]

Part of diasporic writing is its struggle to shift its narrow base in England and America to a multiplicity of centers. The new literatures from Asia, Africa and South America reflect it. Most of the writers who belong to these countries often travel between two worlds and two cultures. Exile sometimes could also mean deprivation, and discussing the alien reality of an artist's existence in exile. Horst Bienek points out: "The exile has a sense of having been cast out, pushed away, isolated . . . and he is right. He continues to write in his native language, the people around him speak a different language. The poet can learn this language, but it is unlikely that it will serve him as an instrument of his creativity. Herein lies the Paradox: the world of exile becomes the alibi of existence."[9]

Their writings have a worldwide perspective, rooted as it is, sometimes in the Western tradition, and sometimes in their own indigenous tradition. Agha Shahid Ali is one such contemporary young Indian poet, who in spite of settling in the West could not wholly imbibe the positive aspects of Western tradition. In *The Half-Inch Himalayas*, a collection of short poems, the setting is his Indian past. In 'Postcard from Kashmir' there is loneliness and despair, the hallmark of most exiles (voluntary or otherwise). "Kashmir shrinks into my mailbox,/ my home a neat four by six inches". Kashmir, his homeland now encapsuled in a postcard is ironically referred to as "The half-inch Himalayas" which he now holds in his hand. He continues, 'this is home and this is the closest/ I will ever be to home.' At a later stage in the unknown future when he might return to Kashmir, 'The colours won't be so brilliant,/ The Jhelum's waters so clean,/ so ultramarine, my love,/ so overexposed.' He concludes with ironic wit, 'And my memory will be a little/ out of focus, in it/ a giant negative, black/ and white, still undeveloped."

This poem sets the tone for the other poems that follow in this collection. Loss, symbolized as his Beloved, appears to be the dominant thread that binds these poems together. If in 'Postcard from Kashmir' the loss is of his birthplace, in 'A lost Memory of Delhi', it is of his parents. In this poem he visualizes the year 1948 when he was not yet born. But it was the year his parents got married, and today all he can recall of his parents is their faded photograph in the family album. 'I want to tell them I am their son' but when he knocks at the door of their house, 'I knock keep knocking/ but for them the night is quiet/ this the night of my being/ They don't they won't/ hear me they won't hear/ my knock drowning out/ the tongues of stars'. This pervasive sense of loss and alienation moves to generations before his parents' birth—to that of his ancestors. 'My ancestor, a man/ of Himalayan snow'. 'His skeleton/ carved from glaciers, his breath/ arctic,/ he froze women in his embrace.' The same arctic coldness passed from generation to generation, 'from son to grandson,/ generations of snowmen on my back'/ 'no, they won't let me out of winter,/ . . . I've promised myself,/ even if I'm the last snowman,/ that I'll ride into spring/ on their melting shoulders'. The desire to escape from an empty historical past into a promising future by disowning it seems to be yet another placebo. The aridity of the past in terms of a historical legacy that should have been enriching and fulfilling, but is not, appears to be a recurrent concern in Agha Shahid Ali's poems. In 'Cracked Portraits' the persona's grandfather 'sauntered into madness' while his great grandfather simply 'disappoints' him, as the only thing he could do to perfection was to whip his servants and his horses in an equally drunken fury. "Story of Silence" is a mute description of the loveless relationship between his grandfather and his grandmother. 'The Dacca Gauzes' presents yet another decadent view of history. The transparent Dacca Gauzes 'known as woven air', was a dead art today, dead for more than a hundred years. The 'heirloom sari' once worn by his grandmother, was later converted into handkerchiefs 'embroidered with gold thread paisleys' and distributed amongst the nieces and the daughters-in-law. Those too were now lost. The devastating conclusion is 'in history we learned: the hands/ of weavers were amputated,/ the looms of Bengal silenced".

Anxiety and separation, the essence of exile, find a voice in 'The Season of the Plains.' 'Separation/ can't be borne when the rains/ come: this every lyric says'. But his mother only said 'the monsoons never cross/ the mountains into Kashmir.'

Anxiety with the past gives way to a desolate concern with the present. While there is no attempt to glorify a 'nostalgic past', neither is there an attempt to idealise the 'grim' present. Poems like 'A Butcher' recreate the impossibility of communication even if the language is the same, but the context different. Exchange of lines from Mir and Ghalib between the butcher and the poet do not cement even a momentary relationship of camaraderie. 'He wraps my kilo of ribs./ I give him the money. The change/ clutters our moment of courtesy,/ our phrases snapping in mid syllable/ Ghalib's ghazals left unrhymed.' 'Chandni Chowk, Delhi' and 'Cremation' dramatise the constricting hold of the past, 'Your bones refused to burn. . ./ who would have guessed/ you'd be stubborn in death' he writes of his ancestors in 'Cremation'. In 'Chandni Chowk, New Delhi' the cry is more insistent 'Can you rinse away this city that lasts/ like blood on the bitten tongue?' Tradition and the past take on a new critical dimension in the evocation of the memory of Begum Akhtar. 'In Memory of Begum Akhtar' is strategically placed alongside the one on 'Homage to Faiz Ahmed Faiz' written ten years later on 20 November, 1984. In the earlier poems, anxiety and loss had been related to the realization of a dead tradition. But with Begum Akhtar, and Faiz Ahmed Faiz, singer and poet, both exponents of the classical Urdu tradition, poetic power and tradition, fuse to engender 'a memory of musk, the rebel face of hope.'

In *The Half-Inch Himalayas* loss is specifically situated in India, in Kashmir, and in the poet's own family. These poems echo the loneliness and the sense of deprivation that exile brings. In this instance, it happens to be physical separation from his homeland. However, he refuses to sentimentalize the past and neither does history paralyse his creative powers as a poet. Creativity is regenerated through the use of memory, which enables him to intervene in history and gain in self-knowledge. Time constitutes a sort of "veritable column to memory, and that memory in its turn, is a backbone of history, as much as in the individual as in the general sense"[10]. In *The Half-Inch Himalayas* there is an attempt to come to terms with the past. The past is a necessary precondition for transition and change. His effort to reach out for a 'usable' past is perhaps exemplified in "Snowmen". His ancestors were exiles from Samarkhand, he in turn is an exile from India. His present exiled condition is a necessary adjunct of the burden of exile that his ancestors carried. By acknowledging and recreating the past, memory is used as a poetic device to exorcise memory itself enabling him to 'ride into spring/ on their melting shoulders'. This painful 're-membering' is thus employed as a literary device to put together the fragments of a dismembered past to articulate the traumas of the present. But tradition is used in a novel way. The traumas perhaps remain unresolved. In "In Memory of Begum Akhtar" the poet states 'I wish to summon you in defense,/ but the grave's damp and cold, now when/ Malhar longs to stitch the rain,/ . . . The rain doesn't speak,/ and life, once again, closes in,/ reasserting this earth where the air/ meets in a season of grief." The positive effect of the exiled condition perhaps lies in the resurgence of one's creative poetic power which seeks to reinfuse a dead tradition with a viable regenerating vitality.

Notes and References

1. *Literature in Exile*, ed. John Glad (London: Duke Univ. Press, 1990), p. x.
2. Bhiku Parekh, "Some Reflections on the Indian Diaspora," *Journal of Contemporary Thought* (Baroda, 1993), p. 106.
3. Abdul R. Jan Mohammed, "'Worldliness'-without-World, Homelessness-Home: Towards a Definition of the Specular Border Intellectual," *Edward Said: A Critical Reader* (Oxford: Blackwell, 1992), p. 97.
4. Edward Said, *Culture and Imperialism* (London: Vintage, 1994), p. 407.
5. Salman Rushdie, *Imaginary Homelands* (Granta Books and Penguin India, 1991), p. 12.
6. Martin Tucker, *Literary Exile in the Twentieth Century* (New York: Greenwood Press, 1991), p. xix.
7. Homi Bhabha, *The Location of Culture* (London: Routledge, 1994), p. 63.
8. Leela Gandhi, *Postcolonial Theory. A Critical Introduction* (Delhi: OUP, 1999), p. 9.
9. Horst Bienek "Exile is Rebellion," Rpt. in *Literature in Exile*, ed. John Glad, p. 45.
10. Jan Vladislav "Exile, Responsibility, Destiny," Rpt. in Glad, p. 14.

All excerpts from Agha Shahid Ali's poems have been taken from Agha Shahid Ali, *The Half-Inch Himalayas* (New Delhi: OUP, 1987).

Conflicts in Consciousness: A Reading of Tejdeep's Poetry

SUMITA ROY

In this brief reading of the poems of Tejdeep, the attempt is to see her works as efforts towards making inroads into consciousness. Therefore, the first part of this presentation deals with consciousness studies as a subtext for her poems. In the second part, specific concerns of the poet as a woman are taken up.

I

Since the title of the paper is "Conflicts in consciousness", it would not be out of place to begin with a definition of consciousness. According to Daniel C. Dennet, a doyen of consciousness studies, "Consciousness is both the most obvious and the most mysterious feature of our minds."[1] It is obvious, therefore, that creative expression is also a reflection of the various levels of consciousness—both existent and potential, the latter especially true of deeply "inspired", "expanded", or "heightened" poetry. Such moments may be fairly common to poets, artists and all those who are used to effortlessly generating ideas from their mind/consciousness. Such "privileged moments", as E.F.N. Jephcott suggests, are creative in some manner or the other. As he says: "There are moments when consciousness seems to expand—when the mind takes in the world with a rare and strange intensity. Such moments are the source of the impulse to create a work of art."[2]

Such a privileged moment, both for the poet and possibly for the reader is in Tejdeep's poem: "If you meet me on the road":

> If you meet me on the road
> Send me home, . . .
> If you meet me gazing at the stars
> send me home.
> If you see me dreaming of butterflies
> send me home. . . .
> But if you can, . . . please
> take me away from the 'Rin' and the Vim',
> where the telephone and the postman don't reach.
> where door-bells do not scream
> where matter does not matter
> and my essence will pervade
> over 'vanillas' and 'Pineapples'
>
> So please don't send me home,
>
> just take my hand and I will take you there,
> where people do not wait in queues,
> consult reservation charts, make enquiries.[3] (*FF*, pp. 41-42)

The portrayal of "home" and "there"—the other place free from the mundane routine—juxtaposed in the above lines is a pointer to a preliminary expansion of consciousness. Here the poetic persona fancies the ideal as freedom from the shackles of *maya* and *lila,* the illusion and the play which is often (or almost always) mistaken for the *only* level of experience. Therefore, the ability to visualize other dimensions of experience different from the available one is obviously a privileged moment illustrative of expanding consciousness.

This kind of a dual external landscape that impinges on the heightening consciousness leads to the next step—internal or introspective analysis. Self-importance is one of the issues that the poet's persona begins to perceive with ironic self-knowledge. The relative insignificance of politically incorrect assumptions of power, position and prestige are dealt with wry humour. As we are told in a poem entitled "Criminal Justice":

> On the eve of transfer,
> they throw an extravaganza,
> call near and not so dear,
> make you stand behind a microphone
> to prattle a few words of thanks (*FF*, p. 5)

Illusions of grandeur generally found at the apex of any social/official hierarchy is the worst form of self-deception possible! This is common knowledge for all who are used to functioning within the framework of accepted structures. It is only the creative sensibility that glimpses the inherent conflict in such situations and uses it as a springboard for leaping into another level of consciousness.

In these glimpses of conflict which abound in the poetry of Tejdeep, one may read recognition as a crucial stage because in it lies the germ of resolution which, in other words, is altering or widening the existent level of consciousness.

For instance, the urge to question concepts that demand conformity is a step in this direction. Tejdeep writes:

> Why does law overtake
> motherhood and bail
> is always conditional? (*FF*, p. 2)

An interesting point to note here is the change/elaboration of the usually limited discourse available traditionally to the role model of mother/woman to include words such as 'bail' and 'law' which in itself provides valuable clues to the conflict arising from conventional and situational conditioning. The ever-present flux of experience reveals further and hitherto uncharted depths which clash with the "accept" or the "expected".

One of the so-called normal courses of action might in itself be a window which looks within and reveals an unconscious/unacknowledged conflict. A key issue is raised in the lines:

> How many channels
> Can you change?
> The news is already
>   three languages old (*FF*, p. 64)

Where technology provides endless engagement for the senses and neglects/negates the evolution of consciousness, where obsessive visual indulgence annihilates the desire/ability for originality—all this finds a telling metaphor in the act of changing channels mindlessly. If poetry is the essence of our experience, then this situation is not really an unfamiliar one.

Another powerful metaphor which reflects one more colour in the spectrum of consciousness and illumines Tejdeep's poetic output is in these lines:

> Time seals memories
> in trunks of trees
> agitates pages in a diary . . .
> Time erodes friendships
> burnishes new friends . . .
> Time just does not leave
> It squats on eyelids endlessly (*FF*, p. 35)

Apparently simple, almost prosaic, yet containing elements of that timeless wisdom which is for ever trying to reach out towards eternity through the flux of time's tyrannical progress. The healing, agitating, eroding, burnishing actions of time are subtle pointers to the core of an existential dilemma. This, of course, may be a point where the process of self-actualisation or recognition of the self as more than the physical/material entity takes shape. According to Abraham Maslow (1964) self-actualisation is the constant striving to realise our inherent potential which proceeds in a hierarchical pattern of motives and needs. Elaborating this, Philip Zimbardo suggests: "According to Maslow,[4] need at the lower levels of the hierarchy are prepotent so long as they are unsatisfied. Once these are adequately satisfied, however, the higher needs occupy the individual's attention and effort.[5]

"Hope" and "poetry" may be two such higher needs in Tejdeep's writings. She says in a poem entitled "Birthday":

> Why can't
> hope thrive
> till life cuts
> another slice? (*FF*, p. 23)

Here the poem's title itself is significant as an actualiser, the birthday marking the beginning of actualisation, and the symbol of "life cutting a slice" is powerfully evocative of conflicts which constitute existence. In an attempt at definition, Tejdeep writes about the quality of poetry as

> Sustaining me at the precipice
> Yet holding me back from
> blowing into smithereens (*FF*, p. 45)

where the relevance of sustaining and holding back—as conflicting actions and yet complementary—needs to be linked with the overall pattern of creative self-expression as a process of searching for and fulfilling inherent potential.

II

Moving on from here to a major category of conflict—of being a woman in a male-oriented world—we come to the second part of this presentation.

In a pioneering study by Clarissa Pinkola Estes called *Women who Run with the Wolves*, the creative potential inherent in the feminine psyche is described thus: "All women have personal stories as vast in scope and as powerful as the numen in fairy tales. But there is one kind of story in particular which has to do with a woman's secrets especially those associated with shame; these contain some of the most important stories a woman can give her time to unraveling. For most women, these secret stories are embedded, not like jewels in a crown, but like black gravel under the skin of the soul."[6]

This perceptive comment can be applied to some of the lines written by Tejdeep to further the present argument that conflict (that is, secrets associated with shame) provides the platform for the evolution of consciousness. To begin with, alienation and marginalisation are the inevitable fate of women in patriarchy portrayed by Tejdeep as:

> it is always male solstice
> If they could the *sun*
> would be spelled *son* (*FF*, p. 9, Italics added)

And again

> hiding a bruised soul
> in six yards of nylon (*FF*, p. 9)

Or

> That hard-earned post-graduation forgotten
> on the husband's name plate (*FF*, p. 9)

In the healing process of unraveling, as suggested by Estes above, Tejdeep refers to her verse as an "antibiotic":

> That has therapeutised my aches
> of ferocious despair
> symbolised my attempts to search
>
> for the broken filament
> in a hundred watt bulb. (*FF*, p. 17)

Gender typing is one of the frightening consequences of conformity to patriarchal norms. The poet's observation puts it in the form of a poem entitled, significantly, "Visionary"

Visionaries at dawn
do strange things
with a handful of
flour or chalk (*FF*, p. 28)

because

with chalk and powder
she must attempt
to hoodwink evil
from under a stranger's spell (*FF*, p. 29)

The powerful subversive tone of "must attempt" makes it clear that the vitality hinted at in the title is noticeable through its absence. One can fruitfully quote Estes again as saying: "When women reassert their relationship with . . . nature, they are gifted with a permanent and internal watcher, a knower, a visionary, an oracle . . . who guide, suggest and urge vibrant life in the inner and outer world."[7] She also suggests: "Women's flagging vitality can be restored by extensive "psychic-archeological" digs into the ruins of the female underworld . . . to recover the ways of natural instinctive psyche, . . . to discern the ways and means of woman's deepest nature."[8] And most relevantly, she adds: "The modern woman is a blur of activity. She is pressure to be all things to all people."[9]

Tejdeep's poetry may be constituted as these "psychic-archeological" excavations amidst the blur of activity which characterises life at present. Being at the focal point of human relationships, seen as a compulsion "to be all things to all people," she realises:

Unlike siblings
spouses have no
blood to match (*FF*, p. 56)

In another poem, wealth is seen as the unnatural barrier to the natural, instinctive response of love:

For the true
marriage of minds
she qualifies
if rich

Cynical though the title "If Rich" is, there is an urge to plummet the dark depths of despair when emotions are dammed.

Continuing on the theme of relationship is another poem entitled "Equation" which says:

Our relationship . . .
Like the relationship
between numbers
One plus one is always two,
One minus one—infinity

Such instances abound in the works of Tejdeep and compel a serious reader of poetry to take note of the underlying significant intent of her verse which at first may appear rather subjective and limited in scope. But the inescapable thrust of her ideas, images and expression provide ample scope for interpretation.

Notes and References

1. D.C. Dennet, "Consciousness," *The Oxford Companion to the Mind*, ed. Richard L. Gregory (New York: OUP, 1987), p. 160
2. E.F.N. Jephcott, *Proust and Rilke: The Literature of Expanded Consciousness* (New York: Barnes & Noble, 1972), p. 11.
3. Tejdeep, *Five Feet Six and a Half Inches* (New Delhi: Sterling, 1997), pp. 41-42. Abbreviated *FF*.
4. See Abraham Maslow, *Religion, Values & Peak Experience* (Columbus: Ohio State University Press, 1964).
5. Philip Zimbardo, *Psychology and Life* (Illinois: Scott Foresman, 1979), p. 577.
6. C.P. Estes, *Women Who Run with the Wolves. Contacting the Power of the Wild Woman* (London: Rider, 1992), p. 374.
7. Ibid., p. 8.
8. Ibid., pp. 3-4.
9. Ibid., p. 4.

Concept of "Tradition" in Sudeep Sen's *Postmarked India*

RAMA NAIR

The contemporary critical climate in India has witnessed the emergence of a number of young poets who are all set to establish a uniquely Indian poetic tradition. The process of assimilation of Western "modernity" into Indian "tradition" has belied the concept of an earlier parochial and prejudiced interpretation of tradition. Most of these younger poets divide their time between India and the West. Their works have a commendable technical virtuosity, coupled with an acute insight into the dilemmas and anxieties of living in two worlds/cultures. Their poems acquire a transcultural and a transnational context, where Indian "tradition" is juxtaposed with Western "modernity". However, these poets consistently delve into their Indian tradition for novelty, modernity, and meaning in their writings. Vinay Dharwadker comments, "For the new poets and story tellers, the individual opportunities, family situations, social practices, economic and political conditions, and cultural institutions that constitute 'everyday reality' are radically different. Colonial India is at best a story, a discourse, an imagined or imaginary homeland, and the post colonial India they know has barely begun to be charted. . . . In the course of the next twenty or thirty years they and their counterparts in the Indian languages functioning as both the sites and the instruments of a larger process of change, will once more alter our conceptions of what 'India' is and has been, 'of what is past, or passing, or to come.' [1]

Sudeep Sen's *Postmarked India* a collection of New and Selected poems was published in 1997. The blurb of this book testifies Sen to be "amongst the finest younger English language poets in the international literary scene." (Gregor Robertson on BBC Radio)

Adil Jussawala in *Debonair* declares Sen to be "an ambitious poet who doesn't fight shy of large themes that involve myth and history." Shiv K. Kumar in *The Hindustan Times* proclaims Sen to be "one of our promising young poets . . . a major voice in contemporary Indian poetry." He continues, "His verse derives its power from the incisive cultural interaction between East and West . . . (he) uses irony as a poetic device to juxtapose cultural polarities."

Sudeep Sen is one of the younger contemporary Indian English poets whose remarkable talent has been recognized by discerning critics both in India and elsewhere. Like many of his contemporaries, Sen divides his time between New Delhi and London. An early exposure to an interaction of cultures marked by an interest in music, literature, art and philosophy, created an eclectic background that is constantly interwoven into the texture of his poems. In earlier Indian English Poetry, primarily in the poetry of the 1960s and 70s (to a certain extent), the main theme generally centred around certain clichéd concepts like the quest for roots, and the search for a meaningful identity. The basic factor was that these poets chose to write in a foreign tongue, English, rather than in their native tongue. Belonging neither here nor there, a sense of rootlessness pervaded their being. The quest therefore, was for a 'usable' past whether spiritual or cultural.

For instance, while A.K. Ramanujan sought to contemporize the past, R. Parthasarathy attempted to neutralize it with images from the present, and these images are contextual. But Ramanujan could neither escape from the past, and nor could he effectively correlate it with the present. As such, in his poems there is no pervasive conflict between self and society as in the poetry of Nissim Ezekiel.

In the poetry of Sudeep Sen, there is a marked tendency to juxtapose Western "modernity" with Indian "tradition". There is no attempt to escape from the past, and neither is there a conscious attempt to come to terms with the present. The title of his volume *Postmarked India* is in itself ironic. It speaks of the new generation of Indian poets in English who did not have to be self-conscious of their past. The poet's sensibility is still rooted in his Indian heritage, but there is no forced attempt to glorify it. 'Postmarked' would suggest that these poems have been routed through India for a wider audience. In other words, they provide a broad spectrum of the paradox and contradiction that India is. Sen's poetry takes for its theme various Indian subjects from legend, myth and folklore to contemporary Indian situations. The political and social realities of India along with the richness of its culture and tradition have had a significant impact on his poetry.

The English definition of 'culture' is inadequate to cover the semantic scope of the cultural situation in India. Multiculturalism is the most durable feature of the Indian way of life. The term 'culture' as used in English can be generally used to describe some common traits of a class or a section in a given society. But an Indian is inevitably bicultural, and lives within a bilingual or even a multi-lingual cultural idiom. Even when he lives within an organic and native social context, he at once lives with many mainstream cultural traditions, and several sub-stream cultures. The traditional terms used to define these states were 'marga' and 'desi'. 'Marga' referred to cultures pervading the entire subcontinent horizontally, with the 'desi' being the vertical, local changing features of one's cultural identity. To these were added the alien traditions of Arabic, Persian, and English tradition. The 'marga' traditions were of Sanskrit, scriptural, and brahminic origin. The 'desi' traditions were of local, indigenous, and regional language origin. The alien tradition in India imitated in part the stylized aspect of 'marga', and in part, the pragmatic aspect of 'desi'[2]. By imitating the 'marga' and the 'desi'

English literary tradition in India developed a compulsion to be Pan-Indian, as well as true to local indigenous traditions. This led to a cultural split which in turn led to an excessive stress placed on some compensatory stylistic features such as irony and humour, stylistic innovations, and the use of myth and legend in Indian writing in English. Indian English style like the texture of Indian culture itself, is woven out of many unconnected strands. Since English does not belong to any geographical region in India, and does not possess the status of a regional language, it is used as G.N. Devy states, on the one hand as a language of 'status' and on the other as a 'static' language. The result is that in order to measure up to the international 'status' of the language, most writers assume a learned ironic tone, but at the same time to rid it of its stasis, burden it with excessive local colour[3]. This tripartite cultural relationship has influenced the course of Indian literature in English to a large extent.

Sudeep Sen's *Postmarked India* consists of a set of new poems entitled *Postmarked India* (1997), and a collection of selected poems from his other volumes entitled *Dali's Twisted Hands* (1995), *Mount Vesuvius in Eight Frames* (1994), *New York Times* (1993), *Parallel* (1993), *Kali in Ottava Rima* (1992), *The Lunar Visitations* (1990), and *Leaning against the Lamp-Post* (1983).

As is evident from the titles, these poems range over a variety of themes, each related sometimes to a particular geographical area. India, Africa, America seem to jostle with Dali, Vesuvius, and Kali. The blending of the existential with the spiritual, and the traditional with the modern encompass the desire to universalize the personal in terms of imagistic verse. The tripartite cultural relationship mentioned earlier seems to be at work here too.

'Bharatanatyam Dancer' is a poem that is an evocation of the sensuous and the spiritual that is so much a part of Indian art. But here again the poet interweaves the 'marga' and 'desi' tradition into the English literary tradition. As one critic Kwame

Dawes observes, "it also displays his [Sen's] sheer talent for formal invention and execution. The abacca—dbdeed . . . fb fggf . . . rhyme scheme maps and mirrors the actual classical dance step pattern and beat of *ta dhin ta thaye thaye* ta."[4] Indian words like *abhinaya, kajal,* Kanjeevaram, the "accompanists'/ intricate raag in this theatre of darkness,/ . . . where oblique memories of my/ quiet kalakshetra days filter" give the poem enough local colour to make it an authentic portrayal of an Indian classical dancer, who 'as the female dancer/ now illuminates everything visible: clear,/ poetic, passionate, and ice pure". In 'Zaragoza Skies' the poet uses imagistic verse to translate the often incomprehensible realities of life into a simple undeniable philosophy of life. The 'glassy Zaragoza skies write out/ a narrative which humans must choicelessly follow,/ even though it may include pain./ But in pain lies unstated happiness,/ a purity of passion/ that remains frozen,/ unborn, but simmering,/ like the melting sky's expansive heat".

Sudeep Sen's poetry is marked by a stylistic plurality that is characterized by novel innovation. Modernism in art in fact turns from realism and humanistic representation towards style, technique, and spatial form in pursuit of a deeper penetration of life. An interesting factor that emerges in such a situation is whether poetry becomes a fusion of autobiography versus imagination. In a letter written to this author on 8 Oct., 1999, from London, Sen had remarked, "For me, it is a combination of both, but more often just imagination, interpretation and re-mapping. Also structure, form, syntax and language interests and excites me—the architecture of language, the way words and phrases are sewn together, its sound and cadence and texture." Sen's fascination with the craft of poetry is offset by his deep involvement with the philosophy and religion of India.

The use of indigenous tradition is reflected in the temple poems. In 'Jagannath Temple, Puri', there is irony and satire in the commercialization of religion. The language is stark, 'we walked in, stripped of all leather and footwear,/ stepping on petals, piss, potholes, and prayer.' The conclusion is devastating, 'your earnestness, gift, or prayer wouldn't teach/ the priests who stand with their sceptre to bless,/ perhaps to erase the unholy, from their own selves."

'Govind Dev Temple, Vrindavan' testifies to the spiritual aridity of the times. Once 'here, under the old sanctum, Krishna's idol was found,/ celebrated, worshipped, rasa-lilas sung by Chaitanya,/ his follower and people.' 'now, the surrounding tenements invade, inching their way into/ every square of the courtyard space, and the pilgrim's walk.' But 'Govind Dev stands steadfastly, propped with monumental/ blocks of red and ochre sandstone.' In spite of the 'pink-buttocked monkeys', the parrots, the resident bees, and the screeching bats, 'Every year on nights when the moon appears full/ . . . the empty temple halls echo . . . "*Radhey, Radhey*"'. Here perhaps faith triumphs, for though perceptions change, the One Reality remains steadfast and permanent.

In 'The Box-Office Hit' the unpalatable reality of everyday existence is replaced with glorious forays into a realm of fantasy. The Hindi films of Bollywood, where the end is determined even before it begins, provide a welcome mode of escapism. The persona overhears a man behind him, 'a factory worker of sorts,/ telling his friend that/ he has seen the film ten times'. And 'As I inch along with this unregimented/ swarm, the same man nudges me and says:/ "*Bahoot baria philum, ek dum dream*—like,"/ nothing like his own life,/ this seven-buck fantasy flight,/ he explains.'

A similar depiction of the moral emptiness of the times is evident in some of Sen's poems that are set in America. In Harlem, 'A boy sauntered around the city/ tripping, smoking pot'. 'The boy, one among others,/ like insects clustering/ around a half-devoured carcass./ Only difference here:/ the boy, the cripple,/ the man, and the whore/ were pecking at the same/ flesh, hung on sale/ on bombed-out ghetto racks.' Decadence and degeneration born of abject poverty, both physical and mental is expressed in equally arresting imagery. In 'Night in Times

Square' 'late nighters like me, amblers, whores,/ all gesture in silence,/ in a language unknown, understanding/ each other with an everyday skill,/ as the chorus of horns drown their murmur'. In 'New York Times' the frenetic pace of modern existence is expressed in equally frenetic language. "In this city, I/ count the passage of time only by weekends/ linked by five-day flashes I don't/ even remember.' 'But somewhere, somehow, time takes its toll,/ malnourished, overburdened, and overutilised,/ . . . After all, how long can one stretch time?'

In 'Kali in Ottava Rima' Sen's ease with the multiple traditions he grew up with is quite evident. The Italian poetic form of the ottava rima is dexterously used to describe the victorious Indian goddess Kali 'As she frees/ herself slowly, crusade-ridden, victorious,/ bedecked, dripping thick in blood'.

In 'Durga Puja' another poem drawn from the 'desi' tradition, the goddess Durga is praised in a language that flows as does the incantatory quality of the recital, interspersed with words and figures that are local and culture specific. The poem ends with Durga whispering in Bengali from the heavens "'*Akhone aami aashi*'—that I'll return once again. . . . *Shashti, Shaptami,/ Ashtami, Nobami, Dashami . . . Shashti, Shaptami, Ashtami, Nobami, Dashami.*"

An awareness of the contemporary Indian political scene is expressed in ironic verse. In 'The Unusual October Heat' the violent aftermath of the 'Mandal Commissions, Rath Yatras, and the students' ire' is expressed ironically in 'sati, I thought, was a ritual only of the past, but this year, a new form of immolation filled the cast.' But ultimately, all that one hopes for is 'for a simple wish, of amity, nothing more'. In 'Mid-Term Polls, Yet Again', the travesty of democracy is violently indicted in a language that is harsh and strident. 'Soon, though only briefly, the same old clowns/ will appear, radiant, from the secretariat/ in shameless gait and white-washed khadi,/ parodying everyone, even the proletariat.'

Sudeep Sen's Indian heritage is very much evident in these poems. English was once looked upon as the language of utilitarian and specific value but never as an organic part of one's cultural legacy. In contemporary Indian English poetry, there is a universalisation of the human predicament in a language that is spontaneous, creative, and natural. The 'marga' and the 'desi' traditions whether social, political, cultural or religious are drawn upon to make thought-provoking observations on the reality around one. In Sen's poetry there is an attempt to synthesize and homogenize the English literary tradition with his own native vision and sensibility. This gives rise to an individuality of the writing self. The instinct is to rely heavily on traditional classical motifs, which in turn are invested with an innovation in technique and form. Tradition and modernity coalesce to create a unique blend of the personal and the impersonal. The past and the present fuse to underwrite the elements of modernity. The poet's creativity and ingenuity lie in his ability to work through language by working on language.

The global amalgam of cultures and identities lead to an interrogation of the term 'tradition' in its limited sense. Today's writers are either transcultural or transnational. In an attempt to preserve one's cultural identity, the infusion of local indigenous colour in terms of ideological and cultural languages lead to a cross-communication between speakers of different ideological/cultural languages. The multi-cultural context of Indian literature in English, in the poetry of Sudeep Sen, has given rise to a style in which the global and the local meet and merge, where international existentialism merges with a sort of national sentiment, ironic or otherwise. Sen's encounter with a wide range of literary traditions led Kwame Dawes to observe that "The central characteristic of this trend is to have an expansive, more global and decidedly less parochial palette from which to create."[5] A concrete definition of 'tradition' in this context remains fluid and evasive. Sen is, perhaps, to be commended for being one of the few poets who have pioneered "a new idiom in Indian literature".

Notes and References

1. *The Oxford Anthology of Modern Indian Poetry*, ed. Vinay Dharwadker and A.K. Ramanujan (Delhi: OUP, 1994), p. 206.
2. See G.N. Devy, *In Another Tongue. Essays on Indian English Literature* (Macmillan, 1995), pp. 14-17.
3. Ibid., p. 15
4. See "Introduction" to Sudeep Sen's *Postmarked India* (Delhi: Harper Collins, 1997) p. 33
5. Ibid., p. 36

All excerpts from Sudeep Sen's poems have been taken from Sudeep Sen, *Postmarked India: New and Selected Poems* (New Delhi: Harper Collins, 1997).

Reflecting Elegiac Tones—An Insight into Ranjit Hoskote's *Zones of Assault*

ANNIE POTHEN

With his maiden venture, *Zones of Assault* published in 1991, Ranjit Hoskote made his foray into the poetic world with a volume that is generally considered the most complex first book in the history of Indian English Poetry. A collection of forty-four poems arranged in seven such groupings, they reflect in an "artful" style the poet's disenchantment with the precarious state of the Indian sub-continent. *Zones of Assault* returns repeatedly to India as a presence in a subtle, modified way.

Hoskote's thematic concerns include historical and political violence and dimensions of the individual perceived with a tough, modernist Romanticism. In this elegiac volume, he mourns the loss of innocence, the death of artists and intellectuals and records the potential for violence in the Indian subcontinent[1]. The title is significant as it deals with specific areas of assault in a world being fragmented steadily by strife and divisive forces. The relevance of the title as a reflection of the present is therefore commendable. Articulating his perceptions candidly and powerfully, Hoskote adopts an elegiac tone in his writing. To be assaulted is, for an individual or an establishment or a country, a matter of anguish and hence the elegiac tone is manifest in all such instances.

The striking tone of an elegy is conspicuous when Hoskote mourns the death of artist Safdar Hashmi assassinated in 1989 on the first of January.

> Smeared with permanent red,
> Revelling in the offering,
> they laughed the laugh of angels.

And wheeling in a magic dance of spring, celebrated Republic Day. The elegiac tone is reiterated when he records plaintively and metaphorically the significant event of "1917".

> When the guns fell quiet
> And the files started moving
> When the teachers stopped talking
> And the students stopped asking
> And prayed together in loyal gloom
> Was it bliss in that dawn
> To be alive?
> Could we tell
> Where the freedom ended
> And the slavery began?

The interrogation in the concluding lines of the poem suggests paradoxically the absurdity of the situation. The devastating aftermath of war is similarly expressed in 'Report of War' when the poet deals with the ravages of war.

> The cindered trees meanwhile let fall
> Their charcoal apples, their branches lopping
> In the bony lethargy of a corpse
> The river has choked on bodies
> Theirs and ours.

The complicity of Hoskote's poetry is found in its images, sound patterns, emotional depth and specific perceptions. His poetry is direct and allusive, realistic and metaphorical. Crucial events become seeds for meditation on universal agonies. Consider the following lines from his poem 'Jerusalem' where the excruciating pain of Lord Jesus Christ is reflected.

> A cross strapped to his back
> Later, nailed to it, he died
> Rubies dropped down
> To the cold Levantine ground

Victims of violence are represented in his poetry with sensitivity. Hoskote's sophistication lies in the fact that he is capable of dexterously blending the personal with the public and political. In 'October Lightburst' the killing of the Manipuri rebel Bedamani Singh by Indian forces in 1981 is numbered and named in song. The political reverberations of this poem are clearly evident as is the gruesome nature of the killing evoking pathos.

The potential for violence in the Indian subcontinent is vividly recorded.

> They shot you in the October light
> It plunged from the trees
> Haloing your head as it fell
> Bombing the rocks, blasting the trees
> Torching the snow where a trail
> Marked your wounds for centuries
> On your native ground

Hoskote has a fine eye for the spirit of a place—Bandra, Central Asia, Hardwar or the Hindukush. His poetry has therefore a concreteness which gives it a rare credibility[2]. Even individuals like Hannibal, Icarus, Leonardo da Vinci and Safdar Hashmi figure both as themselves and as icons modulated into wider narratives. Violent reflections of life become for the poet, a matter of ignominy and anguish. When one reads his poems 'Six Elegies' one immediately perceives the elegiac tone overwhelmingly present in them. A special mention in this respect ought to be made of his poem, "Two Women in Midsummer" wherein he portrays the deplorable plight of widows.

Two women in midsummer
Stare across a many-pillared space
A wordless space, a nameless space.

At an earlier stage in the poem he states:

The courtyard where they had sung
And splashed around in orange and yellow
Is starched and crisp and white

The concluding line reveals the absence of colour in their lives symbolized by the crimson colour, which is conspicuously missing. Incidentally it may be appropriate at this juncture to state that this poem marks one of the rare instances when the poet perhaps deliberately deviates from his typical styles of utterance. For sheer simplicity and directness of expression, it is a refreshing change from the usual style of his writing. Deft understatement, economy of words and phrases invest this piece with a poetic exquisiteness and appeal not found in much of his poetry. So is the second poem in the same series 'Hardwar'.

The Ganga flows
The bathers bathe
And the long accumulated silt
of more than several sins
slowly settles
To the tolerant river bed.
The defiled water moves in
with heaps of other junk
The jettisoned debris of previous lives
which seems to pass
But touching down, circles
And leaves its mark

The post industrial devastation of Bombay is dealt with in many of his poems. In 'Reclamation' he writes:

> the land is a wolf's grey paw reaching out to grab
> Bay and breakwater.
> It grips hurt headlands
> above seabite and claws out
> the grasping promontories of reclamation

His attitude to the city is vaguely reminiscent of Ezekiel as both the poets focus attention on the bleak side of Bombay. Hoskote views life in Bombay as 'the absolute circus in picaresque hues" and the poem is humorously entitled 'The Acrobat'.

In 'Bandra Creek' he reiterates his experience of living in the city as an unenviable one.

> My soles earthquake above
> miles and miles
> of girders clanging on embered tracks
> A red-eyed hymn of war

Therefore it may be emphatically stated that in several of his poems there is a strong under-current of pathos and lamentation. One only wonders why he has chosen to be "artful" in his style, as one critic described it. As Mohan Ramanan states, artful poets are dodgers and usually complicate their utterance by learnedness, obliquity and allusiveness[3]. Hoskote belongs to this category of poets. When the content of his writing is contemporary and relevant it would perhaps have a greater impact if the form were a little less complicated. Somewhere along the way the sincerity of his objectives appear to be masked in the pedantic cloak of his style. Subsequently he seems unable to match his expression with the general content of his writing.

Certainly his best utterances are those in the simple mould of expression where he writes in an easy and relaxed manner.

Notes and References

1. See Mohan Ramanan, "The Sincere and the Artful", a review of Hoskote's *Zones of Assault* in *Indian Review of Books*, 1991.
2. Ibid.
3. Ibid.

   All excerpts from Ranjit Hoskote's poems have been taken from Ranjit Hoskote, *Zones of Assault* (Calcutta: Rupa, 1991).

Debates in Telugu Poetry of the Eighties and the Nineties

ALLADI UMA and M. SRIDHAR

In his editorial to the special issue of *Indian Literature* in 1995 on Telugu writing, K. Satchidanandan says: "Too much reliance on "Movement literature"—and Telugu seems to have been prone to movements from time to time—in spite of the great collective energy the movements release and the opening-up of new areas of experience, can also have a negative impact on individual imagination and linguistic inventiveness, both in fiction and poetry. . . . One positive feature of the Telugu scene today is the visible presence of the assertive female voice both in poetry and in fiction, an area where Telugu equals and at times excels other Indian languages."[1]

Yes, the feminist voice was a very powerful voice in the eighties. The dalit movement was already making its presence felt when this statement was made. Since then there has been the Muslim minority voice and the Madiga voice within the dalit movement. We wish to examine in this paper whether these "movement" literatures really have "a negative impact on individual imagination and linguistic inventiveness."

Neeli Meghalu (1993), an anthology of feminist poetry, stresses the need for the readers to accept new voices and new themes in a language that perhaps has not been used before. Woman's body and her right over it finds expression in the poetry of the feminists. So-called "private" topics like menstruation are dealt with openly. Consider how K. Geeta frankly talks about a woman's pain during her periods in "Nenu Rutuvunaina Vela" ("When I Have My Periods"):

> When the entire body freezes at one point
> when the rock-like self explodes silently
> I try in vain
> to hold the pain in my fist

Many wonder as to how topics like this can be thought of as "poetic material" and question how women can deal with such "blue" material. But the women assert their right to choose their material. In a poem entitled "Neeli Kavitale Rastamu" ("We will Write Only Blue Poems"), Mandarapu Hymavaty asserts women's right to tell the truth and declares that if this truth is considered "blue" poetry, they would not hesitate to write it. They also drive home the point that definitions of poetry have too long remained with the male and that even those male writers who have questioned the traditional notions of poetry have not completely come out of it, for they have continued to write only about the world out there, even if they have attempted to focus on the ordinary things, the ordinary people and on the impact of the harsh economic and social realities on their lives out there. Even these "left" writers are not concerned about the confines of the home and the effect of harsh patriarchal structures on women. Women have therefore felt the need to emphasise their private experiences and their feelings of pleasure and pain. Volga's "Advaitam" ("Monism") expresses the ecstasy a woman experiences through her body and the inseparability of her self and her body. Jayaprabha's "Choopulu" ("Looks") shows how a woman who becomes an easy prey to the prying gazes of men needs to learn to resist and stare back at men with her piercing gazes. Kondepudi Nirmala details the pain of giving birth in "Labour Room." Vasantha Kannabiran talks about a woman's self-realization through her experience of various stages of womanhood in her poem "Aasmita" ("Identity") as also about the romanticisation of motherhood which ignores the difficulties involved in it in "Pass." Even Vimala, a writer committed to the leftist ideology is able to see how women are exploited in the system in her poem "Vantillu" ("The Kitchen").

In the process of redefining their own roles in society, some of these writers re-vision certain existing myths about women. Kondapalli Koteswaramma in "Ashru Sameekshanam" ("Tearful Review") reviews the unhappy side of Sita, Sakuntala, Amba and Draupadi. As women writing in a language which is to a large extent a male construct, these women have tried to subvert the very language given to them. An example of this is Savitri's seemingly simple poem, "Bandipotlu" ("Dacoits"):

> When my brother said,
> "There's my husband in the office!
> He wouldn't grant me leave
> even when I need it most,"
> I began to suspect there and then . . .
> that "husband" meant "one who gobbles up freedom"

Very often the language in their poems, because of their outspokenness, especially of their body parts and their functions, and their desire to expose the hypocrisies of the existing system, is bound to shock people out of their complacency. To term it indecent or unpoetic is to once again use established power structures to judge it. It is all the more shocking that advocates of Naked Poetry like Jwalamukhi, who in no uncertain terms attacked the establishment in a raw and harsh manner, should attack feminist poetry.

One of the charges against feminist poetry is that it is basically middle class, upper caste. As a response to this charge, we can now see poets such as Swarupa Rani, a dalit writer, and Shahjahana and Mahe Jabeen, Muslim writers. While Swarupa Rani writes about the life of a dalit woman, especially of the lower classes, both Shahjahana and Mahe Jabeen voice the specific concerns of Muslim women. While Mahe Jabeen's "Qilwat" deals with the middle/upper class women, Shahjahana's

"Purdah Hatake Dekho" ("Lift the Purdah and See") and "Qabaddar!" ("Beware!") deal with the problems of lower class women.

In this context, it is interesting to note that while Indian writing in English has had a fairly long tradition of women's writing, it has by and large addressed the issues of women belonging to middle or upper classes. One need not be surprised about this because the very fact that these writers use English competently puts them in that class and therefore they tend to bring out those themes and issues that concern them. So they probably have things in common, at least to an extent, with the feminists writing in Telugu. It is this commonness that makes Arlene Zide edit an anthology, *In Their Own Voice,* taking women writers from all parts of India including those who write in English. She insists that they are not "voices" but a "voice," a reference to the unified voice of protest against the patriarchal establishment. But even as we may agree with her reading, while we know that Kamala Das is one of the early writers to emphasise the importance of the body, even while a Rukmini Bhaya Nair talks of the constraints of the Sanskritic patriarchal tradition in a poem like "Genderole," or when a Ruth Vanita writes poems based on the *Ramayana* myth, the forceful voices of Jayaprabha asking for the burning of the "paita" in a poem like "Paitanu Tagaleyyali" ("We Should Burn the *Paita*") or of Kondepudi Nirmala bringing out the trauma of childbirth or of Vimala using the kitchen as a metaphor for women are rare. While Imtiaz Dharker's volume, *Purdah and Other Poems* brings out the constrictions of the Muslim women in a moving and aesthetically pleasing manner, it cannot match the immediacy of Shahjahana's "Purdah Hatake Dekho." Let us read a few lines from each of these poems. In "Purdah I" Imtiaz Dharkar says:

> One day they said
> she was old enough to learn some shame.
> She found it came quite naturally.

Purdah is a kind of safety.
The body finds a place to hide.
The cloth fans out against the skin
much like the earth that falls
On coffins after they put the dead men in.[2]

Let us now read from Shahjahana's "Purdah Hatake Dekho":

Lift the veil and see for yourself
the place where life has been imprisoned behind the purdahs
the place where there are banyan trees of foolish conventions
which try to suppress the already subjugated woman!
Look at my gulmohar women
who disperse the sweetness of the light of freedom and shine!
Having grown up
not having tasted the moonlight not having tasted
rain not having tasted spring
growing up with checks within bounds as a female slave.

While, we are at times aware of Eunice de Souza's Christian background in her poetry, the force with which Shahjahana speaks of her Islamic background is not found.

There has been some criticism that women's poetry in Telugu has become less forceful today. One way of responding to this charge is to see how the movement has extended itself beyond the upper and middle classes as we have already seen. Another way of viewing it is to find women poets trying to express subjects of interest to both men and women in a refreshingly different voice. Consider how Shilalolitha talks about the pain of waiting for the loved one in these lines from "Aina Nuvvu Ravu" ("Even So You Won't Come"): "Silence hurls thousand edged knives/ sound splinters within the womb." The images used to express the pain here can hardly be used by men. Yet another way of looking at the feminist writing today is to see how the strength of the movement has shifted now to the short story.

If the feminist voice has questioned the insensitiveness of the "left" movement to the gender issue, the dalit writers have been upset that there has been a total lack of concern about caste oppression. Many of the dalit writers were originally part of the very movement they are questioning now. The term "dalit" here includes writers belonging not only to the scheduled castes and scheduled tribes but also to the backward classes and to Muslims. They have come together to speak out their minds in their own voices, in a language that is at once shocking and provocative, on subjects that touch their very lives, questioning myths, rewriting them and placing epic characters like Ekalavaya and Shambuka in a totally different perspective. Sivasagar's "Nadustunna Charitra" ("On-going History") is the most powerful voice in this context:

> Sambuka with a smile on his lips
> is executing Rama
> Ekalavya is chopping off Drona's thumb
> with an axe
> Bali with his tiny feet is trampling
> Vamana into the netherworld. . . .
> On the cruel sword of time stands
> the soaring Chandala
> inciting
> four hounds onto Sankara
> That's it!
> The on-going history
> is a very Chandala history

Satish Chander's "Panchama Vedam" is the fifth Veda wherein the poet comes down heavily on the caste system and the Hindu puranic texts. Prasadamurthy's "Tatako Noolupogu" ("A Token Piece for Grandpa") is one of the many poems wherein the writers sing the glory of their traditional occupations. Prasadamurthy writes of the padmasali community, of his grandfather and his ability to weave beautiful clothes, but bemoans the fact that his grandfather could neither clothe his own body nor that of his wife:

Tired weaving the substandard bright cloth of life
the day-weaver would learn lessons from you
Turning the muscle strings around
the spindle of time my grandmother
would show her appreciation for your mastery in her eyes
She would be pained a bit about your poverty
for your inability to cover her naked chest with a blouse

Sikhamani in his "Inupa Paleelu Moluchukostunnary" ("Look, The Steel Nibs are Sprouting") details the very common experience of being constantly reminded of his S.C. background at every step of his academic life. Challapalli Swarupa Rani portrays the anguish of being both woman and dalit in her poem, "Mankena Puvvu" ("Mankena Flower"):

When have I really lived
my life as myself . . .?
If male arrogance at home
gives a resounding slap on one cheek
caste dominance outside
thrashes my other cheek

The tone becomes angrier and even vitriolic in the voice of the male writers at a certain stage in the movement. Denchanala Srinivas in "Swadehalu" ("My Own Bodies") comes down heavily on all religions employing abusive language which offends not just religious sensibilities but also women's sensibilities. In a collection called "Nishani: Dikkara Kavita" ("The Mark: Poetry of Contempt") Paidi Teresh Babu warns the poetic establishment: "As our twelve rupee coolie is our witness we will rape your older and younger sisters." Such language is bound to hurt the sentiments of another oppressed group, women.

Maybe it is pertinent to point out here that the Telugu dalit movement has taken its cue from the Marathi dalit movement. While there have been many individual efforts, Lakshmi Narasaiah has succeeded in giving this trend a very forceful collective voice with the publication of anthologies like *Chikkanavutunna Pata* (1995) and *Padunekkina Pata* (1996). Using the term "pata" ("song"), is one way of emphasising the rich oral tradition of these groups. It is however surprising that there are hardly any 'songs' in these volumes, especially when there is a rich tradition in these communities of folk songs. This first stage of consolidation has led to a questioning within the group.

A Muslim writer like Khaja who has written about his being a dalit in a poem like "Roots" is more emphatic about his being a Muslim in poems like "Jihad" and "Sunti" ("Circumcision"). Muslim writers like him have thus felt the need to voice their specific concerns as a minority group. While empathising with the dalit concern, they have not wanted their individual problems to get submerged in the totalising "dalit" voice. They have felt that their position is different, especially after the demolition of the Babri masjid. That Khadar Mohiuddin's "Puttu Matcha", which raised important questions of identity, of patriotism etc., appeared before the demolition is significant:

Yes, I'm a traitor, am I not?
Yes, it's not a plot
not to see no difference between Islam and Islamabad
it's not a plot
to desire to pull off the earth
from under my very feet
it's not a plot
to make me a hostage in the very land I was born and brought up
It's not a plot
to poison the surroundings and the atmosphere around me

it's not a plot
to slice me into pieces
to annihilate
and build a "Greater India" . . .
My citizenship is
The "holy" game the Constitution has played
Over the question of difference in status

The poem also details the ordinariness of Muslim life through the different occupations they are engaged in such as repairing umbrellas, stitching, repairing clocks, making mattresses etc. The rest of the "Muslimvada Kavitvam" which became a movement after the demolition makes a more concerted attempt to assert not only their Muslimness but also their ancestry, their backward status. It is necessary here to record that the *Kanjira: Poetry Bulletin* was the first to devote a special issue to the demolition of the Babri Masjid. Iqbal Chand's "Aro Varnam" ("Sixth Caste") begins with a reference to a number of them belonging to the "Doodekula" community (Bed Makers). Interestingly, he refers to their having moved from being a fourth (the Sudra), then to the fifth (the Panchama) and finally to the sixth community. Afsar's "Nake Janmabhoomee Ledu" ("I Have No Motherland") also bemoans his not having any status in this country.

The Muslim writers also assert that "Telugu" is as much their language as Urdu, for often especially in Andhra Pradesh there seems to be a notion that Muslims ought to only speak Urdu. They bring out their peculiar mix of language—Telugu and Urdu—their class, the class hierarchy within their own community, their status as a Muslim in India. Powerful poems like Yakoob's "Avval Kalma" ("First Word") and Sky Baba's "Marfa" have appeared from this perspective. Here are a few lines from *Avval Kalma*:

We don't know that we are supposed to call
our mothers *ammijan* whom we address as *oyamma*

and our fathers as *abbu*, *abbajan*, or *pappa*—
How do we know—even our *ayyalu* haven't taught us any of this.

Haveli, *char deevar*, *gilwat*, *purdah*—
How do we who live in bamboo palaces know all this?

We can see how their using Telugu words for the Urdu terms not only brings to mind their converted status from the backward classes among the Hindus but also their class position within the Muslim community. But the anxiety of these poets to fuse the two languages has at times led to a forced yoking of terms which makes comprehension a bit difficult. Perhaps such deliberate usage is inevitable to drive home the point they wished to make. An attempt to bring these voices together are found in collections like *Jihad* (1997) brought out by Virasam (Revolutionary Writer's Association) and *Zalzala* (1997) edited by Sky Baba. The voice in the movement has been predominantly male. It is, however, noteworthy that in poems like Mahe Jabeen's "Qilwat" and Shahjahana's "Qabaddar" Muslim women are writing specifically about their oppression both within the community and outside. In this context it will be in place to write about Muslim male writers' attempt to write about the oppression of women within the community. But ironically their call for the need to lift the purdah is prompted more by the anxiety at their not being able to appreciate the beauty of their women behind the burkha as in Khaja's "Aadhahai Chandrama" ("It's the Crescent Moon") or by the physical distance the purdah creates between them and their women.

A more recent trend in the questioning of the totalising voice of the dalit literary movement coincides with the "Madiga" political movement in the State. The Madigas feel that they are the lowest among the Scheduled Castes, that their specific problems have gone unnoticed and that they have been doubly oppressed. They have felt a need for "Madiga Chaitanyam" ("Madiga Consciousness") and have wished to use "Madiga Literature" as a vehicle for achieving this awareness. Yendluri Sudhakar's "Dandora" and Chitram Prasad's "Chatimpu" present the discrimination of the Madigas by their very brothers, the Malas. Sudhakar says:

> I am writing about the truth
> having experienced it
> that the hierarchy of humiliations
> and the veils of inequality exist
> not just among the forward castes
> but even among my own people

It is interesting to observe that in this poem, Sudhakar, a poet who has established himself in the Telugu poetic scene, decides now to "fling" his earlier beautiful diction and style into the "garbage bin" to write hereafter as himself, as a Madiga. Both "Dandora" and "Chatimpu" refer to loud announcements made to the accompaniment of the traditional drumbeat. Mastaarji, who is better known as a singer, lists the contributions of his community to the history of mankind invoking his ancestry to Kardama, Matanga, Veerabahu, Adi Jambava etc., in his "Evaranukunnaru?" ("Who do You Think We Are?") He reminds us that even the person who provided moments of revelation to Sankaracharya was a chandala. *Madiga Chaitanyam* (1997), a collection of Madiga poetry edited by Nagappagari Sundara Raju, makes it a point to include a few songs. Karra Vijayakumari, Jajula Gowri and M. Gowri are among the few women's voices in this movement. Jajula Gowri in her poem "Nenu Nenuga . . . " ("I, As Myself . . .") shows how the Madigas have been excommunicated at different stages, first by the brahmin controlled caste system, then by the sudras, and finally by their very brethren. While she talks of their being oppressed by other communities, their being oppressed as women finds its expression in M. Gowri's "Pandina Chetulu" ("Ripe Hands") where, drawing on her strength as a woman used to doing hard labour, she throws a challenge to the men from other communities who try to take physical advantage of her. Karra Vijayakumari's "Sombuvva" is the poignant tale of a Madiga widow who is shabbily treated by the landlord:

> I've been ordered
> to make three pairs
> for the master mistress and the brother
> in the remaining skin if at all
> I see the pitiful face of my young one
>
> Hoping they may give at least some *sombuvva*
> straining my back
> beating with an iron pestle till my hands ache
> collecting all my drained strength
> to make holes with an awl and stitch the slippers
>
> When I carry the slippers in a pewter vessel
> apply castor oil on your soles
> and put the slippers on
> the master says throw her some food
> For my hardship
> The mistress brings
> and throws into my pewter vessel some stale *sombuvva*

While individual poems have come out about these concerns, the anthology *Madiga Chaitanyam* brings these voices together to drive home the point. One may wonder what will happen to movements such as these once their immediate political ends have been achieved. In this context, we can remind ourselves that though the policy of reservation has existed since long, it has not completely rooted out the social evils of the caste system. Therefore, it is only natural that the literature of protest will take different shapes. While it may be true that each of these movements we have discussed has arisen out of its conflict with an earlier movement, it is heartening to find that there exists a sense of solidarity between them on many issues of common interest, a moral commitment to fight questions of oppression and a healthy respect for real democratic values.

Whether it is dalit writing or Madiga writing or Muslim writing, all these have emerged from the grassroots. All these are responses to existing movements, to political needs of the groups at particular historical junctures. Therefore, it is not surprising that we do not find such writings in works written by Indians in English. It is perhaps not an exaggeration to say that except for the nationalist poetry, some "feminist," "gay" and "lesbian" poetry, not much has been written from a political perspective. Some consider this lack of the political as a positive quality, for they feel that it does not dilute the aesthetic quality of poetry by turning it into "protest" or "propaganda". But we wonder how any writing can be devoid of the writers' immediate historical necessities.

We have focussed mainly on the more prominent movements in the last two decades in Telugu poetry. Left poetry which has a long history in this soil continues to be written, albeit less forcefully. Similarly, Telugu writing has responded to the "post-modern" tendencies and there is a considerable body of poetry of this kind. We have confined ourselves only to the more prominent "movement" voices here.

Notes and References

1. K. Satchidanandan, "Reflections." *Indian Literature*, Vol. 166 (1995), pp. 5-8.
2. *Nine Indian Women Poets. An Anthology*, ed. Eunice de Souza, (Delhi: Oxford University Press, 1997), p 50.

All translations in the paper except of Sivasagar's poem are our own unpublished ones. Sivasagar's poem has been translated by Archana Chowhan and the translator has given us permission to use her unpublished translation.

The Dalit Woman at the End of the Millennium: Her Representation in Telugu Poetry

G. TIRUPATHI KUMAR and ALPHA JOSEPH

The Dalit poets interrogate all kinds of oppression. They strongly reject the Brahmanical construction of monolithic India, which people like Vivekananda, Gandhi and Raja Rao have been doing. These poets perceive Brahmanism as the root cause of all forms of oppression on them. They reject Hindu Gods, rituals and symbols, and they successfully show how they are against them, and how they function in degrading them as sub-human beings. As Brahmanism affects every walk of life of a Hindu and non-Hindu, these poets do not limit their attack on to the priestly class only, but endeavour to expose its much complex ramifications in other fields also. Thus, they question the role of Indian-Nation-State, bureaucracy, judiciary, media and various cultural forms, like music and literature. In their view, the Indian-Nation-State is highly casteist and biased towards higher castes with a strong prejudice against the untouchable and Shudra Castes. They see an unholy nexus between Indian-State and capitalist imperialism. They are greatly agitated at the way the "mainstream" treats their women. Some of the well-known collections which deal with these issues are *Chikkanavvuthunna Pata, Bahuvachanam, Padhunekkina Pata, Memo, Megi, Chittaruvu Videe Akasham* and Satish Chander's *Panchama Vedam.*

'Mainstream' literature never thought that the Dalit woman is also a fit subject for their narrative construction. In fact it completely ignored women in general, leave alone Dalit women. We find woman in these writings as the one who is delicate, tender, and thus graceful; she is so delicate that she cannot even bear the weight of her own broad and round breasts. She is never seen as a human being with flesh and blood. That is why when feminists in Andhra Pradesh intervened and talked about themselves as women, the reaction to it was only venom in mainstream literature. Feminists were picturised as "*Gayyaalulu*"—strong-headed, ungraceful and shameless creatures and their poetry was termed immoral and 'Blue' (yellow). Even a progressive writer like Raavi Shastri[1] is no exception to this mudslinging and spitting of venom. As a reaction to this condemnation, feminists with vengeance brought out their collection of poetry called "Neeli Megalu" in 1993.

But even the feminist poets failed to portray the real life of a Dalit woman. The leading feminists in Andhra Pradesh are either Brahmins or other upper-castes, and they failed to understand the complex nature of caste. Being progressive, these women sympathized with Dalits, and condemned caste atrocities on them. But the important point for any artistic creation is the empathy and one's willingness and ability to study the life of the subject from various dimensions, and feminists coming from "upper castes" failed to do so. It is a fact, which they themselves admit. Their caste background did not allow them to understand the problems of a Dalit woman in totality. They did respond to the cause of the Dalit woman, like the tradition of the Jogins, but it was limited to the periphery.

The advent of Dalit women poets is a major breakthrough in Telugu Literature. They brought to the forefront many issues, which were hitherto ignored and suppressed. The Dalit men did construct poetic narratives on caste oppression in various forms, including oppression on their women, but they could not think of the oppression they themselves were perpetuating on their women as males. If male Dalit poets failed to recognize the importance of gender question, the upper-caste feminist women poets did not address the caste question, which inherently also has class and colour dimensions. None other than the Dalit woman fills both these gaps. This paper aims at throwing light on the specific issues they raised as Dalit women.

At a time when the whole world is geared to celebrate the end of the millennium in a big way, the poem "*Pani Pilla* (A Little Maid)" by G. Vijaya Lakshmi at once shatters the shallowness and the media hype, and brings us down to earth again. She narrates in first person a telling story of a little girl who ekes out her living as a maid. There is no romanticism attached to her childhood. The poem starts with a powerful evocation of her misery.

> Since I opened my eyes
> I filled in them only tears
> Instead of calling mother, mother
> I used to weep uttering landlord, landlady,
> Caste is my colour
> Bitter poverty is my pallav[2].

The poet believes that the root cause of the sorry state of the maid is her caste. It is the caste which determines her life. Her assets are her coarse hands, which became thus due to constant scrubbing of the vessels in the landlord's house. At a very tender age, she becomes the victim of the landlord's lust. From here on the poet brings out sharply the casteist nature of society. Though the girl is too young to understand the implications of the sexual act, she is made to believe that she is the arbitrator. She does not enjoy any sympathy from the public and when she goes into the streets crying for justice, the accused, the landlord himself, appears on the seat of judgement. Her burning heart is priced at a hundred-rupee note and thus dispensed with. The climax is that the village does not find any fault with the landlord. If this act only exposed the patriarchal nature of the society, the poem would have been merely feminist. But the poet does not stop there. She as a victim of caste knows the other dimension of the act as well; it has the caste colour too. Thus when the landlord disposes the girl with a mere hundred-rupee note, the landlady goes a step further, and spits on the girl with vengeance. Though a woman herself, the landlady never sympathizes with the little maid. And even when her husband ruins the girl's life, she takes the side of her husband. All this happens because what is prominent in our society is caste, and it is a bigger evil than gender. It affects all walks of our life. Thus the poem ends with the maid's mourning:

> Sky is my village
> Darkness is my abode
> Insults are my food
> Dangers are my company
> Womanliness is my cry.

Vijaya Lakshmi is not the only poet who recognizes the role of caste even in the gender question. Challapalli Swaroopa Rani further elaborates this point in her poem "Mayyamma" (My Mother). She does not go by the mainstream feminist understanding that all women are one and all of them have the same problems. Instead she is bitter with feminists and exposes the shallowness of their understanding and practice. Addressing her mother in this poem she discloses what happens in a city-based women's movement.

> There in the bobbed-hair movements
> In silk sari struggles and sleeveless speeches
> Your coarse saree
> Meets only embarrassment.
> There, respected Mahalakshmamma, Ankalamma, Seetharamamma
> Deliver speeches till their mouths ache
> Demanding

Annihilation of oppression on women
Sexual rights
And economic independence:
However in the end,
Their speeches urge
That the Dalit woman too should be uplifted[3].

A similar opinion is expressed by Darise Shashi Nirmala, but more vehemently. In her poem "Ninda Chedindanni Nene" (I am the one who's lost everything), she comes down heavily on upper-caste women and feminists. This is directly addressed to them. She sees a sharp and unbridgeable divide between herself and them. She questions:

When your husband
Made me a featherless hen
Do you remember
What you said?
In your own house
And in your own tongue
How many times
Did I become cheap and a street walker
Do you know?

You may say anything
I am inferior
And you are superior
There is nothing that you have done for me[4].

The poet points out the distance between two communities. The upper caste women talk about democracy and equal rights, without being democratic. Though they themselves are victims of patriarchy, they look down on women who come from lower castes. They talk about the importance of uniting women, but in practice they practise the politics of divide. That is why there is no strength in the movements that they lead. They may challenge patriarchy, but cannot overthrow it. They don't have enough strength, because they dwell in comfort and luxury, and are scared of any sacrifice and hardship. Only Dalit women with coarse hands and sunburnt black skin are ever ready to sacrifice and face any hardship to fulfill this dream. Till then in Nirmala's words: "let them speak"[5].

The severity of the problems of Dalit women is much more than those of the upper-caste woman. Their problems are basic. They want water, food, clothing and shelter. They want to lead a life of dignity and respect. They want protection for their men and for themselves. Though poets like Darise Shashi Nirmala and Swaroopa Rani denounce male chauvinism, they do not break their ties with their brethren. In fact Shashi Nirmala sees a conspiracy to bifurcate Dalit women from their men, and she exposes this plot in her poem "Muttu Gudda Kapputhunna" (Covering with Menstrual Cloth). It is the conspiracy to strain away "Hotness from the Sun"[6]. She plans to move ahead for the liberation of her community in the path of "Alissamma", a witness to the brutal killings in Karamchedu, but with the symbolic smearing of Anil Kumar's blood on her body, who is another victim of caste brutality in Chundur.

The Dalit women poets do not rejoice only at rejecting Brahmanism like their brethren, though they see it as their principal enemy. For them all religions are means of oppression. In her poem "Sawal" (Challenge) Vijaya Lakshmi declares:

> We do not want any temples
> We are expelling all cunning gods.
> In any religion
> We are the ones who are suppressed[7].

The Dalit movement in general has broad understanding and friendly relations with the minorities. That is why, we do not see such harsh statements like the one above in the poetry written by Dalit men. Dalit women are harsher, perhaps because they are doubly suppressed.

The Dalit women poets reject mainstream symbols. In mainstream society, there is a lot of importance attached to the white colour. It symbolizes purity and peace. At the same time black colour is condemned as something deplorable and offensive. Interestingly the majority of Dalits are black, and they are subjected to humiliation for their body complexion. It is believed that Dalits are ugly because they are black. Mainstream literature perpetuated this idea, and Dalits themselves for a long time believed that they were ugly. But the new consciousness given by the Dalit movement empowers them to assert themselves. J. Indira proudly writes:

I am born from the earth
My colour is black
White colour
I definitely hate
But I am more enraged
At those who
Take away my earth[8].

The other prominent symbols that come under their attack are "Lord Rama and Krishna". There is a lot of work done on Rama in this regard, but rarely is Krishna mentioned. But in the poem "Pandina Chethlu" (Ripened Hands) written by M. Gouri, Krishna comes under a different treatment. Lord Krishna is famous for his exploits, and the poet here like a *Gopika* invites him to play with her. But the place is not Brindavan, but *Madigavada*, a Dalit street.

Our street contains blood and flesh
Extricating buffalo's horns as easily
As cutting nails is our child's play
We shall play
Will you come once?
But not the coward games like
Moving around on the backs of animals
I shall show you

The daring game of slitting open
The lusty bull!
You who drank the milk and killed Rakshasa Matha
O warrior Krishna

I will show two lumps flesh and a pot full of blood
Can you stand without fainting?[9]

The poem moves on interrogating the images attached to Lord Krishna. The poet does not feel sorry for being born as an untouchable. Instead she takes great pride in her birth, and presents how productive her caste is, (which has the ability to convert "dirty skin" into a great musical instrument like "the mrudanga".)

These poets have laid their hands on varied themes. "Dirty Merit" by Vasantha deals with the hypocrisy present in the concept of merit, while "Modern Arundhati" by Vijaya Lakshmi portrays a Dalit woman who is neck deep in problems because of her intercaste marriage. Nakka Vijaya Bharathi in her poem "Kula (Caste) College" brilliantly uncovers the casteism practised in colleges when she points that "the college is typically like her village divided into castes and castes"[10]

The poem "Mankena Puvvu" by Challapally Swaroopa Rani sharply brings out what Susie Tharu calls "everyday Casteism"; it portrays vividly the every day predicament of a Dalit woman in this modern, emancipated and educated world at the end of this millennium.

I am trapped in a thorn bush
Like the blue-jay
Which ever way I turn, the
Thorns poke only me,
These are not to-day's thorns
But those, that were
Built from ages around
Me like chains of slavery. . . .

Swimming against all currents
Of insults, I educated
Myself and got a job
And went to office, and there
People started to murmur
"Reservation Category". I felt
like pouring hot lead into
my ears to block the comments.

When patience gets exhausted,
Even a blade of grass becomes a bodkin

I cannot race anymore
I shall wash myself in the flames of suffering
And blossom like a wild flower in the forest
Over-taking forests of difficulties and bouncing
Like a brook.[11]

If this were the predicament of an educated Dalit woman, then one can only imagine the gravity of caste. Her counterpart in villages would, at best become Mahadevamma, Alisamma or Muttavva. At the turn of the century when the whole world is moving towards an egalitarian philosophy let Indians treat Dalits at least as human beings.

Notes and References

1. Jaya, "An Interview with Raavi Shastri", *Rachana*, Qtd. in *Neeli Megalu—A Collection of Feminist Poetry* (Hyderabad: Swecha, 1993), p. 215.
2. G. Vijaya Laxmi, "Panipilla" (A Little Maid), *Padunekkina Pata: Dalit Poetry*, ed. G. Laxmi Narasaiah (Vijayawada: Dalita Sana, 1996), p. 9.
3. Challapalli Swaroop Rani, "Mayamma", *Padunekina Pata*, p. 23.
4. Darise Shashi Nirmala, "Ninda Chedinadanini Nene", *Padunekina Pata*, p. 5.
5. Ibid., p. 6.

6. Darise Shashi Nirmala, "Muttu Gudda Kaputhunna", Ibid., p. 17.
7. G.Vijaya Laxmi, "Saval", *Chitharuvu*, ed. Thatiparthi Bala Swamy and G.Vijaya Laxmi (Vijayawada: Andhra Jesuit Social Action, 1977), p. 16.
8. J. Indira, "Dalitha Sthree Agenda" (Agenda of the Dalit Woman), Ibid., p. 17.
9. M. Gouri, "Pandina Chetulu ", *Madiga Chithanyam*, ed. Naggappa Gari Sundararaju (Hyderabad: Madiga Sahithya Vedika-A.P. U of Hyderabad, 1997), p. 15.
10. Nakka Vijaya Bharathi, "Kula College", *Meme—A Collection of Dalit Bahujan Poetry* (Nalgonda: Gosangi, 1996), p. 2.
11. Chalapalli Swaroopa Rani, "Mankena Puvvu", *Gunde Dappu—A Collection of Dalit Poetry*, ed. Patteti Rajashekar and Nagappa Gari Sundara Raju (Hyderabad: Dalitha Sahitya Vedika, University of Hyderabad, 1995), pp. 1-2.

Contemporary Trends in Bangla Poetry

TUTUN MUKHERJEE

The word that has been reiterated since the beginning of this seminar on "Contemporary Trends in Indian English Poetry" is "anxiety". Poets as well as readers of poetry have talked about the "anxiety" of writing Indian poetry in English: the "anxiety" of Indian-ness and of Indian literature, especially poetry, as the repository of many anxieties. As Harold Bloom once suggested, "How do we understand an anxiety? By ourselves being anxious,"[1] anxieties provoke this paper too. And I have let them initiate in this discussion an exploration of intra-poetic relationships.

The first anxiety, strictly personal, is about the relevance of discussing the trends of Bangla poetry in a seminar devoted to poetry in Indian English.

For many of us here, English is one of the several languages used in our daily interactions. While some of us use it for the purposes of functional communication, others discover the range and depth of the expressive properties of the language to articulate their imaginative perceptions. But has English been able to enchant and seduce us away from the culture to which we were born? Has it alienated us from our social ethos? Today, English is considered as much a part of Indian milieu as any of the other languages. How is it possible, then, to wax eloquent about the achievements of Indian Writing in English exclusively with total disregard or indifference for the entire literary spectrum of multi-lingual India?

It is true that in the last fifty-odd years, during the period of reconstruction, social reorganization and post-imperial realignments, there have also been cultural redefinitions. Cultural sectors have become marked. While on one hand, borders of nationality have been breached and writers as agents of culture have registered a presence in the global community; on the other hand, another effect has been the tightening of linkages that bond together linguistics or regional blocs and the intensification of old conflicts of allegiances. When nationalist or regionalist desires are expressed, very often consciously or unconsciously the writer becomes the agent of these forces. Thus the politics of culture that has always been with us, has acquired special significance in these times when art and literature can be used as the means, as an instrument or even as a weapon, for the articulation of new consciousness. Yet the balkanization of Indian literature is a problem of perception rather than reality. Relationships of filiations and affiliation abound in modern cultural history and one should not lose sight of the double and perhaps even multiple angles of vision that a writer in India is inevitably gifted with—of being able to weave one's locality into the national, even international fabric. One can choose to simultaneously belong to several blocs and feel not entrapped but enriched by this. So the poet writing poetry in Indian English looks outward toward the global community forging new linkages yet never loses touch with the local. The lilt, rhythm and nuances of regional languages and the aspirations of regional literatures inform his writing. Therefore, I think perhaps a paper discussing trends in Contemporary Bangla poetry is not so out of place in this context after all.

The second anxiety is cultural—related to the findings of this paper based upon the study of the state of and the trends in Bangla poetry in the last few decades.

In spite of the general shrinking readership of poetry in a world driven by prosaic materialism and gross consumerism, poetry writing and reading in Bengal has not been terribly affected. This is mainly because new writing has been encouraged and sustained by little magazines and smaller presses. Festive occasions such as Durga Puja, Nabo Barsho (New Year), Panchisey Baisakh (Tagore's birthday), Boi Mela (Book Fair) are celebrated with special commemorative issues and provide a forum for new writers. Indeed this has been the special strength of the cultural interaction in Bengal.

Poetry is in good health and is thriving in Bengal. Young poets exhibit reflexivity and vitality that certainly bodes well for Bangla poetry. This paper focuses attention on the recent trends in the style of new poets.

II

The poets of the thirties and the forties were greatly influenced by the High Priests of Modernism and the poetic style of Pound, Eliot, Baudelaire, Mallarme, Rilke and Auden. For several decades the western concept of "ennui" and "angst" dominated Bangla writing.

First Phase: Modern Bangla poetry was the outcome of a turbulent ethos devastated by a sense of disintegrating values, scepticism, bitterness and a pervasive feeling of nothingness. There was also a deliberate attempt to break away from the poetic conventions of the earlier decades. If the earlier poetic values were imagination, subjectivity and lyricism and the stalwarts were Rabindranath Tagore, Madhusudan Dutta, Dwijendranath Tagore, Biharilal Chakraborti, the new taste was for absorption in the subject, impersonality and objectivity in thematic treatment, sophistication and technical finesse as exemplified in the poetry of Jibanananda Das, Bishnu Dey, Premendra Mitra and Buddhadeb Bose. Yet, the severance between the romantic and the modern poetic tradition was never complete. In the deeper sense, both the older and the avant-garde styles reflected the search for epiphanic moments of truth, the spirit of experimentation with theme and structure, the attempt to understand the supra real or the surreal, and a preoccupation with the pervasive I.

It would appear that what prevailed was a kind of "poetic misprision". As Harold Bloom has said, "poetic history is indistinguishable from poetic influence, since strong poets make that history by misreading one another so as to clear imaginative space for themselves."[2] Indeed, one such strong poet is Jibanananda Das who marked the path for the later generations to follow. For Das, modernity signified "the perpetual search of the human mind"[3]:

"Banalata Sen"

I have walked the paths of earth for thousands of years,
from the Sinhala ocean in midnight dark to the Malay sea
I have circled much, in Bimbisara and Ashoka's ashen sphere
I was there, in even more distant dark in Vidarbha city;
I am an exhausted soul, all around me life's foaming ocean,
two moments' peace I was given by Nator's Banalata Sen.

Her hair like dark Vidisha's night of long before,
her face Sravasti artistry, when on the ocean for distant
the sailor who had broken his rudder and lost direction saw
nothing but the land of green grass within the cinnamon island
so I saw her in the dark; she said, 'where were you all these days then?'
raising her bird's nest-like eyes at me, Nator's Banalata Sen.

Like the sound of dew at a full day's conclusion
evening comes, the kite wipes away the smell of sunshine from its wings;
all of earth's colours fade, then for manuscripts make preparations
to twinkle with fireflies colours for the sake of storytelling;
all birds come back home—all rivers—all give and take in this life end;
only dark remains, sitting face to face with Banalata Sen.

(Trans. Anand Lal)

"Thousands of Years Merely Play"

Thousands of years merely play like fireflies in the darkness.
Pyramids all about. The smell of coffins.
Moonlight upon sand. Here and there the shadows of date palms
Like disintegrated columns. Assyria stands dead—humbled.
Stench of mummy on our bodies: all of life's business is finished
'Remember?' she asked. I queried merely, 'Banalata Sen?'
(Trans. Clinton B. Seely)

The unique fusion of European modernism and indigenous history and allegory was a distinctive feature of modern Bangla poetry, though at times there was a tendency towards waywardness and nihilism. According to Abu Sayeed Ayub, two obvious characteristics of the writing of the time were the absence of a sense of joy and surprise and the predominance of evil and the horror of life.

Second Phase: The publication of the poetry journal *Krittibas* in 1953 marked the next phase in the development of modern Bangla poetry. It was a mouthpiece for the reactionary response to the imitators of the early Modern Masters. Sunil Gangopadhyay, the founder-editor explained that their attempt was to demythisize the poets and to demystify the act of writing poetry. In his words, "poets are not warranted to utter sagacious truisms. . . instead of singing paeans of artificial beauty, they should hold up the mirror to the reality of our existence. We discovered that in poetry colloquial words and slangs could easily be blended with pure Sanskrit words. Like the French, we did not, however, brand our literary movement with a particular label. "But broadly, the poems of the *Krittibas* group came to be dubbed as 'confessional poetry'. . .". Reflecting the politics of the time, the crisis of the war years, Independence of the country, growing contact with China, Russia, France and Turkey, the poems of Sunil Gangopadhyay, Subhas Mukhopadhyay, Samar Sen, Nirendranath Chakraborty, Alokeranjan Das Gupta moved closer to the daily rhythms of life:

"My Task": Subhas Mukhopadhyay

I want my words
to stand straight on their feet.
I want every shade
should have eyes
I want every static picture
to walk.
I don't want to be
called a poet.
I want to walk
shoulder to shoulder
till my last day.
I want to put down my pen
beside the tractor, and say
now I'm free–
Brother, may I have a little fire? (Trans. Surabhi Banerjee)

"Perestroika": Alokeranjan Das Gupta

Perestroika's three butterflies came to me,
With their medium of dance they sought
To gather crucial news from me.

Horrible riots and violence
Raged in Armenia and Azer Baijan
In between we were the only tourists.

After giving all our provision
We were also penniless. We were thinking
How could we possibly return.

Then the three butterflies suddenly
Breaking their glossy wings vanished.
Were they perhaps hungry
In spite of the war? (Trans. Subhoranjan Das Gupta)

"For Neera": Sunil Gangopadhyay

Neera, take the purity of the noon
Take the distance of the night
Take the sandalwood breeze
The soothing simplicity of the soil on the river shore

The lemon-odour within the fist
Neera, turn your face towards me
I've preserved the most colorful sunset of the year
For you.

Take the smile of the beggar boy
The fresh verdure of the deodar tree
The marvel of the green-beetle's eyes
The whirlwind on a lonely afternoon
The tinkling chime of buffaloes in the woods
Take the silent tears
The wakeful loneliness at midnight
Neera, let the dewy shiuli shower on you
Let a solitary nightbird whistle
For you. (Trans. Surabhi Banerjee)

Third Phase: Growing up with the poetry of Jibanananda, Buddhadeb, Sunil and Subhas, the poets of the seventies stepped away from the tug of war of reaction and retaliation and tried to create a poetry of connectedness—bringing them closer to the cultural roots of the region. Difficult, lucid, impassioned, intense, whimsical, lapidary: these are some of the words that come to mind when reading the poems of Shankha Ghosh, Sukanto Choudhury, Shakti Chattopadhyay, Arun Mitra, Joy Goswami, Shamsur Rahman, Dibyednu Palit.

"Home": Shankha Ghosh

I've been looking for a home, for long –
In my mind
When would I be swept by liquid light?
Have you found a home?
I have found a home long ago –
In my mind
I long for a haven in the outer world.

(Trans. Surabhi Banerjee)

"Grief's Weight Entire": Shakti Chattopadhyay

Grief's weight entire is in grief itself.
Not in happiness or terror, not in enlightenment—
Grief's weight entire is in grief itself.
Under the heart lie sunlight and shadow both
The cloud is here to lie curled up like a dog
Not leaving when shooed, simply floating at night.
Grief's weight entire is in grief itself.

(Trans. Jayanta Mahapatra)

Poets of the nineties talk about everyday experiences. Women poets like Mallika Sengupta, Suchitra Bhattacharya, Nabaneeta Dev Sen, and Mandakranta Sen enrich the poetic output by focussing on female experience. There may be still an anxiety about style as well as the anxiety of influence but when we open a volume of verse these days we hear a distinctive voice, a new voice talking about experiences or even notions which every reader has felt, or is persuaded she has felt.

The declared intention of the poets of the nineties has been to reflect the social problems, cultural changes and complexities of postmodern life. However, there were serious accusations levelled at it. First, there was concern about the diminishing use of language resources, as there seemed to be an alarming increase in the use of linguistic and syntactic imports (mostly colloquial English terms) for the sake of contemporaneity. Second, poems seemed to have become more esoteric and solipsistic.

Anxieties may remain but as long as poetry continues to be written and read, anxieties of all kinds can be addressed and resolved. The taste for poetry—of different kinds—may be taken as the sign of good health of any culture, and the innate strength of a living language.

Notes and References

1. Harold Bloom. *The Anxiety of Influence: A Theory of Poetry* (London, New York: Oxford University Press, 1975 rpt.), p. 96.
2. Ibid., p. 5

Some of these translations have been taken from *Modern Poems from Bengal*, ed. Surabhi Banerjee (New Delhi: UBS, 1996).

Recent Oriya Poetry: Some Trends

SACHIDANANDA MOHANTY

There are a number of socio-cultural reasons that must explain the perception of the predominant use of the poetic form by creative writers in Oriya. Although short stories and fiction in general, regularly find a place in the various literary journals and periodicals, it is undoubtedly poetry that seems to be valorized by the literary-cultural establishment in Orissa. For all their mass appeal, many Oriya fiction writers regularly lament that their work does not receive due appreciation or recognition in the institutional context in the state. Further, the politics of literary awards in Orissa, some complain, seem to disproportionately favour the poetic form.

One reason for this perception is that in a largely feudal set-up, literary role models are of some consequence for the neophytes; and coincidentally, some of the writers that have received conspicuous recognition and generally come to mind at the state and at the national level happen to be poets. Ramakant Rath, Sitakant Mahapatra, Rajendra Kishore Panda and Haraprasad Das—all are members of the coveted All India Civil Services. Because of their service background, the vantage point and the institutional attention they can command, some argue, their achievements get magnified by the reading public. This is of course not to minimise or belittle their own intrinsic merit and excellence, but only to point at the larger socio-cultural matrix within which a literary work is inevitably produced and disseminated.

Whatever be the reasons, the poetry scene in Orissa is extremely active and vibrant. Different forms and experiments in the poetic form are constantly attempted. As elsewhere, here too, the traditionalists have given way to the modernists. A few of the earlier poets of the older generation like Sachi Routray still write and publish; the man generally acclaimed as the founder of literary modernism in Oriya poetry, Guruprasad Mohanty no longer does so. But his followers clearly reign supreme. While a large number of them employ their own idiosyncratic mode, it is also possible to discover underlying patterns in some of this poetry. This is what I shall attempt to do in my paper; firstly, I shall attempt to indicate dominant trends and significant voices, and secondly, I shall try and underscore their achievements in style and technique through a comparison with some of the earlier practitioners. Most of the leading Oriya poets are all well-known and appear regularly in journals and anthologies. Some of them are award-winners, others are equally distinguished. Sitakant Mahapatra, J.P. Das, Ramakant Rath, Sourindra Barik, Rabi Singh, Haraprasad Das, Rajendra Kishore Panda, Haraprasad Parichha Pattnaik, Jayanta Mahapatra, Mamata Dash, Pratibha Satpathy and others have all made a mark in recent Oriya poetry. They are all basically from the middle class. It must be mentioned here that despite having a large tribal population, there is hardly any Oriya poetry of consequence that deals with the tribal experience, comparable to say what Gopinath Mohanty did in his novels like *Paraja* or *Amritara Santana*. Similarly, there is glaring absence of the Dalit or Subaltern tradition of poetry in Orissa. The reason is simple: Education in Orissa is still a matter of social and economic privilege, and protest poetry of the political kind hardly exists.

It is true that earlier, progressive poets like Sachi Routray expressed rage and indignation in their poetry, as poet Rabi Singh does even today. But these isolated voices can hardly constitute a tradition. Another caveat I wish to offer at this stage is that despite the presence of many short story/fiction collections, there is a dearth of anthologies of contemporary Oriya poetry.

Adhunika Oriya Kabita (Cuttack: Janashakti Pustakalya, 1968) and more recently, *Adhunika Oriya Kabita Sambhara*, edited by Jatindra Mohan Mohanty (Bhubaneswar, 1998) are perhaps two of the better known. (Mention may be made here of anthologies edited by Sitakant Mahapatra and J.P. Das respectively).

Most of the poetry produced is also not translated into English, and for a survey of the present kind, the critic has to depend on individual anthologies of the various poets in Oriya.

II

A good way of initiating a discussion of recent Oriya poetry is to signal its difference from the earlier kind. The latter tradition was represented in Oriya in the form of the Oriya literary Romanticism: Mayadhar Mansingh, Radha Mohan Gadnaik, Ananda Shankar Ray, Kalindicharan Panigrahi, Nityananda Mohapatra, Bidyut Prabha and others represented what is known as the tradition of the *Sabuja* or The Green. The use of a primarily lyrical mode, rhyme scheme, love of the Romantic kind, a celebration of Nature and the countryside, a valorisation of intuition and imagination—all formed the bed-rock of this poetry. The break came by poets like Guruprasad Mohanty whose *Nutana Kabita*, 1955 and *Samudra Snana*, 1970 are regarded as landmarks. Some like Benudhar Rout and Sachi Routray also became transitional figures. Some of the poems they composed are also of the intermediate kind, betraying both the Romantic as well as the modernist sensibility. This becomes clear by looking at just three poems: "Malayara Atmahatya" ("The Suicide of Malaya") by Benudhar Rout, dated 1948 and two poems by Sachi Routray and Guruprasad Mohanty under the same title "Alaka Sanyal".

In "The Suicide of Malaya" (1948) from the collection of *Pingarlara Surja* (first published in 1967), poet Benudhara Rout effectively reverses the Romantic expectations of spring. Instead of the festival of gold that spring generally entails, we find the cry of anguish, the reality of poverty, and heaps of skeletons and bone that populate the urban landscape. The maiden here carries no arrow of cupid in her gaze.

The bow of flowers associated with *Madana*, the God of Love, must give way inexorably to the "rotten odour" and the "forlorn cry" of the dispossessed. The early rays of the sun only bring in the warmth of the blast furnace and the reality of the smoky chimney. Such is the backdrop that must serve as Malaya's funeral.

If death, desolation and decrepitude pervade many poems of the collection *Pingalara Surjya* such as "The Grief beneath the Waves," then the contrast between the two "Alaka Sanyal" poems also reveals the working of a modernist sensibility.

To begin with, "Alaka Sanyal" by Sachi Routray employs a language and idiom that are colloquial and casual:

> When I first saw you O Alaka Sanyal
> It was in the palace of Videha
> amidst a pile of hide
> of a million golden deer.

The poet-narrator has clearly embarked upon a search after Alaka Sanyal that takes on mythical overtones. The shift from the here and now to a world evocative of Nalanda "Chitraratha Gandharva", "Barunabantha", "Kalinga Cuttack" and the "Island of Spices" shows the working of both the mythical and the modern.

On the other hand, the poem by Guruprasad marks a clear-cut break. It is deliberately down to earth. The reference to the earlier poem by Sachi Routray is unmistakably clear in the opening line itself: "Perhaps Sachi babu spotted you once/I am not sure of this O Alaka Sanyal." Much of the imagery that follows, such as the "hide of the golden deer" is reminiscent of the earlier poem. However, the similarity ends there. The series of later stanzas that capture the life of Alaka Sanyal are evocative less of the mythical world and more of the modern cityscape a la T.S. Eliot. There are references to the ritual of domesticity, to female sexuality, to the "buttoning of a blouse", to "hot water", "shoe straps", "cigarette smoke," allusions to "contemporary holocaust," to the "riots at Noakhali," the "photos of Netaji and Nargis" and the cry of crows and bats. Clearly, this Alaka Sanyal is not of a pure or the pristine kind. As the poet-narrator says, "I have seen in your body the hand bill of cinema!" The deliberate evocation of levity and the mundane commonplace is clearly suggestive of a deromanticized temper: the treatment of the heroine and the characteristic idiom used are also to be found in another poem of Sachi Routray called "Pratima Nayak". Pratima of Routray is not moulded in the Romanticism of the earlier kind. Her listless profile full of pallor and pockmarks, devoid of a vibrant sexuality, is reminiscent of the women in "The Love Song of J. Alfred Prufrock" who "come and go"!

III

Like Sachi Routray's treatment of Alaka Sanyal, recent Oriya poetry is also characterized by the powerful use of myth. There are at least two full-fledged books that deal with mythological themes. *Sri Radha* (1985; 1990) by Ramakanta Rath that won him the Saraswathi Samman award and *Sabari* (1991) by Pratibha Satpathy.

Speaking about his poem on Sri Radha, Ramakant Rath says in the epilogue:

> The poems in this book are about Radha. One might feel that it is unnecessary and unreasonable to compose so many poems about a Puranic character. In fact, these creations are based on the ordinary circumstances of someone who finds a notable mention in the Purana and popular folklore. Of course there is no dearth of reasons not to like these poems. I am certain that I have not been able to articulate all that I wanted to say about Radha. Most often, I have not succeeded in finding an adequate expression. (Translation mine, p. 121)

Again:

> The love story of Radha and Krishna are plainly different from other such annals in world literature. In most other tales, the loving couple manage to get united at the end, or would have got united if the story had taken a somewhat different turn ; if others had understood them correctly or refrained themselves from evil action. Radha and Krishna had no such possibility. By the time they got to know each other, Radha was already married. Involved as they were, there was no question of their starting a household together. The outcome would have been no different even if the others had aided them. Undoubtedly, Radha would have been aware of this. If she persisted despite this, then she would have continued fully realizing that there would be no concrete outcome to this relationship. (Translation mine, pp. 123-24)

Rath attempts the sense of the inarticulate experience regarding Radha in many places. One of the opening stanzas provides a characteristic instance.

> That dawn, at the river front,
> Bathing, I gazed at my feet
> It was not my feet, not mine,
> I thought:
> This body is not mine,
> Nor is it the history of my hopes,
> my despair my own.
> Spouse, home, herds of cattle
> None of these are mine.
> My life not my own.
> And death?
> When it comes one day,
> Is not death.
> I shall remain a destitute.
> Always!
> Between my stretched arms
> I am a soaring emptiness.

After all,
it is the fate of some
to remain as a gap
for ever. (Translation mine)

At times, the love story employs an idiom and expression redolent of a contemporary domesticity:

Yesterday, my husband
pulled my hair,
and dashed my head
again and again.
Where did I spend
last night?
He demanded a confession
It pained me,
certainly it did.
But when he went
through each part
of my limbs, in detail,
I could not
suppress my laughter.

I said,
what a foolish husband!
On my forehead,
he looks for
signs of my infidelity.
That too
At day time. (Translation mine)

Like Ramakant Rath, Pratibha Satpathy in "Sabari" makes her own statement in prose in the epilogue of the book. As she remarks:

Is it a dream or reality? Frankly I do not know. I do not know whether I entered into her being or she enveloped

> mine; if this was a dream, then to realize its truth, this must be a well chosen path. But why did I select her among all the characters of the *Ramayana*? Perhaps because of all the characters, who were adorned full of vanity and arrogance, she stood out alone and self-collected. Because I spotted that eternal presence within the body of an ordinary woman. (Translation mine)

Such mythopoetic imagination finds expression in many other contemporary Oriya poets as well.

Many poems of Sitakant Mahapatra, skilfully interweave the mythic with the modern. The contemporary world of poverty, destitution, pain and suffering is not discarded. Instead, there is a reworking of the older myths in a renewed modern context. Such poems, built on a carefully structured pattern lead eventually to an unexpected *tour de force*. Such an approach seems to be integral to much of Mahapatra's poetry. As he explains in his Jnanpith Award speech:

> I hear my own recitation of the Oriya Bhagavata in the inner room of the house where so many gods were installed in a small wooden chariot. I hear the voice of Achyut Yashovant and Bhima Bhoi's bhajans at the tiny temple at one end of the village. I hear the stark fearsome voices of silence in the dark night of the village with cholera raging everywhere and the voice of the rain, of numerous deaths of remembered loves and the passing of seasons, punctuating births, sickness and death.

Thus, the opening stanza of the poem "Cuttack", for instance, magically transforms the familiar cityspace in sterile summer into the epic battle-ground of the *Mahabharata*:

> Even on crowded hot afternoons
> the fiery sun's Bhima like roar
> sends a million Duryodhana—in the Vyasa Sarovara of the Chandi temple

the afternoon shows and the offices.

Similarly, in the poem "Cock Fight" a commonplace sporting event involving roosters "awkwardly armed to the teeth" at the village square takes on dangerous overtones of the *Mahabharata* war:

The village trembles
in mild bursts
of shouts and battle cries
Pandavas and Kauravas
ranged in the battle field
of Kurukshetra.

Likewise, the poem "The Song of Jara the Hunter" makes an effective use of the famed myth in the *Mahabharata*. The poem, an eloquent elegy sung by Jara for his unwilling act of killing the Lord, is built on a monologue. There is a series of interrogations that carry both mythic as well as modernistic overtones.

If you are beyond birth and death,
If your existence is beyond history,
Why then the blue waters of Jamuna
weep for you, and for the fall of Kadamba flowers
the Govardhan hill, the flute tune
empty wavering

In the same manner, in the poem "Death of Krishna", an ironic transition in the middle of the poem creates an abrupt disjunction between the world of mythical festivity, of frolics and rasas, moonlight nights, "the myriad deceits on river banks" and the suddenly incongruous evocation of the metropolitan world: newspaper flashing "hurried obituaries", meetings that condole "the sad demise" and declare "another public holiday"!

In contrast, recent poetry by Oriya women shows a marked preference for themes and concerns related to the female identity. The tone is often reflective and many poems express them selves through a primarily lyrical mode. Brahmotri Mohanty's

1988 poem "Darpana" for instance, draws up a sharp contrast between identity based on the image of a mirror and identity rooted to the inner self, "this majesty of my own being". And hence, the fact of "not recognizing myself". As the opening lines suggest:

> That image of mine only a mirror can reveal
> amazes me, this majesty of my own being
> so much light, so much radiance,
> yet I never recognize myself. (Trans, Jayanta Mahapatra)

There is here a fear that after the initial "familiarity of praise" one may be left with "declaration devoid of brilliance."

Consequently, the mirror does not induce self-love or narcissism. And the poet declares:

> I step away from myself, unable to taste this reality of mine
> How can I experience the essence of an indivisible experience? (Trans. Jayanta Mahapatra)

Similarly, poet Pravasini Mahukud's lyrical study of loneliness is marked by a set of insistent questions:

> Where is this loneliness I heard where does it live?
> Inside my agony?
> Beyond, in the possibility of love?
> Further on, in a lake of tears?
> Or in the fear of death? (Trans. J.P. Das and Arlene Zide)

"This voice of loneliness" is redolent of images of a forlorn world: "abandoned castle", "gray marbles", "desolate forest" and "empty sky".

However, the loneliness paradoxically marks the presence of the other. As the poet says aptly "even in the scent of the Mahua, carried on the breeze/a frail voice reaches me".

Similarly, in "My Whole Life for Him", Manorama (Mahapatra) Biswal plays on the theme of waiting. For the female self, all waiting is a matter of anxiety and anguish. How, for instance, is one to know that "I am not here any longer" if he were "to come under a silent sun" or a "heavy downpour". Difficult though, his search would not be without helpful clues, the neem tree and mustard flowers would surely remind him of the lost childhood. The interesting question comes at the end of the poem:

> But how would she know
> for whom
> A whole life passed
> waiting, waiting. (Trans. J.P. Das and Arlene Zide)

Recent Oriya poetry is distinguished by other voices as well. In "This Day" and "Photograph" that appear in the translation form in *Kavya Bharati* (No. 9, 1997 issue) poet J.P. Das seems to celebrate ordinary commonplace moments and objects. "This Day" for instance becomes sacred and eventful for the persona simply "because/you appeared for a while/in my morning dream." Consequently, there would be no news in the papers "except your face". All the phone calls and letters would be "from you" only, and "all the knocks on my doors/would be yours alone." If the work ended due to some cataclysm and "only a fraction of man's dreams remained" even then there is the certainty that

> You will come to me . . .
> assuming the wholeness of the relics
> of that dream. (Trans. Niranjan Mohanty)

Equally striking are some of the poems of Rajendra Kishore Panda. "A Poem for My Daughter" seems to be a reworking of W.B. Yeats' "A Prayer for My daughter". The experience is appropriately Indianized. The fate of an Indian daughter is depicted with a sense of irony and detachment:

> If your in-laws spit out
> the well-cooked food
> served to them, you will
> suppress your sobs and smile instead.

If the destiny is ominous then the suggestion is:

Do not let yourself grow old daughter
you won't curse yourself, nor your fate.

The poem ends not on a note of despair. It is not the model of Sita, to be swallowed up by the mother earth that is being urged by the father, but an alternative mythological model full of creative possibility:

Never ask the earth to crack up
dear daughter, rather, you yourself
burst like Devaki and open the door
for the birth of God. (Trans. Rabindra K. Swain)

Like J.P. Das, another Sahitya Akademi award winner, Haraprasad Das too has made a mark for himself. The producer of many collections, Haraprasad too concentrates in many poems, on day-to-day events of domesticity. The poem "Farewell" provides a good example. The opening line begins on a dramatic note: "I shall not be there at dawn".

It will be futile for the wife to unfathom the mystery of the husband's disappearance. For has he not said that many times?

I shall go away,
Surely!
Haven't I said that
While again and again
removing the bone
from the fish
or swallowing
my saliva
or while beholding
the black spot
on your thigh. (Translation mine)

Clearly, she paid no heed to such threats. Now that he has gone to the other side of the road, from where he came, he offers a round of advice:

do not search for me
or open the door to anyone else. (Translation mine)

Like Haraprasad, there are many other poets in Oriya with powerful individual voices: Rabi Singh, Sourindra Barik, Pramod Mohanty, Soubhagya Kumar Mishra, Haraprasad Parichha Pattnaik, Mamata Dash, Bibek Jana, Deepak Mishra, Saroj Ranjan Mohanty, Bansidhar Sarangi, Surya Mishra and others easily come to mind. They have considerable achievement behind them. A survey of the present kind can hardly do justice to such a large variety of truly worthwhile poetry. An absence of translations is also a major hurdle for the interested non-Oriya reader. Hopefully, this lacuna will be overcome in future.

To sum up: Recent Oriya poetry is active and buoyant. It speaks in many voices. Its limitations are obvious. Largely middle-class, it has not been able to cover a wider gamut of experience. It is not bereft of the political, but the political is not a dominant trend here. Rich and many-hued, this poetry is sure to blossom more expansively in the next few decades.

Selected Bibliography

Adhunika Oriya Kabitaa Sambhara (A Treasury of Modern Oriya Poetry), ed. Jatindra Mohan Mohanty (Bhubaneswar, 1998).

Anthology of Modern Oriya Poetry in English Translation, ed. Sitakant Mahapatra (New Delhi: Vikas, 1984).

Kavya Bharati (Translation issue), No. 9, 1997 (Madurai: American College).

Shatabdira Srestha Kabita (Best Poetry of the Century), ed. Chintamani Behera (Bhubaneswar: Orissa Sahitya Akademi, 1979).

Under a Silent Sun, ed. J.P. Das and Arlene Zide (New De7lhi: Vikas, 1992).

Women Writing in India, 2 Vols, ed. Susie Tharu and K. Lalita (New Delhi: Oxford University Press, 1991; rpt. 1995).

A Note on Indian Urdu Poetry

S. KHALID QADRI

During the last twenty years, both literature and literary theory have undergone drastic changes. It has also triggered strong reaction and in some cases hot debates. One may welcome some of these recent literary trends and subscribe to the postmodernist views or reject them but one can certainly not afford to ignore them altogether.

For some, poetry too, after the seventies, has been marked by a kind of intellectual chaos. It is, for them, the poetry of mediocrity and spiritual decadence. However, for some others, it is an age of genuine artistic search and true creative freedom reflecting an entirely new poetic vision.

Preferring a more modest and a less startling statement, one would be inclined to say that the poetry of the last two decades, unlike in the past, has been considerably free from any broad ideological bias. It may be so perhaps because ideology is no longer an issue or because ideology is a concept now so diluted and dispersed that it seems to emanate and spill out from every kind of discourse let alone poetry or literature. Hence the poetry of our times, although it may not be categorized as being progressive or regressive, revivalist or futuristic, democratic or fascist, it has managed to survive as an art form against all odds. It succeeds in projecting a post-modernist vision and holding its own in the cramped corridors of capital markets and consumerism.

Quite like the literature of other languages in India, Urdu poetry too, of the recent times, is striving to retain its own identity against heavy odds. In the process it is shorn not only of its soft and soapy hues but also of such labels as classical, progressive and symbolist. It may be said to serve now truly as a voice of harmony in an era of discontent and disharmony. It is an authentic document of the spirit of modern times and its transcendental demands as well as a reverberation of the psychic and emotional reaction of mankind to the present day realities and circumstances.

In the recent past, during the days of the progressive movement, Urdu poetry was said to be sounding like a community chorus wherein there was hardly any room for individual creative expression to thrive. Majaz, Makhdoom, Saahir, Sardar Jafri and so many others of the same tribe were writing as if under a kind of pact to churn out identical compositions. Describing the poetic scenario of his time, Josh Maleehabadi had wittily but quite aptly called it 'a carnival of frogs'.

Strongly reacting to it, the poets of the modern movement in Urdu poetry chose to be so individualistic, personalized and self styled that they began to make use of obscure metaphors, complex symbols and such vague ideas that, at times, it was difficult to disambiguate their writings. However, from the same bizarre crowds emerged masters of modern Urdu verse of the calibre of Meeraji and Akhtar-ul-Iman. Among others who earned a name for themselves during this period, it will be apt to name poets like Khaleelurahman Azmi, Balraj Komal, Bani, Qazi Saleem, Shaheryar, Mohd. Alvi, Adil Mansoori, Moghni Tabassum, Shaz Tamkanath, Zahida Zaidi, Moshaf Iqbal, Tauseefi, Zubair Rizvi, Nida Fazli, and Basheer Badr. These and a few others contributed significantly to the modern movement in Urdu poetry by way of exploring new possibilities and breaking fresh ground. Several of them, though slowed down a bit, are still active creatively. A few specimens of their writings would suffice to suggest that their voices still lend credibility to the contemporary poetic scenario in India:

For centuries, I have been waiting for your call,

When would ye summon me—
The ocean of my blood. (Khaleelurahman Azmi)

To see him at home—the whole city is amazed
One who is being sought so frenziedly all over the wilderness. (Shaheryar)

I stared at her thirsty lips
knowing not
That the clouds had come swelling to drown my boat.
(Moghni Tabassun)

I regret so having built this house
Now—as I am in the house,
The house is in flames. (Mohd Alvi)

Though a humble particle of no consequence,
I accompany the gust of wind
As it soars towards the skies. (Adil Mansoori)

The clay of my being has yet to dry
Oh! lend me a shape
I am yearning to come to life. (Shaz Tamkanath)

Come! let is inscribe our names
On dry leaves
And proceed onwards
With the wailing winds. (Moshaf Iqbal Tauseefi)

What else is your body
than a disintegrating composition
Who am I—but a sad spectacle turning into ashes. (Bani)

Whose voice escapes from the sulking waves?
Listen! Some one is waiting, at the bottom of the river.
(Basheer Badr)

Among the multiple forms practised, 'ghazal' is the one which has cast a huge shadow over the landscape of Urdu poetry for more than a century. The form of 'nazm' which has got a relatively late genesis, is the other dominant form of verse practised side by side. However, in contemporary Indian Urdu poetry 'ghazal' and 'nazm' both have undergone large scale transformation not only in terms of their themes and substance but also in the kind of poetic devices used, and in the linguistic idioms evolved. (The case of a peculiar brand of Urdu poetry—the populist poetry of Urdu 'Mushairas'—Poets' gatherings—is entirely different and needs to be considered separately).

Among the younger generation of Urdu poets of the post-modernist era there are several noticeable voices that hold the promise of further ripening and maturity in the days ahead. To recall a few, one can name poets like Salahuddin Parvez, Irfan Siddiqui, Azad Badayuni, Jayant Parmar, Faiyyaz Rafat, Fazal Tabish, Farhat Ahsas, Ain Rasheed, Mahtab Haider Naqvi, Asha Prabhat, Shahid Kaleem, Abdul Ahed Saz, Sajid Hameed, Jamal Ovaisi, Ameen Ashraf, Javed Akhtar and Zaki Bilgrami.

The poetry of many of these poets reflects a new sensibility and seems to speak to us in a different voice. It is also successful, quite often, in echoing the social and the spiritual concerns of the modern man.

However, the name that stands out here and deserves a special mention is that of 'Salahuddin Parvez'. He may be truly called 'the poet with a difference'. He seems to have cast aside all the norms of conventionality brilliantly carving out for himself a unique poetic diction, and a superb style of his own. It is no wonder, therefore, that his poetic compositions are marked by a strange freshness, an amazing vitality and a strong aesthetic appeal. His poetic sensibility seems to constantly oscillate between a physicality which is close to chastity and a transcendence which is not so far off from the natural and the material. In spite of the fact that it is not a very auspicious time for writing poetry, it will augur well for contemporary Urdu poetry in India, if a few more poets are to approximate the poetic genius of poets like Salahuddin Parvez. Given below are a few specimens of contemporary Urdu poetry in translation.

What if I have managed to arrive in the land of spring

On the way,
I had to surrender my being
To the wilderness of autumn (Azad Badayuni)

I have been treasured like a showpiece
In the house of beauty
But the mirror mocks at me like a vampire.
There is no Christ to redeem me
Though all the doors are ajar
I can find no outlet. (Asha Prabhat)

O house of agony! your humble dwellers have arrived,
Can't ye recognize us,
We have returned home before the nightfall. (Irfan Siddiqui)

O God! Cut us off,
sever all our bonds and
make us sow the seeds of kinship
in infertile lands.
Bestow us with wars
and the gifts of hostility.
O God!
Let not the flowers of love
blossom on any of our trees. (Fazal Tabish)

These maidens—how they are transformed into flowers
At the touch of thorns
Their necks—adorned by garlands of beads
They keep picking up tears
In the corridors of dreams.
The wailing cloud, as it appears in the skies
they rush out to help it—
wailing and crying along with it. (Salahuddin Parvez)

Note

Translations of verses from Urdu to English have been done by the author.